Aging Heroes

Aging Heroes

Growing Old in Popular Culture

Edited by
Norma Jones
Bob Batchelor

ROWMAN & LITTLEFIELD
Lanham • Boulder • New York • London

Published by Rowman & Littlefield
A wholly owned subsidiary of The Rowman & Littlefield Publishing Group, Inc.
4501 Forbes Boulevard, Suite 200, Lanham, Maryland 20706
www.rowman.com

Unit A, Whitacre Mews, 26-34 Stannary Street, London SE11 4AB

British Library Cataloguing in Publication Information Available

Library of Congress Cataloging-in-Publication Data

Aging heroes : growing old in popular culture / edited by Norma Jones and Bob Batchelor.
p. cm.
Includes bibliographical references and index.
ISBN 978-1-4422-5006-2 (cloth : alk. paper) — ISBN 978-1-4422-5007-9 (ebook)
1. Older people in mass media. 2. Older people in popular culture. 3. Heroes in mass media. I. Jones, Norma, 1972- editor. II. Batchelor, Bob.
P94.5.A38A55 2015
305.26—dc23
2014049733

∞ ™ The paper used in this publication meets the minimum requirements of American National Standard for Information Sciences Permanence of Paper for Printed Library Materials, ANSI/NISO Z39.48-1992.

Printed in the United States of America

Contents

Acknowledgments

Let me first thank the "Godfather," or Bob Batchelor. Words cannot adequately express my gratitude. Please let me say, simply, thank you for giving me your trust, support, encouragement, and guidance.

Next, I also want to acknowledge my dissertation advisor and mentor, George Cheney. I appreciate you for being willing to advise someone a bit off the beaten path and sticking around, voluntarily, when you did not have to . . . thank you, thank you, and thank you again. I am learning to not only be a better scholar, but a better person, from you.

I also want to extend my gratitude to Stephen Ryan at Rowman & Littlefield, for all the things that Bob mentions below, in addition to providing us these amazing opportunities. Thank you!

As Bob acknowledges, these edited volumes are collaborative efforts, and this one would not have been possible without our contributors. Thank you, each and every one, for taking time to share your thoughts and work with us. I hope that together, we will help with how aging is thought of and studied now and in the future.

Let me also thank A. Bowdoin Van Riper. Thank you for lending me your ear, experience, and great advice!

As always, I want to thank my wonderful family: the Chus, Murphrees, Joneses, Rayburns, Yaghmaeis, Yangs, Chens, Changs, and Lipscombs.

And, of course, all credit to my best friend, my soulmate, and my awesome husband, Brent Jones. None of this would have been possible without your love and support.

—Norma Jones
Fort Worth, Texas

I would like to take a moment to acknowledge the outstanding work done by my coeditor Norma Jones. Without her intellectual leadership, stick-to-it-ness, and strong editing skills, this collection would not exist. Norma and her husband Brent Jones have developed into friends and colleagues over the years—and often coconspirators. What a fantastic trip.

Norma and I have had the great pleasure of working with a fantastic group of collaborators. Going out strong with a new collection of essays when little guidance exists is not always easy, even for accomplished scholars. We would like to thank them for their insightful analysis and thoughtful work.

Thanks to Stephen Ryan, our amazing editor at Rowman & Littlefield, for his continued support. His publishing acumen and deep knowledge of contemporary popular culture is invaluable, from brainstorming right on through to publication and marketing. Also, thanks to the entire Rowman & Littlefield team. They produce great books with superior covers and all in the spirit of collaboration so necessary in today's competitive publishing market.

My list of mentors and friends grows with each new project. I would like to thank the following for serving as role models in my own academic journey: Phillip Sipiora, Don Greiner, Gary Hoppenstand, Lawrence S. Kaplan, James A. Kehl, Sydney Snyder, Richard Immerman, Peter Magnani, and Keith Booker. Many friends offered good cheer: Chris Burtch, Larry Z. Leslie, Kelli Burns, Thomas Heinrich, Anne Beirne, Gene Sasso, Bill Sledzik, George Cheney, Josef Benson, Ashley Donnelly, Sarah McFarland Taylor, Kathleen M. Turner, Heather Walter, and Tom and Kristine Brown. A special thanks to the popular culture all-star team: Brendan Riley, Brian Cogan, and Leigh Edwards!

My family is wonderful. Thanks to parents Jon and Linda Bowen, who provide great support. I could not ask for a better wife or daughter. Kathy is an amazing scholar and soulmate, while Kassie is smart, funny, artistic, and beautiful. My days are filled with love and joy because of Kassie and Kathy.

—Bob Batchelor
Munroe Falls, Ohio

Introduction

Bad Abides: Jeff Bridges, Ideal Aging Hero

Bob Batchelor and Norma Jones

In a book of essays about aging heroes in popular culture, it might seem odd to call out one figure over another. The notion certainly grows more questionable when many of the stars featured are puffed up, real-life screen superheroes, like Sylvester Stallone and Arnold Schwarzenegger, or revered Hollywood icons, such as Clint Eastwood or John Wayne. Heck, even Superman is placed under the cultural magnifying glass! At seventy-seven years old, Superman may just be our most important aging superhero, important for his endurance and central place in cultural discourse, yet not really growing older like those of us in the three-dimensional world.

For our money, however, we would like to nominate Jeff Bridges (born December 4, 1949) as the ultimate representation of the aging hero, particularly as this character continues to dominate contemporary American popular culture. It is Bridges—more than counterparts Stallone, Kevin Costner, Bruce Willis, or the dozens of others who continue to ply the action hero trade—who sets the standard for what an aging hero can be or should be within the larger dynamics of the Baby Boomer generation. Bridges has achieved this laudable position based on a steady churn of critically acclaimed films as he has grown older, from the offbeat Jeffrey "The Dude" Lebowski to his more recent Academy Award–winning turn in *Crazy Heart* (2009) and Academy Award–nominated role in *True Grit* (2010), the latter reprising the Rooster Cogburn character made famous by John Wayne, who was a spry sixty-two years old in 1969 when the film appeared.

What Bridges and other Baby Boomer (and older) actors demonstrate is that despite the increasing number and variety of aging portrayals in film, television, comics, and other mass media channels, much of the cultural understanding has been limited to outdated stereotypes. Often the labels include portrayals of weakness and frailty (for example, the infamous infomercial tagline: "I've fallen and I can't get up") or soon dying (the urgent tone of commercials reminding people that it is time to buy life insurance). In a popular culture–saturated world that almost aimlessly caters to the eighteen- to twenty-five-year-old demographic, older people are often conveniently used as props in the lives of young people, which makes it easy to resort to the basest stereotypes about older people.

Simultaneously, though, given the simple fact that the Boomer population is enormous and growing older (with a greater percentage of disposable income and buying power), one sees more and more advertising, products, and other goods and services directed to them. The seemingly nonstop Viagra commercials and other pharmaceutical wonder pills reveal the convoluted nature of modern consumerism. In other words, those in power want to direct popular culture toward younger audiences, but it is the Baby Boomers who control the nation's purse strings. Thus, it makes sense for a star vehicle to star fifty-something Brad Pitt, or even seventy-something Robert De Niro, each a comfortable choice for aging audiences. Pitt, De Niro, and their contemporaries may be aspirational for older viewers or simply provide the kind of personas that they are used to experiencing as filmgoers.

Spurred on by the large Boomer demographic and its headlong consumerism, popular culture is shifting in response. As the population ages, some portrayals of older Americans in the media are becoming more multidimensional. With every sly wink from a Michael Douglas character when he shows that wisdom can overcome youth, or every close-up of Stallone centering on a T-shirt-ripping bicep, these mediated stereotypes become more influential in the daily lives of aging adults, as well as on how younger generations interact with or perceive older Americans. We note that the older heroic figure now spans comic books, stage, and the music industry. Also, more aging male and female actors are taking leading roles in movies, or collaborating in big-budget ensemble films such as *The Expendables*, *RED*, *Gran Torino*, *Grudge Match*, *Escape Plan*, *Space Cowboys*, *Taken*, *Mamma Mia*, *Wild Hogs*, and *X-Men*.

Although so much of our popular culture universe focuses on television and film, the interest in aging is hastened by the large cadre of cultural producers who also fit in this demographic, from critics and producers to directors and writers. So, too, the vast majority of the nation's professors, teachers, doctors, lawyers, and engineers comfortably fit in the "aging" demographic. These audiences are not only consumers of the new ideas about aging heroes, but often they also produce the ideas that have changed attitudes. As they think about their own roles as producers and consumers of culture, the notion that older people have to fit a tidy stereotype are falling away.

An aging population that has spending money and is living longer, healthier lives based on medical and technological innovation has far-reaching consequences. As a result, this book is one of the first to reveal the varied and multidimensional portrayals of aging in mass media. Instead of falling into some existing negative stereotypes, these depictions show that aging does not equal feeble; rather, the new-age heroic figures can be vibrant, wide-ranging, and strong. In a plethora of blockbuster ensemble films, aging heroes are showing that growing older does not just result in weakness or disease. Instead, they are smarter, wiser, faster, and (in some cases) even stronger.

The idea that wisdom matters is one that other nations, particularly in Asia, have known for centuries. The force of nature that is the Baby Boomer population is expanding this notion, most noticeably in film and television, but across contemporary culture. Returning to Jeff Bridges, our ultimate aging hero, we encounter a man who exudes grand understanding of himself and his place in society. And, because we see Bridges as an authentic person, we allow this foundational trait to seep into the characters he occupies. Writer Chris Nashawaty explains this vibe, saying, "He seems to have a knack for finding wonder in everyday things like Ferris wheels, and sharing that awe with whoever's along for the ride."[1] As a matter of fact, the idea that we know or comprehend the actor on some deep level is part of the acceptance process that Bridges and his cohort employ as a means of altering the perception of aging heroes.

CRAZY HEART

Crazy Heart (2009) opens on long shots of the majestic American West.[2] The breathtaking mountains and windswept plains represent the continuity of life in the region, as well as its boundless opportunity, particularly when examined from an overhead, sweeping perspective. When the camera moves from the broad to the specific, however, the viewer gets her first glimpse of Otis "Bad" Blake. Then, life starts to look more real . . . messier.

Approaching sixty years old during the filming, Bridges oozes Bad, the broken-down country singer—once a star—struggling with inner demons and alcoholism as he travels across the grand but wilting Southwest and West, chasing dollars down the neck of a bottle. When Bad arrives at another small-town stop, a bowling alley of all things, he is polite and earthy. Soon, though, the singer is asked to pay for his own drinks at the bar and turns surly. His reputation for heavy drinking precedes him.

Bad is a grizzled, good-looking man, despite his drinking challenges. When he gets on stage, he has star presence and dominates the small stage. Initially the singer seems okay, but quickly degenerates into a wheezing, stumbling drunk. Going from bad to worse, he completely loses it in the second half of the show. Too drunk, Bad runs off the stage, out the back door, and throws up. He returns, sweating, shirt and armpits soaked. The depths of his despair are symbolized by the decision to sleep with a middle-aged fan.

Early in *Crazy Heart*, there is nothing heroic about Bad Blake, a washed-out musician. As portrayed by Bridges, though, the audience knows that these depths will be scaled. The down-and-out star who finds redemption is a trope that filmgoers understand, just as they comprehend that Bad's trek across the West is in fulfillment of the age-old adage, "Go West, Young Man."

Rooting for Bridges/Bad, the audience also realizes that his salvation necessitates a redeeming relationship. Enter Jean Craddock (Maggie Gyllen-haal), an enterprising young music journalist who sees Bad as a great feature story. When she asks, "How did you learn music," the singer offers up the typical up-from-the-bootstraps musician's tale. While serving up rote an-swers, though, Bad reveals his vulnerability that oozes as countrified charm. He is comfortable in his degeneration, eating in front of Craddock with his shirtfront open and then leans back, letting his ample gut hang out. Bad flirts with her, but does not like being asked personal questions and shies away or flatly refuses to answer.

After the concert, things heat up between Blake and the decades-younger Craddock (Gyllenhaal was thirty-two years old when the movie was re-leased). They drink together, and she wears a revealing, low-cut tank top. They sit close together and flirt more, but she leaves kind of mysteriously. As audience members might anticipate, the next night Bad is more energetic and engages with the adoring crowd. Several times he is actively scanning the crowd for the younger woman, but she does not show up. They meet later "for a drink" and the ruse of a follow-up interview. Comfortable with one another, they sit together on his hotel bed and drink. Later, they sleep togeth-er.

Bad is living the Boomer/aging hero dream—getting the girl and showing sparks of his former, more powerful (younger) self. All this takes place while Bad displays few redeeming qualities as an individual, which shows that the aging hero does not have to make wholesale transformations to achieve suc-cess. The one area in which he does seem to shine is in dealing with Buddy, Jean's four-year-old son. Despite a checkered past with his own child, now a man, Bad buys the youngster toy cars and takes him to the aquarium when the mother and son visit the singer at his home in Houston.

Next, a kind-of bad guy is introduced, Tommy Sweet (the then thirty-three-year-old Colin Farrell), Bad's former band member who has rocketed off on a solo career. Tommy looks heroic (and young) in comparison to his erstwhile mentor, but in a corporate "new country" way with slicked-back hair, earrings, and jet-black shirt. Even their transportation is old versus new: Bad's beat-up pickup truck, dubbed "Old Bessie," versus Tommy's new, shiny SUV. For Boomer audiences, Tommy is the personification of corporate sellout, which they understand, even as they navigate their own 9-to-5 jobs in cubicle farms across the nation. By standing in juxtaposition, Bad is a rambling hero with a heart of gold.

In a move that certainly touches a nerve for viewers, the older star stands as the opening act for his protégé. Bad is forced to put his tail between his legs for the pot of money that the gig promises. He justifies the act by rationalizing that he can use the money to win the heart of his sweetheart. The concert is exactly what Bad (and moviegoers) anticipate—in the battle of old country versus new, the fans barely recognize or acknowledge Bad. They only cheer when Tommy makes a guest appearance and sings with him.

Bad still has a bit to fall before hitting rock bottom, which occurs when Jean and Buddy visit him in Houston. On a day trip downtown, the older man loses Buddy after stopping into a bar to get out of the Texas heat. When he loses Buddy, he is hobbling around and sweating, which makes people he approaches in his frantic search think he is a lunatic or crazy. The scene symbolizes the way society often looks at old people. Bad is supposed to be fifty-seven years old, but looks older and disheveled. Naturally, Jean realizes just how bad Bad is and leaves him.

The final straw of what could have been in both losing Buddy in a crowd and the relationship with Jean tears at Bad, but also gives him cause for turning his life around (perhaps the message being "it's never too late"). The most important step in rehabilitation is going into a recovery program. Also, back in Houston, Bad cleans up his yard and tries to get his house back in shape (shown obsessively scrubbing the stovetop, which betrays years of neglect). When Bad reaches out to Jean, admitting, "I'm changing everything," she won't take him back.

The film pushes ahead sixteen months to reveal the deep changes in Bad's life. Tommy Sweet is an even bigger star, singing the songs Bad has written. The cleaned-up older man exudes contentment. He runs into Jean outside a venue, and they exchange heartfelt words, but she is marrying another man, which Bad abides. Opposed to the candy-coated happy Hollywood endings so prevalent in contemporary film, *Crazy Heart* fades out on a somewhat bittersweet note. Bad transformed his life, but did not get the girl. His final atonement is giving Jean the large royalty check he just received to put toward the boy's future—a way of thanking her for her role in turning his life around.

As a star vehicle for Bridges, *Crazy Heart* won critical acclaim based on his strong, sorrowful performance as a man on the brink, but able to recover. Bad is a believable hero based on story narratives that audiences understand. Bridges's accomplishment, based on the personal authenticity as an actor and musician that he brings to the part, uncovers the complexity of aging heroes in contemporary popular culture. Certainly, one message is that love can turn a bad man good. Gyllenhaal's Craddock is young and beautiful, but not in a conventional sense, and her grace empowers him to transform. The attempt to win her back fails, but Bad wins at life. Rather than a pathetic figure, Bridges employs his star power to show the singer as human and fallible, able to overcome deep adversity to regain his soul.

THE BIG LEBOWSKI

In the hands of Ethan and Joel Coen, Jeff Bridges transformed into "The Dude," the penultimate 1960s stoner trying to get by in the last days of the go-go 1990s. As a result of the Coens' brilliant writing and amazing acting by Bridges and an all-star cast, *The Big Lebowski* (1998) is a nostalgia-laced gambol through the Bush I era that turns into a comic, LA neo-noir whodunit. While the film did reasonably well at release, its rise as a cult classic brings to light its true significance. As a result, the film, its stars, and its tangled meanings have entered the national cultural climate.

As The Dude, Bridges is the film's heart and soul, melding his personal gravitas as an actor with the character into a powerful fusion. The Dude is a zenlike, quotable hero, hooked on bowling, marijuana, and the ever-present White Russian. It takes the combination of Bridges's comedic timing and large doses of his personal authenticity to pull off The Dude, a character that on paper might seem somewhat obnoxious and perhaps repugnant to some audiences. Even Sam Elliott's mysterious cowboy narrator does not know quite what to make of The Dude, explaining his hazy persona: "I won't say a hee-ro, 'cause what's a hee-ro?—but sometimes there's a man."[3]

Bridges is the right man to bring The Dude to life, demonstrating the character's ability to be heroic in the face of modern society's Machiavellian nature. The Dude remains somewhat aloof to the conniving taking place around him. His sensibility harkens back to the activism of his college days, but the materialism of the 1990s shelves his hopes of engaging with the system. The Dude's mental standing is in the earlier era, a time when he showed promise as an individual, but ultimately found himself beaten down by the system that the "real" Jeffrey Lebowski supports and epitomizes as part of the power elite. The Dude, in contrast, is a true believer. As a matter of fact, he is an architect and author of "the original Port Huron Statement," not, as he tells Maude Lebowski, "the compromised second draft."[4]

One of the questions at the heart of *The Big Lebowski* is whether or not it is possible to be a hero in the Gulf War I era as orchestrated by George H. W. Bush. Perhaps the primary query is whether or not any kind of aggression abides. The Coen Brothers are asking the 1998 moviegoer to reconsider the film's early 1990s time frame and ask what price the nation paid for the war in the Middle East. This question has remained important as *Lebowski* transformed from box office middle fare to cult classic. Furthermore, in a post-9/11 world, viewers are asked to constantly renegotiate these ideas.

Although on one level a farcical neo-noir, the Coens' film takes the question of what it means to be American in the late twentieth century beyond the war in Iraq and asks filmgoers to reassess their place in that world. The Western setting in and around Los Angeles symbolizes the demographic movement of people and power from East to West since World War II. Pitting heroic "little people" versus the corporate and police state, viewers are presented a bleak portrait of real-world power and hegemony. In other words, what takes place in Iraq also occurs on the city streets and its suburban neighborhoods. Using LA as a backdrop and its status as the creative epicenter of America's illusion industry, *Lebowski* tackles the nation's many contradictions, from economic inequality to the role of law in a police state.

While a bumbling hero, the Dude is also contradictory, just like many other characters in *Lebowski*. Often, these masks are purely illusionary, ranging from the Big Lebowski's faux wealth to Jackie Treehorn's supposed respectability. The blurring lines between illusion, self-delusion, and reality combine to highlight the clashing ideas at the heart of the film. The Dude, for example, is remembered as a laid-back stoner, with his outer appearance accentuating his mental outlook. Yet, his exterior as a paragon of zen beliefs is betrayed by erratic, bewildering behavior. He is often angry, exasperated, or downright coldhearted.

The viewer sees this alternative performance in The Dude's decidedly distant reaction to Donny's death, particularly in the nonchalant manner he brushes off the episode in the film's final scene. After condolences from the bowling alley bartender, the Dude replies, "Yeah. Well, you know, sometimes you eat the bear, and, uh . . . "[5] The Dude often trails off when speaking, unable to articulate his thoughts, which might be chalked up to excessive weed, but certainly not excessive care. Ultimately, The Dude and Walter are complicit in Donny's death, which stemmed from their schemes that led to the perilous situation with the nihilists.

As a hero, the Dude is a mixed bag, which represents the difficulty of being heroic in the 1990s, an era obsessed with hyper-capitalism, aggression, and hegemony. What one understands is that The Dude is a new hero for a new age, as the cowboy narrator explains, "The man for his time'n place, he fits right in there."[6] As he would later do in *Crazy Heart*, though, the authenticity Bridges incorporates in the role fills the audience with a yearning to like the character, even when he loses his temper, swears, or places his own needs ahead of those around him. The Dude clearly is not a Superman figure with incredible strength and unwavering ideals. He is vulnerable and twists and changes with the day's needs. This is the new heroic character, super in his daily machinations, and seems in line with the Boomer/aging version of heroism where one becomes "heroic" for recycling, being concerned about the environment, buying green products, and the like.

Even as we argue that Bridges is the consummate aging hero, perhaps the more pressing concern is how we untangle the idea of heroism in contemporary popular culture. A strong argument could be made that "real-life" heroism rarely exists today, which results in wildly fluctuating visions of aging heroes across mass media. Certainly the notion of heroism has undergone sharp change, ranging from the national debacles of Watergate, Vietnam, and the Great Recession to the patriotism/heroism in the wake of 9/11 and the War on Terror.

Our notions of heroism change, too, as the nation suffers through scandal after scandal, promoted by an increasingly sensationalism-based mass media and millions of self-styled pundits given a platform via the Internet. The consequences are evident. Anyone held up as a hero soon faces relentless, unyielding scrutiny, as if the media's portrait of the public downfall and resulting humiliation would be found much more satisfying than the hero's rise to glory. President Barack Obama is another case study in the hero's rise and fall (depending on one's political bent) as he moved from savior to villain over the course of his term in office. One can look back even further, citing President Bill Clinton's impeachment. As a result, contemporary American history is a series of crises and personal missteps by so-called leaders.

On the other hand, the media and public drop the "hero" label pretty arbitrarily on the military, police officers, and firefighters, but concurrently does little to help these individuals once the gun is put down or the uniform hangs in the closet. The hero gets a parade down Main Street USA or holds the flag at an NFL game, appearing on TV for twenty seconds, but is later left jobless, without benefits, and unable to cope with mental and physical ailments. Our convoluted ideas regarding the definition of hero plays a role in the looseness of the term and how it is applied across popular culture. Maybe what our culture needs is an evolving array of potential heroes, rather than the traditional patriarchal politician or other leader. Bridges and his roles in *Lebowski* and *Crazy Heart* certainly represent this newfangled hero, which is so intricately tied to the aging population that controls and produces mass media. What our aging heroes demonstrate is that we no longer expect a superhero to save us. Maybe the focus is better understood from the perspective of everyday acts of heroism or just common decency.

* * *

For those readers who like to jump from essay to essay, a brief overview is necessary to provide a better understanding of the book and its purposes. The reader finds four thematic groupings that provide form, although these parts overlap. The parts begin with examinations of aging in film. Next, the contributors analyze aging heroes based on diversity concerns. Then, the book turns to issues of masculinity. Finally, we conclude by focusing on specific aging individuals in popular culture texts.

In part 1 we examine aging across film genres, including "Heartland" films, Westerns, action-hero movies, and space travel blockbusters. In "On the Silver Screen: Aging Heroes in Film Genres," Cynthia J. Miller discusses "better" role models for aging from films set in the American Heartland. Next, Mei-Chen Lin and Paul Haridakis review aging stereotypes and how they are portrayed in the venerable Western genre. Norma Jones then examines movie action heroes as they age, or do not age, in action films. In this part's concluding essay, "Under the Wide and Starry Sky: Hollywood and Aging Astronauts, 1996--2000," A. Bowdoin Van Riper provides an exploration of aging astronauts in turn-of-the-millennium space exploration films.

In the second group of essays, the contributors explore diversity, including sexuality, race, and gender. Gust A. Yep, Ryan Lescure, and Jace Allen read Liberace in HBO's award-winning *Behind the Candelabra*. Next, in "Overcoming the Villainous Monster: The Beginnings of Heroic Gay Male Aging," Dustin Bradley Goltz offers a historical review of how aging and gayness have been portrayed in mainstream media. We next explore race and aging as Carlos D. Morrison, Jacqueline Allen Trimble, and Ayoleke D. Okeowo discuss Tyler Perry as Madea. Then, Emily S. Kinsky and Amanda Gallagher show us the power of aging in *Maya & Miguel*. Caryn E. Neumann concludes this part with "Babes and Crones: Women Growing Old in Comics," an examination of women and aging in comic books.

In part 3, the contributors analyze masculinity and aging. Patrice M. Buzzanell and Suzy D'Enbeau lead with a case study of the irascible Roger Sterling from AMC's hit television series *Mad Men*. Next, Nathan Miczo explores Superman and Wolverine as aging superheroes in *Kingdom Come* and *Old Man Logan*. Itır Erhart and Hande Eslen-Ziya continue the superhero theme in "Mr. Incredible, Man of Action, Man of Power: What If He Loses It All?" Guilliaume de Syon then concludes this part with his discussion of male pilots in advertising.

In our last and most specific grouping, the contributors focus on individuals as they age, both on and off the screen. Barbara Cook Overton, Athena du Pré, and Loretta L. Pecchioni first examine Helen Mirren, as well as other aging women. Anna Thompson Hajdik explores the extraordinary career of Peter O'Toole as a hellraiser, dandy, and eccentric. Next, in "The Betty White Moment: The Rhetoric of Constructing Aging and Sexuality," Kathleen M. Turner provides an assessment of the incomparable Betty White. Salvador Jimenez-Murguia then concludes this part with a review of Danny Trejo as aging *bricoleur*.

Whether assessing a specific iconic figure or examining heroic images as represented across popular culture, our goal is to begin conversations that enable readers to look anew at issues regarding aging that run the gamut from identity and semiotics to sexuality and diversity. This collection, the first to hone in on how aging heroes are portrayed in our culture and what this means for us as viewers, consumers, and culture makers, fills a gap that grows more fundamental to understanding the continuing evolution of popular culture in the contemporary world.

NOTES

1. Chris Nashawaty, "The Ballad of Jeff Bridges," *Entertainment Weekly*, January 8, 2010. http://www.ew.com/article/2010/01/01/jeff-bridges-likely-oscar-contender (accessed November 15, 2013).

2. *Crazy Heart*, directed by Scott Cooper (2009; Burbank, CA: 20th Century Fox Home Entertainment, 2010), DVD.

3. Ethan Coen and Joel Coen, *The Big Lebowski* (London: Faber and Faber, 1998), 4.

4. Ibid., 107–8.

5. Ibid., 139.

6. Ibid., 4.

I

On the Silver Screen:
Aging Heroes in Film Genres

Chapter One

Twilight Heroes

Old Age and Unfinished Business in Four
"Heartland" Films

Cynthia J. Miller

Our understanding of the heroic is rooted in its mythic past—brimming over with adventure, uncertainty, and danger. Warriors such as Ulysses and King Arthur, even at an advanced age, ventured off to pursue quests, conquer lands, defend honor, and beat back enemies—or die glorious deaths in the process. This myth of the heroic animates legend and folklore, but also persists to the present day and shapes contemporary narratives and readings of heroes at any point in the life course, with little to no consideration of the contextual changes created by their advanced years. Aging heroes in contemporary film and television are typically crafted and evaluated using the same criteria as youthful heroes. Agility, reflexes, endurance, and technological savvy serve as the primary framework for comparing and contrasting new heroes with old, and actors such as Sylvester Stallone, Arnold Schwarzenegger, Bruce Willis, Billy Bob Thornton, Mickey Rourke, Liam Neeson, Pierce Brosnan, and others portray aging figures bent on proving that they've still "got it"—that they can compete and win in a young man's game—or that their experience allows them to circumvent contemporary norms and succeed specifically because they are uniquely "old school." But do the characters they portray simply reinforce a stereotype that, in truth, is irrelevant for aging heroes? What constitutes the heroic for aging characters? If we understand the heroic as exhibiting courage, making outstanding achievements, and displaying noble qualities, what does that mean in the context of aging?

A small cluster of films set in the American heartland speaks to these questions: *The Straight Story* (1999), *Get Low* (2009), *Jayne Mansfield's Car*

(2012), and *Nebraska* (2013) are all small-town tales about cranky old men whose greatest challenge is being able to face the world on their own terms as they grow old. Their lives are quiet, understated, and tinged with depression. While many aging heroes continue to battle their way into their twilight years, the old men in this cluster of films are actually better, more realistic role models for aging male viewers who are never going to be warriors. These characters are frustrated, have regrets and unfinished business, and they meet all of that the best way they can, learning things about themselves and those around them in the process. They may be on a quest, but unlike mythic heroes and those modeled after them, their quest involves finding peace, not war.

IN SEARCH OF ULYSSES

Time may have dimmed popular memory of the heroes of old, but their legacies live on in contemporary expectations surrounding the heroic, as the tales of one generation continually inspire those of the next. Myth, legend, and folklore are animated by strong, fearless, virile heroes who are tested— by battles, magic, riddles, quests, or temptation—and who, even if they initially falter, rise to the occasion and emerge victorious. Jason . . . Achilles . . . Hercules . . . Ulysses . . . these and many others follow a traditional heroic archetype, displaying courage and self-sacrifice in the face of danger, and providing moral examples for the listeners and readers of their tales.

Most often called into being as a warrior, defender, or protector, the classic hero of myth and legend has been given pride of place in most analyses of traditional tales, from the early work of Vladimir Propp in his *Morphology of the Folktale*, through notable work by Lord Raglan, Alan Dundes, Claude Lévi-Strauss, and of course, Joseph Campbell.[1] Each has carefully examined the figure of the hero and the narratives in which he or she is featured, exploring the nature and function of the heroic character. Identified as an archetype with at least some degree of universality, the hero is most often understood by commonly recognizable actions and achievements—quests, trials, victories—and not by any unique personal attributes or depth of character—and most certainly, not by his or her stage of life. Across these studies and analyses, all heroes are shown to have been created relatively equal, including those of advanced age. Timeworn and battle weary, archetypal aging heroes still venture forth in search of glory, dreading a mundane fate that would lead them to "rust unburnish'd, not to shine in use."[2] They return from their quests only to chafe at the quiet, wondering if "some noble work of note may yet be done."[3]

Ulysses was one such hero, and echoes of his character type can still be seen in contemporary notions of the heroic. Known to the Greeks as Odysseus, the character's adventures were first narrated in Homer's *Iliad* and *Odyssey*. King of Ithaca, and descendant of the god Hermes, he was one of the most influential figures of the Trojan War. Clever, brave, and powerful, Ulysses was a champion of the battlefield and a restorer of order. It was he who devised the ruse of the Trojan Horse that allowed the Greek army to sneak into Troy, but his renown through the ages owes more to the story of his epic quest than to his prowess in battle. Mythic chronicles of his decade-long voyage home from the great war spin tales of magic and wonder, as he and his crew encounter and best monstrous and powerful enemies: they blind the Cyclops Polyphemus, escape the witch-goddess Circe, resist the call of the Sirens, and nearly meet their deaths in the jaws of the six-headed Scylla. Time and again, the hero and his crew, with the help of the gods, magic, and their own daring, narrowly evade certain death, although they do pay dearly for foolhardiness and other moral offenses along the way.

But Ulysses/Odysseus is not a young man. The quest to return home from the war has seen him transition from a mature warrior to an aging king. In Tennyson's eponymous poem, set at the end of the hero's life, Ulysses has completed his journey home to Ithaca and reasserted his rightful place as king, by slaying the houseful of suitors who had laid siege to his wife during his long absence. He quickly grows restless and discontented, however, and longs for his heroic past:

> Tho' much is taken, much abides; and tho'
> We are not now that strength which in old days
> Moved earth and heaven, that which we are, we are;
> One equal temper of heroic hearts,
> Made weak by time and fate, but strong in will
> To strive, to seek, to find, and not to yield.[4]

Whether Ulysses departs on his final quest, or as critics suggest, Tennyson's entire poem represents a *monologue intérieur* that takes place on the hero's deathbed, the significance of the verses remains: He is an aging hero, clinging to an identity that was forged in his youth, compelled to carry out a role typically fulfilled by a decades-younger man. There is no attractive model of an elderly hero to which he might adapt his imaginings of glory and honor. Full of youthful ambitions in an old man's body, he is bored in Ithaca, and refuses to "yield" to the limitations of old age. He longs, instead, to set off on one final adventure and die a glorious death—in a manner defined by the goals and abilities of decades-younger men.

In this, the character of Ulysses has become one of the dominant models of the heroic for characters that are long past their prime. He epitomizes the aging adventurer who cannot stop seeking adventures, even when physical ability, mental acuity, and everyday obligation would dictate otherwise—he is powerless to define himself otherwise, despite occupying other valuable social roles of husband, father, and king—and is destined to end his days pursuing a quest for glory and honor that speaks to the goals and needs of young men half his age. We see his unrelenting legacy in latter-day fictional characters who cling to youthful heroics well into later adulthood: Alan Quatermain, Peter Devereaux, Indiana Jones, Rocky Balboa, and James T. Kirk, as well as in aging comrades-in-arms such as the Wild Bunch and the Expendables. These figures of the masculine heroic are compelled to battle the ravages of time, often in greater measure than any enemy. Their strength, courage, determination, and skills are routinely called into question—their virility and relevance challenged—as they time and again challenge the phrase, "old man." As they reach back in time to evoke heroics of old, these characters affirm that there is but one model for the hero, throughout youth and old age: a model that privileges physicality, fearlessness, self-sufficiency, and the refusal to accept limitations. We are always, it seems, in search of Ulysses.

INTEGRITY OR DESPAIR

Philosophers, poets, storytellers, and scholars have attempted to map the terrain of the human lifetime, exploring its peaks and valleys, contemplating its light and shadow. Advancing years are variously framed as "golden" or "twilight"—the culmination of a lifetime of wisdom and experience, or the lamentable descent into deterioration and despair—all, in a sense, measured against the vitality of youth. "Older, but wiser," "past their prime," and similar descriptors color common understandings of aging, and the tension between the gains of a life well lived and the changes framed as losses brought about by the aging process is apparent in countless narratives. Shakespeare, in his elaboration of the seven roles or "ages" played by all men and women over the course of a lifetime, from infancy through death, described the elder years—the sixth age—as a visible diminishing of both stature and life force, the elderly withering away, taking leave of the world, an inch at a time:

> The sixth age shifts
> Into the lean and slippered pantaloon,
> With spectacles on nose and pouch on side;
> His youthful hose, well saved, a world too wide
> For his shrunk shank; and his big manly voice,
> Turning again toward childish treble, pipes whistling.[5]

The fearful anticipation of such an impotent departure from the world, characterized by shrinking, withering, and weakening, is made palpable in the work of poet T. S. Eliot, whose verses evoke an image of aging and death that is similarly inescapable and without glory:

> I have seen the moment of my greatness flicker,
> and I have seen the eternal footman hold my coat, and snicker,
> and in short, I was afraid.[6]

The teachings of the Buddha, however, instruct that as a wise man ages, "his form changes and alters, but he does not fall into sorrow, lamentation, pain, distress, or despair over its change and alteration."[7] Here, change is not equivalent to loss—it is merely the outward signifier of a new state of being. In this, and in many other spiritual traditions, the attainment of old age heralds the achievement of honor, heightened insight and enlightenment, and the final stage on the path to the divine, the casting off of worldly cares. The physical and social losses that accompany aging are seen as part of a positive process of relaxing one's grasp on the illusory values of youth, in favor of eternal gains.

Approaching the life course from a stance that shifts the focus away from a comparison with youth, psychologist Erik Erikson has situated aging in its social context, focusing instead on the nature of relationships that are developed and maintained, understanding one's place in the world, coming to terms with the past, and fulfilling a role of helping the next generation move forward. Aging, in this view, is neither a diminished remnant of youthful vitality, nor a refinement and polishing of youth's rough edges; it is a unique status, with its own cluster of challenges, expectations, and achievements, with goals not measured by the desires, ambitions, or abilities of youth. In his foundational study of personality development, Erikson contends that individuals proceed through a series of eight hierarchically ordered stages. Associated with each stage is a developmental conflict or "crisis" that must be resolved, or further development is impaired. The final stage, later adulthood, turns on the dawning awareness of mortality, and the review of one's life—determining it to be a success or failure. If an individual has successfully reconciled earlier life stages, he or she carries forward into late adulthood hope, will, purpose, competence, fidelity, love, and caring; if not, the final stage of the life course may be marked by their absence, and fraught with mistrust, doubt, guilt, isolation, and low self-esteem. For Erikson, the aging process seeks to resolve issues that are distinctly social in nature, and is a function of context, rather than biological processes. This framework for thinking about aging, then, views it as a unique period, best understood by its own unique criteria and characteristics, rather than being "greater than" or "less than" another unique stage of life, such as youth.

Erikson argues that as individuals grow older, they tend to slow down their productivity—not as a result of an inability to produce, but as a gradual shift from an identity as a worker to that of a retired person—exploring a shift of priorities away from the economic and toward the existential and relational. It is during this time that individuals contemplate their accomplishments, measure the impact of their lives on others, and develop an inner sense of integrity, or wholeness, when they conclude that they have led a successful life. On the other hand, if the individual views his or her life negatively—as unproductive, unsatisfying, or unsuccessful—or feels guilt or remorse about past, increased age often leads to dissatisfaction, alienation, and despair, resulting in depression and hopelessness.

"Success" in the context of aging, Erikson contends, leads to wisdom— the "informed and detached concern with life itself, in the face of death itself."[8] Wisdom, in turn, enables an individual to look back on his or her life with a sense of closure and completeness, and accept death without fear. The mature adult develops and displays integrity: he or she trusts, is independent, and dares to venture into the new and unknown. Erikson elaborates by arguing that successfully aged individuals have found well-defined roles in society, and have developed self-concepts with which they are happy. They do not seek to recapture their youth, nor do they place themselves in competition with the young that surround them; they accept their position in the life course and do not equate the changes that accompany aging as "shortcomings." They can be intimate without strain, guilt, regret, or lack of realism, and are proud of what they have created—be that children, work, or hobbies. If one or more of the earlier psychosocial stages have not been resolved, Erikson warns that individuals may view themselves and their lives with disgust and despair—what Kierkegaard referred to as the sickness unto death.[9]

GRUMPY OLD MEN ON A QUEST

If not despair, then at least dissatisfaction, is the driving force behind the aging heartland characters in *The Straight Story*, *Get Low*, *Jayne Mansfield's Car*, and *Nebraska*. They are approaching the end of their days, ornery, obstinate, and burdened with unresolved issues. Before their time on earth has passed, they each seek—some subconsciously, but others in more self-aware fashion—to make peace with their lives and those around them, and come to terms with their places in the world. This is their quest, as understated as it might seem: to live out their days on their own terms.

The first of this small cluster of films, *The Straight Story*, also offers the closest tie to traditional heroic quest narratives, chronicling seventy-four-year-old Alvin Straight's (Richard Farnsworth) epic journey across Iowa and Wisconsin, riding a lawn mower. When the elderly World War II veteran learns that his estranged brother Lyle has had a stroke, he sets out, amidst doubt, ridicule, and protests from those around him, to make amends before his brother dies. His failing eyesight prevents him from driving, so Straight presses his old riding mower into service, and towing a small home-made travel trailer, sets off down the road. When his first attempt fails, he shoots the mower's gas tank (sending it to the hereafter in a ball of fire) uses his life savings to purchase a new "steed" (a refurbished John Deere), and begins his quest anew.

Based on the true story of Straight's real-life 1994 trek, the film spins a tale of the elderly man's adventures in the heartland. He makes camp under the stars, witnesses the wonders of a cycle race, faces near disaster when his brakes fail, and avails himself of the kindness of strangers along the way. Straight never wavers, however, in pursuit of his goal: reconciling with his sibling and making peace while there is still peace to be made. His senses of autonomy, agency, and accomplishment all rest on this task, and at its end, when he reaches Lyle's house and the two brothers—one supported by a walker, the other, by two canes—meet in silent kinship, his wholeness is restored.

Another aging character hinting at underpinnings in myth and legend is Felix Bush, the mysterious hermit at the narrative center of *Get Low*. Loosely based on the real-life 1930s story of Tennessean Felix Breazeale,[10] the film spins a tale of pain and alienation at the end of a lifetime of regret. Living deep in the woods, the cantankerous Bush (Robert Duvall) strikes fear into the hearts of local children, who dare each other to approach his house, and is the subject of rumor and speculation in the community. Is he a murderer? In league with the devil? Perhaps not, but the gruff loner certainly has his demons. Estranged from the community, and burdened by a painful secret of love and death from his past, Bush struggles with his troubled image as the end of his life approaches. The prospect of death, as one critic notes, "brings him back into the life of the community."[11] He uses his life savings to commission a "funeral party"— inviting the entire community to attend and tell their stories about him. When no one displays interest in attending, a lottery is established, with Bush's property as the prize. The entire community turns out, and at the urging of a local preacher, the dark secret that has haunted Bush is revealed in a public confessional. His burden lifted, Bush is reunited with those around him; relieved of his suffering, he is visited by the figure of his long-dead lost love, and dies.

The process of reconciliation—with the past, as well as the present—is even more fraught for Jim Caldwell (also played by Robert Duvall), the bitter elderly patriarch in *Jayne Mansfield's Car*. Caldwell's family, his home, and the rural southern landscape around him are all in decay. Surrounded by his offspring, he is neither physically nor socially alone, but is nonetheless emotionally isolated and brimming over with contempt since his wife divorced him for another man. Caldwell's pain and anger seep into every crevice of his life, and so, when the news of his ex-wife's death in England reaches him, it precipitates not only an emotional crisis, but a social crisis as well, as her new British family—headed by the man for whom she left him—arrives in Alabama to honor her dying wish to be returned to a final resting place in her American home. When the two elderly rivals meet for the first time, the antagonism and awkwardness between them is palpable. On the surface, they could not be more dissimilar in both background and demeanor, Caldwell's gruff, working-class bluntness standing in sharp opposition to Kingsley Bedford's (John Hurt) well-educated, understated British social grace. But as the pair gradually become acquainted, their generational commonalities—as frustrated patriarchs, World War II veterans, and aging men whom the world is quickly passing by—overshadow Caldwell's jealousy, resentment, and the sharp edges that often held those around him at bay. As he grows closer to Bedford, Caldwell reconciles with the past, makes peace with himself, and opens his heart to his children and what remains of his time on Earth.

This small group of films ends with another quest—or in this case, a fool's errand. Woody Grant (Bruce Dern) has received a letter informing him that he has been awarded a million-dollar sweepstakes prize. The letter, of course, is a marketing scam, but Grant, elderly and vulnerable, is convinced that he has finally struck it rich. Unable to drive any longer, but undaunted by the 900-mile journey from Billings, Montana, to Lincoln, Nebraska, he sets off down the road, on foot, to collect. Like a child caught running away from home, he is retrieved by his son David (Will Forte), who is frustrated by his parent's gullibility. After intercepting his father several times, David finally agrees to drive him to Lincoln, and the two begin a road trip that forces Grant to confront not only the fraudulent nature of his windfall, but the fragility of his status as a capable, self-determining man. Time and again, he attempts to reestablish his social value, only to meet with resistance, injury, misfortune, and humiliation. Still, he continues to push onward, until even he can no longer deny the futility of his quest. The "treasure" at the end of his journey represented his final remaining opportunity to validate his life in visible economic terms, and his value as a husband, father, and provider, and its loss leaves him in despair. That value is restored, however, when his son realizes the meaning of Grant's perseverance, and conceives a plan to make his father a "winner" in his own eyes, as well in the eyes of those around him.

REDEFINING AGING HEROISM

How, then, do we make sense of these struggling, bitter, alienated characters in the context of a volume focused on aging heroes? At first glance, they seem the antithesis of heroic, and little that happens during the course of the narratives in which they are featured alters that image. Even when they assert their own agency, there is little glory, adventure, or prowess involved; frequently, they fail miserably, reinforcing that, for these grumpy old men, those days have long since passed. In fact, they often echo that conclusion themselves. When asked about the worst part of being old, Alvin Straight responds: "remembering when you was young."

That, however, is because these characters are written into being in the same cultural context that created Ulysses, King Arthur, Allan Quatermain, Indiana Jones, and so many others—a culture that privileges youth, and lacks a strong model for the true aging hero that valorizes behaviors and characteristics appropriate to the final stage of the life course. Traditional mythic hero types present a constellation of qualities such as power, control, and confidence that, as Kimmel notes, "imply authority and mastery."[12] Joan Mellen describes these cinematic and literary heroes as "indomitable males":

> The stereotype of the self-controlled, invulnerable, stoical hero who justifies the image of unfeeling masculinity as a means of winning in a world that pounces on any sign of weakness. . . . Male heroes pontificate platitudes such as that invoked by an elderly John Wayne in *The Shootist*: "I won't be wronged, I won't be insulted, I won't be laid a hand on."[13]

As a result, we routinely expect our aging heroes to simply perform as older versions of youthful heroes—perhaps just a bit more limited due to the ravages of time—rather than reconceptualizing the "heroic" in terms that are true measures of heroism for *them*.

If we think back to Erikson's discussion of late adulthood, we find cues as to what those measures might be. The most highly valued qualities at this stage of life include the ability to successfully develop and maintain relationships, come to terms with the past, understand one's place in the world, and develop an inner sense of wholeness. In other words, to feel, when looking back at the end of life, a sense of satisfaction that one has come to terms with shortcomings and mistakes, reconciled wrongs and estrangements, and maintained a sense of integrity. These are the challenges and obstacles—sometimes harrowing—that must be overcome late in life in order to achieve success.

Each of the characters featured in the quiet, understated heartland stories discussed here struggles, throughout the films' narratives, with the attainment of these end-of-life goals. For them, there is no signpost indicating that expectations of them have changed as a result of their advanced age—that traditional understandings of masculine success have been replaced. Instead, these new goals have grown up alongside more familiar measures, creating a dynamic tension between the world of youth and the world of the aged, and leaving them foundering for appropriate ways of being in the world.[14]

For Alvin Straight and Woody Grant, this results in the undertaking of a physical "quest"—a journey that will yield satisfaction and reconciliation of their respective regrets. While their goals are, in fact, driven by their stage in life, the manner in which they each embark on these quests underscores the influence of the "monomyth" of the hero's journey and traditional conceptualizations of masculinity.[15] For each, the journey is a test—a task from which they cannot be dissuaded, and during which they feel diminished by the acceptance of help. They set off alone, unaided, only to falter and reluctantly accept assistance. Straight, a widower with a mentally challenged adult daughter, is used to his role as a self-reliant male and caretaker. He camps out and repays every favor he receives, rather than accept the subordinate role of "guest" and create social debt along the way, even insisting on paying for the use of a telephone when his mower breaks down. Grant, on the other hand, is long accustomed to a diminished masculine role. Chided by his wife and infantilized by his children, he desperately needs the winnings promised in his prize letter to reaffirm his ability to provide and re-establish himself in the hierarchy of his family and community. He is willing to accept his son's help in accomplishing the quest, because his sense of himself as a "failed man" is so pervasive from the outset.[16] In the end, only subterfuge on the part of his son satisfies the stereotypical masculine measure of success for Grant: After his son secretly purchases a secondhand truck and tells his defeated father that he managed to obtain it from the sweepstakes company that scammed him, the pair ride slowly through Grant's hometown, with the unlicensed Grant beaming at the wheel until they clear the town limits. It is a façade of success designed to repair the elder Grant's diminished image. The true success of the journey is the renewed connection between father and son.

For Felix Bush and Jim Caldwell, the quest to shed their resentments and regrets and finish out their days whole is more metaphorical. Both harbor pain from old loves torn away, and have turned the shards of their fragmented emotions outward toward the world around them. Bush has isolated himself ever since the day he was unable to prevent the tragic death of the (married) love of his life, after their affair is discovered. Shrouded in guilt and anger, he has lived through years of grief and bitterness, misunderstood and feared by those around him. His funeral party, attended by the entire town, ultimately takes the form of a grand rite of passage, as Bush achieves layers of transformation: from hermit to community member; from anger and remorse to forgiveness and release; and, ultimately, from life to death.

Caldwell, surrounded by family, is no less emotionally isolated. Ever since his divorce, he has existed in bitter silence, wallowing in self-pity and allowing his anger and intractability to drive a wedge between himself and his children. He is the epitome of Erikson's unsuccessful aging: fearful, aggressive, intolerant, and filled with a self-loathing that projects onto those around him. When forced to confront his nemesis—his ex-wife's second husband—Caldwell must also confront his inner demons. As the two patriarchs form a tentative relationship, the tension between the archetypal masculine pride and posturing of youth and the mature drive to attain closure and resolution is palpable. Caldwell comes to understand the ending of his marriage, and recognizes a degree of kinship with Bedford. An initial olive branch—venturing out together to view the car in which actress Jayne Mansfield was decapitated—leads the two to a camaraderie and mutual caretaking that earlier would not have seemed possible.

CONCLUSION

For each of these heartland characters, the ultimate "prize" at the end of their trials is peace. The events of their pasts have not allowed them "golden" years, but they each struggle to brighten the "twilight." Whether trekking across the country on a lawn mower or delivering a public confessional, confronting failing bodies or failed relationships, they are all undertaking journeys, overcoming daunting obstacles, wrestling with demons, and slaying dragons. The world around them simply fails to recognize their challenges as such, because our shared tradition of mythic heroes illustrates that heroic tests—even when moral or ethical—are manifested externally, and typically take spectacular form. If, following Erikson, however, successfully inhabiting the state of late adulthood means coming to terms with one's life—letting go of those things that are inconsequential or ephemeral, reflection and positive self-evaluation, resolving conflicts and restoring relationships, and understanding one's place in the world—then surmounting the obstacles to that, built up over a lifetime, may indeed be viewed as heroic.

Considered together, the tales of these four ornery old men shuffling and cursing their way toward the close of their lives illustrate that there is clearly more to aging than "remembering when you was young." There is work to be done—heroic work—in order to end one's days with a sense of satisfaction and completeness. Unlike the heroes of myth and legend, however, that work is often not public, colorful, nor destined to inspire epic songs. It is quiet, small, and sometimes desperate. Buried beneath the story of each of these elderly men's lives, just out of view, is another story of their struggle to come to terms with those lives, in their own ways, rather than those prescribed by mythic archetypes who were never asked to hand over their car keys.

NOTES

1. See, for example, Vladimir Propp, *Morphology of the Folktale* (Austin: University of Texas Press, 1968); Otto Rank, Lord Raglan, and Alan Dundes, *In Quest of the Hero* (Princeton, NJ: Princeton University Press, 1990).

2. Alfred Lord Tennyson, "Ulysses," 1842. http://www.poetryfoundation.org/poem/174659 (accessed November 2, 2014).

3. Ibid.

4. Ibid.

5. William Shakespeare, *As You Like It*, in *The Complete Pelican Shakespeare* (Baltimore: Penguin Books, 1969), II:vii: 157–163.

6. T. S. Eliot, "The Lovesong of J. Alfred Prufrock," in *T. S. Eliot: Collected Poems, 1909 – 1962*. San Diego, CA: Harcourt Brace Jovanovich, 1991), 6.

7. Gautama Buddha, SN 22.1, Nakulapita Sutta, in *The Connected Discourses of the Buddha*, ed. Bhikkhu Bodhi (Somerville, MA: Wisdom Publications, 2000), 855.

8. Erik Erikson and J. M. Erikson, *The Life Cycle Completed* (New York: Norton, 1982), 61.

9. Soren Kierkegaard, *The Sickness Unto Death* (Princeton, NJ: Princeton University Press, 1941).

10. In the 1930s, reports indicate that Breazeale threw himself a "funeral party" before his death, featuring storytelling, musical entertainment, and a raffle. A. O. Scott, "Movie Review: Get Low," *New York Times*, July 30, 2010, C14.

11. Ibid.

12. Michael S. Kimmel, *Changing Men: New Directions on Research on Men and Masculinity* (Newbury Park, CA: Sage 1987), 13.

13. Joan Mellen, *Big Bad Wolves: Masculinity in the American Film* (New York: Pantheon, 1977), 5.

14. Kimmel, *Changing Men*, 9.

15. Joseph Campbell, *The Hero with a Thousand Faces*, 3rd edition (Novato, CA: New World Library, 2008).

16. See Robert Bly's *Iron John: A Book about Men* (Boston: Da Capo Press, 2004).

Chapter Two

Golden Agers, Recluses, and John Wayne

Aging Stereotypes and Aging Heroes in Movie Westerns

Mei-Chen Lin and Paul Haridakis

How do we think of aging or older adults? How do our perceptions of aging affect our communication with them? How do these age stereotypes affect older adults? Social psychologists and communication scholars have devoted extensive research attention to understand relationships between age stereotypes, communicative behaviors, and their social consequences. In this chapter, our purpose is to provide a very brief overview of some of the social scientific research on age stereotypes and communication to help readers gain a general picture of this topic, at least in the U.S. context. Then, we move into the primary context of this book, popular culture, and review some empirical studies on how aging and/or aging characters are portrayed in the media. We conclude this chapter by discussing aging characters, specifically aging heroes, in a specific genre: movie Westerns.

BRIEF OVERVIEW OF RESEARCH ON AGE STEREOTYPES

Our perceptions of objects and people are organized hierarchically, with several subcategories subsumed under the general idea of that type of person or object. Take older adults as an example. When we think about older adults, we may have different types/categories of older people (grandparents, colleagues, professors, neighbors) in mind and different types of personality traits or traits we attribute to them (active, loving, wise, stubborn, vulnerable, depressed). These descriptions may not all be attributed to one older person in particular, but they may be attributes we use as a stereotype of *older people*, with different types of older adults associated with different traits. For example, we may have an aging grandparent whom we think is loving and kind. We may also have an aging neighbor whom we think is fragile and grouchy. Age stereotypes, thus, are part of our social knowledge, loosely grouped together in clusters of attributes that we draw on in a given context. Researchers, therefore, have conducted studies to investigate the stereotypes we have about aging, the ways in which they are organized in our knowledge structure, and our attitudes toward these stereotypes. [1]

Hummert and her colleagues extended previous research on age stereotypes and identified three positive age stereotypes and four negative age stereotypes. [2] Positive stereotypes were "golden ager" (traits such as active, independent, capable, happy, sociable), "perfect grandparents" (traits such as kind, loving, family-oriented, wise, trustworthy), and "John Wayne conservative" (traits such as patriotic, religious, nostalgic, proud). Negative stereotypes were "severely impaired" (traits such as slow thinking, incompetent, feeble, incoherent), "despondent" (traits such as depressed, sad, hopeless, afraid), "shrew/curmudgeon" (traits such as complaining, ill-tempered, prejudiced, demanding), and "recluse" (traits such as quiet, timid, naïve). These age stereotypes suggest that we do have multiple representations of aging, and that they range from extremely positive to extremely negative.

Even though people hold both positive and negative age stereotypes of old age, negative age stereotypes tend to have more influence than positive ones. Negative age stereotypes also have been found to be more accessible than positive age stereotypes, especially for young people, [3] and they are more prominent in people's minds. [4] In addition, Hummert suggests that young people tend to think of negative stereotypes more characteristic of older adults than positive stereotypes when the target of the stereotype is female and much older (seventy-five or over). [5] In other words, age stereotypes may begin to skew to the negative side with target age. For example, when we think of older adults in their sixties, we may be more likely to think of them as active and wise. These positive traits may be more likely to be replaced with negative ones such as senile and feeble when we think of older people in their eighties.

What are the consequences of stereotypes? Both positive and negative age stereotype traits have been studied in examinations of communicative and social consequences of intergenerational communication, confirming that negative age stereotypes usually lead to young people's age-adapted speech (e.g., patronizing talk). [6] This means that young people may use a speech style such as baby talk when speaking with older adults. Patronizing talk is oftentimes spotted in the hospital settings where endearment terms or directive instructions are used to older patients. Adopting this speech style can constrain older interactants' opportunities to engage in adult-like conversation, which in turn, reconfirms the existing negative age stereotypes.

The effects of age stereotypes can be strengthened or altered depending on the context. For example, when we see an older person sitting in a wheelchair in a hospital, we are more likely to engage in age-adapted talk (e.g., being overly nurturing or directive) versus when we see the same person in a community center doing volunteer work. Detrimental consequences for older people repeatedly exposed to these negative age-adapted conversation patterns include loss of self-esteem, poor performance in tasks, increased dependence, or decreased communication satisfaction with the interlocutor (e.g., physicians, younger people, and nursing home staff). Thus, the key issue is not the existence of both positive and negative age stereotypes; rather, it is the differing strength of their influence on people's expectations of how the conversation would unfold and how they respond in the encounter.

In short, it is nothing new to learn about the pervasiveness of age stereotypes in our culture and that it affects our attitudes toward and perceptions of aging. It is imperative, though, to take the research further to understand the ways in which these positive and negative stereotypes work together in different contexts to influence our behaviors toward older people and its long-term social consequences. Now, let's turn to one of these contexts, media portrayal of older people and aging, a source where our stereotypes of social groups are formed, reinforced, and activated.

MEDIA PORTRAYALS

Questions have consistently been raised about the extent to which media portrayals of older adults contribute to such age stereotypes and/or perceptions of the elderly, and the identity-related effects of these media portrayals.

One of the earlier large-scale research projects on the effects of media portrayals was the Payne Fund studies during 1929–1932.[7] Although not concerned with age stereotypes specifically, the project identified stereotypical traits of characters in movies, and examined the physical and physiological effects children displayed after watching feature films. The findings suggested that much of the content of these films affected children's sleep patterns, emotions, attitudes, and behaviors. Further, many of the characters in these movies, such as heroes and villains, were portrayed in stereotypical ways, and often in ways that made them bad role models.[8] Since then, media effects, including the portrayal of stereotyped characters, have remained a major scholarly interest and public concern.

An area of ongoing scrutiny by media effects researchers is how media portrayals (e.g., in television programs, newspapers, TV commercials, films) of a social group (i.e., demographic, ethnic, racial) influence perceptions of the group in real life—that is, how these media depictions are translated into viewers' knowledge of the group. This inquiry is important because media portrayals of members of a social group provide information (whether it reflects or creates social reality) about the social standing of this group,[9] and can affect the well-being of its members and intergroup communication and relations.[10]

So, in the following section, we will discuss media portrayals of one such group—older adults—by reviewing selected studies illustrating how the elderly have been portrayed in various media fare. In particular, three tentative research points are made here. First, aging characters are underrepresented, and are less likely to be cast in central roles. Second, older adults are portrayed both positively and negatively, with older women suffering ageism more often than older men. Third, the use of humor or positive attributes in these media portrayals may have unintended consequences.

UNDERREPRESENTATION OF ELDERLY AND AGING ADULTS

Older adults are underrepresented across media, when compared with census data. For instance, Gerbner and colleagues found this to be the case with prime-time television programming from 1969 through 1978.[11] In an analysis of prime-time TV programming published in 1995, Robinson and Skill found that less than 3 percent of the characters were sixty-five years old or older, and only 8.8 percent of them were cast in leading roles.[12] In magazine advertisements, only 8.9 percent of the characters were over age sixty, whereas that age group comprised over 16 percent of the population.[13] Tom Robinson and his team studied older characters in teen movies from 1980 through 2006, and found that aging characters were present in two-thirds of the movies; however, older females were underrepresented (39 percent in these movies versus 59 percent in the population) and portrayed less often than older males.[14] Disney may have done a better job in recent years by including slightly more older characters in their movies than before (i.e., from 2.0 older characters per film in the 1950s–1970s to 3.8 older characters per film in the 2000s).[15] However, such improvement is slower than the real increase in the aging population in the United States, and representation of older females was, again, much lower than the representation of older males.

In short, there are more aging characters in particular types of media fare in recent years. However, the overall pattern remains disappointing. Media have been very slow in recognizing the increase in older populations,[16] and when older characters are present, they tend to be placed in minor roles.[17]

What are the potential social consequences of these portrayals? One consequence is that the presence, or lack thereof, of a social group in the media—in this case older adults—denotes the vitality of that group in society.

When older people are peripherally featured in the media, viewers may easily discount their significance in the real world, and this effect may be more likely for viewers who have little contact with older people, such as children or younger adults.[18] Moreover, heavy viewers, those who consume a lot of media content, may gradually perceive the real world through the lens of the mediated one.[19] Therefore, at least among heavy viewers, perceptions of aging populations may be inaccurate.

Another potential social consequence is the identity threat to older adults themselves. People tend to select programs that feature members of their own group (age, race, gender, etc.) for identity gratification reasons.[20] Media consumption, therefore, provides support for individuals' social identity needs. That is, we look for and view media content that supports positive images of who we are as social groups. However, as people move into old age, it becomes more difficult for them to find programming or media content that are geared toward their age group. Older adults now may be able to turn to alternative or new communication technologies to help meet their identity needs. However, the mere fact that their "presence" in the mainstream media is not readily available creates a threat to the well-being of their age identity.

RANGES OF PORTRAYALS OF ELDERLY AND AGING ADULTS

A second research point is that aging characters are portrayed in the media both positively and negatively, and in a stereotypical manner, and aging female characters are more likely to be cast in a negative light than their male counterparts (less serious, less successful, less good, less attractive, less intelligent, lower socioeconomic status).[21] For instance, older characters in animated television programs were cast in positive roles such as worker/boss, teacher/instructor, or grandparents.[22] However, 13 percent of them were in negative roles such as villains. Positive or neutral portrayals were found in teen movies.[23] They were also found in advertisements.[24]

A positive portrayal of older adults in advertisements could be attributed to the nature of the central message of advertisement—to sell products. However, the implicit message of old age embedded in these ads could be troublesome. For example, during the presidential elections from 1960 through 2000, the inclusion of older adults in political ads has surged since 1996.[25] However, when older adults were present in the ads, the visual images of these older adults conveyed a sense of helplessness and in a situation where they had to depend on the government for assistance. Even though the overall tone of the ads was positive, use of these aging portrayals was for the purpose of political party campaign—Democrats used them as fear appeals to attack

Republican opponents, whereas the Republican camp used them to reassure the voters of a better future.

The increase of positive portrayals of older adults does not cancel the effects of negative portrayals. In many instances, they were described as angry, grumpy, or forgetful more often than other traits. When cast in positive or neutral roles, they were usually nonessential to the story plot, and therefore, produced little effect in changing audiences' negative perceptions of aging. Moreover, in media contexts such as advertisements (older adults shown as active, healthy, outgoing), the underlying messages usually suggests that aging is not something to look forward to ("anti-wrinkle" or "anti-aging" products; products to help with dementia or arthritis). Therefore, while we should be encouraged to see more positive illustrations of older adults in the media compared with those in the past, the pervasiveness of negative stereotypes and implicit messages embedded in those portrayals warrant continuing concerns.

Moreover, women tend to suffer a cultural ideology of beauty or attractiveness and are marginalized when older. When present in the media, they tend to be associated with negative stereotypes more often than are men.[26] When they are portrayed positively, it is usually corresponding with stereotypical traits associated with women (kind, warm, not ambitious, not career-oriented). Therefore, the message about aging, for women, is about conforming to the expectations of the cultural standard (nonthreatening, supportive of the family or spouse).

SOME UNINTENDED CONSEQUENCES OF HUMOROUS/ POSITIVE PORTRAYALS

The use of positive portrayals and humor in portrayals of older adults may have unintended consequences for older adults' sense of self or societal perceptions. For instance, when asked to evaluate portrayals of older adults in magazine advertisements, older participants were displeased with the images of older characters as "comic foils" when the ads targeted younger consumers, and as out of touch or objects of ridicule.[27] Therefore, advertisers should recognize the unintended consequences of commercials and be sensitive about aging stereotypes in advertising. While some humorous portrayals are obviously offensive, some portrayals that are overly positive are in fact rejected by older adults. For example, images of older people being happy and enjoying life, affluent and content, were perceived as unrealistic. Comical older characters, when viewed as "whimsical" or "playful," were also more likely to be criticized as undignified.[28]

A media context in which humor is often used in the portrayal of older adults is situational comedy. Shows such as *The Golden Girls, Everybody*

Loves Raymond, *Hot in Cleveland*, *Frasier*, and *King of Queens* have aging characters in major roles (which is good), and jokes targeting the characters' ages are central to the dynamics we see among the characters. For example, in the sitcom *Frasier*, when the punch line suggesting that the older character may be mildly cognitively impaired, study participants made overall negative judgments of that older character (e.g., cognitively impaired, complaining), despite the fact that the conversation prior to the punch line suggested that the character was an alert and competent older person.[29] The entertainment function of these older characters is to target their elderliness.[30] In essence, they are put on the shows to be laughed at.

Therefore, humor, when it is done at the expense of older adults' dignity, or by violating age stereotypes (e.g., being sexually active, or being physically strong, aggressive, or powerful), may be temporarily funny or may challenge the cultural frames of aging, but in fact reinforces existing age stereotypes—particularly the negative ones—in the long run.[31] Moreover, whether positive, humorous, or negative, older adults seem to have a set of images of what aging "should be," and deviation from that norm garners criticism from elderly viewers. As we discussed earlier, media portrayals provide members of a given social group with an understanding of their social standing and vitality. When older adults measure their reality against that in the fictional mediated world—a limited set of portrayals, even though seemingly optimistic and socially worthy—they may not be gratified because these portrayals do not fit what they believe aging should be.

Though valuable in identifying various age stereotypes and the effects of positive and negative age stereotypes, research to date has not really focused specifically on heroic depictions of older adults and the appeal of such depictions. The aging hero is a special "older adult" stereotype category that has seldom been explored in communication research. Therefore, we do not know all of the positive and negative effects of such portrayals, or the extent to which they correspond to portrayals of older adults identified in other media genres. However, certain media and media genres routinely present older heroic characters, and they are popular with audiences.

STEREOTYPICAL PORTRAYALS OF THE AGING HERO IN MOVIE WESTERNS

Hummert and her colleagues asserted that "stereotype schemas are loosely structured constellations of traits that perceivers recognize are variably true of individual members of a category" and that *older adult* is really "a superordinate category subsuming several subcategories or stereotypes of different types of older adults."[32] The media, of course, can present stereotypical portrayals that support, refute, and/or contribute to audience members' schemas. Here, we discuss how one of those arguably stereotypical "older adult" categories has been presented in one specific media genre: the aging hero in movie Westerns. The movie Western is a relevant genre on which to focus in exploring this topic, because in "many ways the idea of the Western is inextricably entwined with the concept of the hero. Early Westerns centered on a hero of impeccable moral fortitude, rugged masculinity, and superhuman abilities. While later Westerns muddied the waters of morality, the central Western figure remained somehow stronger, smarter, and faster than regular folk."[33] In addition, the American Western in the second half of the twentieth century, in particular, is a movie genre that has provided a place for the aging hero to appear, often as a central protagonist.

This movie genre is rife with examples of the aging hero. Generally, they are heroes because they possess the traits we expect and admire in a stereotypical hero—traits to which we also aspire (e.g., justice, honor). But, they are not superheroes. They are human heroes, stripped of some of their physical and/or emotional strength that comes from a lifetime of trials and tribulations. The aging hero may have previously missed his chance to accomplish something great. He may have lost his former glory. He may have lost some of his toughness. But, somehow he finds the strength to take on some noble task and, ultimately, succeed. Clearly, he has inadequacies. But the mere fact that the aging hero can transcend his human weaknesses, some of which we all have, makes him perhaps a hero with whom we can identify. We can relate to him as another human being, or even think of someone we have met in life reflecting those characteristics.

Given the limited space available, we will discuss some of the features of portrayals of aging heroes, citing representative Westerns. The examples referenced are not exhaustive; because the Western has so embraced the aging hero, it would be impossible to discuss them all in a single chapter. Thus the discussion is not intended to suggest that the portrayals discussed here represent the way these characters are always presented. However, the traits shared by aging heroes in these illustrative examples are common stereotypical traits these characters share across movies, and the settings in which the aging hero is situated represent common plot themes in many Westerns.

Representative Settings

The settings in which the aging hero is situated in the movie Western permit us to see him rise to the occasion, overcoming his flaws and meeting the expectations we have of heroes. He is a "mythic and not an historical figure."[34] The myth is believable, because the historical characters on which the myth is loosely based could be real U.S. Western characters. For example, he can be a cowboy (*The Cheyenne Social Club*, 1970); a sheriff (*High Noon*,

1952); a gunfighter who cannot escape his past reputation (*The Shootist*, 1976); a stranger helping a person (*True Grit*, 1969); family (*Will Penny*, 1968); or town (*High Noon*); and even an outlaw (*Ride the High Country*, 1962; *The Wild Bunch*, 1969). In each case the hero is somehow fighting for justice.

In some ways the setting itself is a stereotype. Two settings or plot schemes are exemplary: the aging gunfighter (both the outlaw and the lawman) who must have a shoot-out, and the aging hero caught between two worlds.[35] In the latter setting, the plot involves an older America giving way to a more modern one. The qualities of the past with which the aging hero is comfortable are either presented as something that has to be discarded, or as qualities so important that they should be adopted and incorporated in a newer modern America, and the aging hero serving as the bridge. He is a representative of all of us and an exemplar, really, of American national character. The aging hero is confronting the trials of the modern world (*Bronco Billy*, 1980; *Lonely Are the Brave*, 1962) armed with an older moral code. It is the aging hero who grapples with the change for us and helps us conclude whether the qualities on which this older moral code is based are outdated in a more modern society or something that should be embraced as a continuing social compact in a newer social order. The moral tale is the contemplation and ultimate decision about how we do or do not make room for the characteristics of the hero in this new social order.

Another classic plot theme in which conflict between law and order or old and new ways is played out is the gunfight. As Turner describes it, "The shoot-out also metaphorically addresses another central issue of the Western as a genre, that of the conflict between law and lawlessness. The gunfight establishes moral law and moral right. . . . Moral law, unfettered by effeminizing civilization, is ultimately the highest law in a Western. It is expressed through masculine violence in the shoot-out, a violence that becomes necessary when the rules of civilization are too rigid or ineffectual to solve the problem."[36]

In the case of the gunfight or shoot-out the aging hero is often outnumbered (*True Grit*; *The Cheyenne Social Club*; *High Noon*). He takes on these odds that seem insurmountable. Those he confronts generally are characters who have few if any redeeming social values, but the law or society has not brought them to justice. That task is left to the aging hero. Like most Western movie heroes, "Standing alone, he acts as a barrier between civilization and barbarism."[37] Regardless of tack taken, because the hero is acting on behalf of order and in defense of the civilized, the hero is presented in such a way that even "vigilante justice" is acceptable.[38]

Representative Traits

In these and similar settings, the aging hero must meet the expectations and exhibit traits that the stereotype demands and that we expect in heroes. The myth is part of our identification with the values with which these traits are linked. As West suggests, some Western heroes "cling to characteristics we admire."[39] These include, for example, wisdom, honor, bravery, mentoring, knowledge of oneself, regenerative abilities, rugged individualism, a commitment to freedom, a commitment to justice, and a commitment to a moral/ethical code. Even when the motivation is vengeance, it is framed in a characterization that makes even vengeance acceptable, if not necessary.

These values are often tested in the settings in which the stereotypical aging hero must confront the obstacles or task he assumes. We learn from and accept or modify his rugged individualism. Thus, the choice is not necessarily dichotomous. Often, his rugged individualism is necessary for the health of the society/community or specific person or group of people he protects. Without the aging hero the civilized and civilized society would not survive. For example, in *High Noon*, aging Marshal Will Kane (Gary Cooper) is retiring to go on his honeymoon with his new young wife. However, the main villain in the movie is arriving on the noon train to reconnect with his gang. Confronted with the realization that no one can or will stand up to the gang, Kane decides to face the gang alone in a climactic shoot-out. Of course the town does not deserve Kane, yet he saves it. Even when he goes to the church to try to get help, no one steps up; so much for an ordered society! It is vulnerable and tenuous. It is the hero's bravery and individualism that is necessary for its continuation.

However, if the aging hero is too individualistic, he must adjust or suffer dire consequences, sometimes even death. In this scenario, even if he exhibits traits we admire such as guile, wit, wisdom, bravery, honor, intelligence, and the like, he suffers or dies because he cannot conform and adapt his too-extreme individuality (*Lonely Are the Brave*) to new circumstances, or he chooses death rather than adapt to a more modern era (*The Wild Bunch*). In *Lonely Are the Brave*, for example, protagonist Jack Burns (Kirk Douglas), a drifting twentieth-century cowboy who returns to New Mexico after learning that an old friend has been jailed, cannot stay out of trouble because he cannot conform. In a world of cars and trucks, he still gets around on his trusted horse. He breaks out of jail, is chased by the sheriff, and ultimately dies alone on a highway after he and his horse are struck by a truck while running from a pursuing sheriff in a world where horses and motorized vehicles do not mix (similar to a scene in *The Shootist* in which the hero's horse is spooked by a horseless carriage). In *The Wild Bunch*, a group of aging outlaws ultimately choose to go out in a blaze of gunfire (and glory—

at least in their minds) rather than succumb to a world of order where they are no longer able to lead their outlaw way of life.

What these stories have in common is that regardless of the consequences of the aging hero's individualism, it is ultimately up to us, the viewers, to decide the proper balance between the values of individualism and those of an ordered society. As West asks, for example, "We claim to admire both individualism and order, but what if one conflicts with the other?"[40] The traits and values the aging Western hero exhibits help the viewers reach their conclusion.

Another trait the aging hero often exhibits is self-knowledge. The stereotypical aging hero knows himself.[41] He maintains his dignity by not deviating from who he is.[42] For the aging hero this often means living and dying on his own terms. In *The Shootist*, for example, the aged hero, J. B. Books (John Wayne in his final role), chooses to die in a gunfight he sets up rather than succumb to the ravages of cancer that will kill him in a way that he sees as ignoble. In *Ride the High Country*, the main character, Steve Judd (Joel McCrea), dies in front of a majestic mountain in the high country, content to know that he has achieved his last true goal: "To enter my Father's house Justified." In both of these examples, the aging hero exemplifies the ultimate goal of a life fulfilled.

Another illustrative trait of these aging heroes, even if they are loners, is that they understand (or come to understand) the value of relationships. Often these relationships are more important to the hero's quest than is the goal of the journey that he is on. Often this is a relationship with a traveling companion who is a younger person—a character that permits the hero to serve as a teacher and mentor (*The Shootist*; *The Searchers*, 1956). But it sometimes could be with a buddy of similar age (*The Cheyenne Social Club*), or an older person whom they help, such as a parent (*Junior Bonner*, 1972). Although the hero may be a loner, he needs another person, or a person to help, in order to do the heroic things he is called on to do.

In many instances the aging hero wrestles with exhibiting these values, ultimately coming to embrace them after an internal struggle over whether to do so. For example, Rooster Cogburn (John Wayne) in *True Grit* starts out searching for a killer for selfish reasons (the reward money the murdered man's daughter offers). However, during the course of the film he does the right thing. He helps the young girl find the outlaw who killed her father and serves justice. In the movie's final scene, after visiting her father's grave with her, he says to her, "Well, come see a fat old man sometime," and jumps his horse over a fence, rejuvenated, as he rides off.

This reformation is poignant in *Ride the High Country*. The movie starts with Gil Westrum (Randolph Scott) intending to rob his old buddy, Judd, of a gold shipment the latter is transporting for a mining camp—an intent that lasts through most of the movie. However, in the end, Gil ends up siding with

Judd during a shoot-out with a gang intending to steal the gold for themselves. When Judd is dying from wounds he sustains during the gunfight, Gil
promises his old friend to get the money back. In response to Gil's promise,
Judd says "Hell, I know that. I always did. You just forgot it for a while,
that's all."

These illustrative traits are part of a body of traits that are shared by those
we describe as heroes. These traits enable them to support important values
such as honor, justice, social relationships, and serving others, while retain-
ing valued individualism.

Problematic Presentations

The aging hero has been a popular figure in movie Westerns. While we have
relied on a small number of examples, the movies and characters referenced
are part of a larger body of movie Westerns in which the aging hero has been
showcased. In general, the heroes in these movies are guided by a moral
code. The traits and values they exhibit and the settings in which they exhibit
them are undergirded by a moral obligation they have to meet. Consequently,
the stereotypical portrayals of the aging Western hero are generally positive.
At the same time, these heroes display characteristics related to their age that
are somewhat consistent with the way aging characters are portrayed in other
media genres and reflective of stereotype schemas people often have of the
aged—some of which the research suggests may be less than positive. Thus,
prior research on stereotypes of older adults suggests that some aspects of the
aging hero stereotype may be problematic. First, aging heroes in Western
movies are almost exclusively men, supporting prior research that suggests
older women are underrepresented in the media.[43] Second, these films sometimes present a negative view of age. At times the aging hero is out of his
element—having incompatible views of modern society or life with others.
At times, age itself is not a strength, but an infirmity that he must overcome
to accomplish something heroic. The aging hero succeeds in spite of his age,
not because of it. Third, sometimes, the hero dies sacrificing himself to save
others—suggesting that it is okay for him, or maybe expected of him, to
make this sacrifice, because he is old. He has lived his life, and the lives of
those he saves are of greater value for the future. Although the sacrifice is
often voluntary—as the hero's last chance to be visible in a heroic fashion—
old age, once again, is marginalized.

Consistent with characteristics of what Hummert and her colleagues
called the John Wayne stereotype, the aging hero can be hardheaded to a
fault, particularly in movies in which he meets a tragic end.[44] In movies such
as *Lonely Are the Brave*, *Tom Horn* (1980), *The Wild Bunch*, and countless
others, the aging character could have or should have changed, but wouldn't.
In some ways, the message is that although there are good values attached to

older ways of life that the hero exemplifies, some of the old ways must go, and if you cling to them, you must go, too. Sometimes the way the aging heroes cling to notable values that we all support makes them heroic. However, their almost pathological clinging to the past renders them tragic heroes.

One of the more problematic aspects of the stereotypical portrayal is that the aging Western hero often winds up alone after the job is done. As the stereotype often requires of the loner, he rides off into the sunset (or walks off into the sunset, as in *The Searchers*). They often end up alone because they don't necessarily fit anywhere, like a marshal tied to his job (*True Grit*), an ex-lawman who wanders the West (*Ride the High Country*), an aging gunfighter who has no family or home (*The Shootist*), or an ex-soldier who never made it back home after the war (*The Searchers*). The viewer is sympathetic to that but also sad, because belonging is a basic human need, and older people in particular often end up alone. Although this is acceptable and perhaps even expected for the movie hero, who is necessarily different from common people, such a characterization could also be interpreted as one of the unavoidable traits of old age—a fate experienced by many older adults.

CONCLUSION

There may be positive and/or problematic consequences that emanate from the portrayals of the aging hero in movie Westerns. To reiterate, the aspects of the aging heroes in movie Westerns discussed here are not exhaustive. However, together, they do promote a stereotypical characterization of these popular movie characters. Because of the popularity of the aging hero in movie Westerns, the stereotype in this genre deserves greater attention in future research. What, for example, are the effects of portrayals of violence often perpetrated by these heroes, and how do we judge the valence of these violent acts? Certain theoretical frameworks, such as social cognition theory, suggest that media violence, when perpetrated by heroes and seen as justified (often a formula in movie Westerns), is more likely to be modeled or seen as acceptable.[45] At the same time, several traits exhibited by these aging heroes and referenced above (justice, honor, morality, integrity, individualism) are admirable, and we can identify with them. Identification with media characters and the traits they exhibit also can enhance effects of these portrayals. Thus, greater attention to such effects should be studied in future research.

In addition, age is often marginalized or treated as a negative characteristic of older adults. While the older hero's age in movie Westerns often is not an impediment in the stereotypical portrayal, at times it is portrayed as a weakness. The hero often is portrayed as overcoming his age. Future research therefore must assess, on balance, whether age generally is a positive or negative attribute of the aging hero, and the effects of both types of representations of age in this movie genre.

Similarly, research should also consider the extent to which women may be marginalized in these movies. Because virtually all of the aging heroes in movie Westerns are men, we should consider whether this popular movie genre, because of the dearth of female heroes, contributes to the marginalization of women that prior research suggests has occurred in other media portrayals, or whether these movies feature women in positive roles that detract from such marginalization.

In short, the aging hero stereotype in movie Westerns is somewhat unique and not easily classified into age categories identified in prior research on age stereotypes. He has traits that fall in several of the categories of older adult stereotypes identified in prior research. Accordingly, the popularity and effects of the portrayals may also be unique. As is the case with all heroes, it is not easy to generalize the effects of these fictional stereotypes to those of us in the general population of viewers. What is clear, however, is that they have been popular characters in movie Westerns over the years. In recent years the Western went through a period of relative unpopularity. The genre was featured in fewer movies and TV series than in past decades. Despite the relative paucity of Westerns, however, the few that were produced did not desert the aging hero. For example, 1990s Westerns such as *Unforgiven* and *Maverick* featured aging movie stars (Clint Eastwood and James Garner, respectively) in roles in which they played Western heroes similar to those they played thirty years earlier. Thus, the aging hero continues to be a featured character and a viable stereotype in movie Westerns today. Thus, studying the effects of these portrayals remains a viable subject of scrutiny.

NOTES

1. Marilynn B. Brewer, Valerie Dull, and Layton Lui, "Perceptions of the Elderly: Stereotypes as Prototypes," *Journal of Personality and Social Psychology* 41, no. 3 (1981): 656–70; Marilynn B. Brewer and Layton Lui, "Categorization of the Elderly by the Elderly: Effects of Perceiver's Category Membership," *Personality and Social Psychology* 10, no. 4 (December 1984): 585–95; Mary Lee Hummert, "Multiple Stereotypes of Elderly and Young Adults: A Comparison of Structure and Evaluations," *Psychology and Aging* 5 (1990): 182–93; Mary Lee Hummert, Teri A. Garstka, Jaye L. Shaner, and Sharon Strahm, "Stereotypes of the Elderly Held by Young, Middle-aged, and Elderly Adults," *Journal of Gerontology: Psychological Sciences* 49, no. 5 (1994): P240–49; Daniel F. Schmidt and Susan M. Boland, "Structure of Perceptions of Older Adults: Evidence for Multiple Stereotypes," *Psychology and Aging* 1, no. 3 (1986): 255–60.

2. Hummert, "Multiple Stereotypes;" Hummert et al., "Stereotypes of the Elderly."

3. Mary Lee Hummert, Teri A. Garstka, Ellen B. Ryan, and Jaye L. Bonnesen, "The Role of Age Stereotypes in Interpersonal Communication," in *Handbook of Communication and Aging Research*, edited by Jon F. Nussbaum and Justine Coupland (Mahwah, NJ: Erlbaum, 2004), 91–114, on 102.

4. Mary Lee Hummert, Teri A. Garstka, Laurie T. O'Brien, Anthony G. Greenwald, and Deborah S. Mellott, "Using the Implicit Association Test to Measure Age Differences in Implicit Social Cognition," *Psychology and Aging* 17, no. 3 (2002): 482–95.

5. Hummert, "Multiple Stereotypes," 190–92.

6. Jake Harwood and Angie Williams, "Expectations for Communication with Positive and Negative Subtypes of Older Adults," *International Journal of Aging and Human Development* 47, no. 1 (1998): 11–33; Mei-Chen Lin and Jake Harwood, "Accommodation Predictors of Grandparent-Grandchild Relational Solidarity in Taiwan," *Journal of Social and Personal Relationships* 22, no. 4 (2003): 537–63.

7. Everett M. Rogers, *A History of Communication Study: A Biographical Approach* (New York: The Free Press, 1994), 190–92.

8. Herbert Blumer, *Movies and Conduct* (New York: Macmillan, 1933).

9. Michelle Ortiz and Jake Harwood, "A Social Cognitive Theory Approach to the Effects of Mediated Intergroup Contact on Intergroup Attitudes," *Journal of Broadcasting and Electronic Media* 51, no. 4 (December 2007): 615–31, on 617–18.

10. Jake Harwood, "'Sharp!' Lurking Incoherence in a Television Portrayal of an Older Adult," *Journal of Language and Social Psychology* 19, no. 1 (March 2000): 110–40, on 133–35.

11. George Gerbner, Larry Gross, Nancy Signorielli, and Michael Morgan, "Aging with Television: Images on Television Drama and Concepts of Social Reality," *Journal of Communication* 30, no. 1 (Winter 1980): 37–47.

12. James D. Robinson and Thomas Skill, "The Invisible Generation: Portrayals of the Elderly on Prime-Time Television," *Communication Reports* 25, no. 1 (Summer 1995): 111–19, on 111.

13. Priya Raman, Jake Harwood, Deborah Weis, Judith Anderson, and Grace Miller, "Portrayals of Older Adults in U.S. and Indian Magazine Advertisements: A Cross-Cultural Comparison," *Howard Journal of Communications* 19, no. 3 (July–September 2008): 221–40, on 232.

14. Tom Robinson, Mark Callister, and Dawn Magoffin, "Older Characters in Teen Movies from 1980–2006," *Educational Gerontology*, 35 (2009): 687–711, on 694–95.

15. Tom Robinson, Mark Callister, Dawn Magoffin, and Jennifer Moore, "The Portrayal of Older Characters in Disney Animated Films," *Journal of Aging Studies* 21 (2007): 203–13, on 206.

16. Jake Harwood, *Understanding Communication and Aging* (Thousand Oaks, CA: Sage, 2007), 150–56.

17. Latika Vasil and Hannerlore Wass, "Portrayal of the Elderly in the Media: A Literature Review and Implications for Educational Gerontologists," *Educational Gerontology* 19, no. 1 (January 1993): 71–85.

18. Susan Fox and Howard Giles, "Accommodating Intergenerational Contact: A Critique and Theoretical Model," *Journal of Aging Studies* 7, no. 4 (1993): 423–51, on 436–39.

19. Michael Morgan, James Shanahan, and Nancy Signorielli, "Growing Up with Television: Cultivation Process," in *Media Effects: Advances in Theory and Research*, edited by Jennings Bryant and Mary Beth Oliver (New York: Routledge, 2002), 43–67.

20. Jake Harwood, "Age Identity and Television Viewing Preferences," *Communication Reports* 12, no. 2 (Summer 1999): 85–90, on 85–86.

21. Doris G. Bazzini, William D. McIntosh, Stephen M. Smith, Sabrina Cook, and Caleigh Harris, "The Aging Woman in Popular Film: Underrepresented, Unattractive, Unfriendly, and Unintelligent," *Sex Roles* 36, no. 7/8 (April 1997): 531–43; Gerbner et al., "Aging with Television"; Robinson and Skill, "The Invisible Generation"; Vasil and Wass, "Portrayal of the Elderly."

22. Tom Robinson and Caitlin Anderson, "Older Characters in Children's Animated Television Programs: A Content Analysis of Their Portrayal," *Journal of Broadcasting & Electronic Media* 50, no. 2 (June 2006): 287–304, on 294.

23. Tom Robinson et al., "Older Characters in Teen Movies."

24. Jake Harwood and Abhit Roy, "The Portrayal of Older Adults in Indian and U.S. Magazine Advertisements," *Howard Journal of Communications* 10, no. 4 (October–December

1999): 269–80; Darryl W. Miller, Teresita S. Leyell, and Juliann Mazachek, "Stereotypes of The Elderly in U.S. Television Commercials from the 1950s to the 1990s," *International Journal of Aging and Human Development* 58, no. 4 (2004): 315–40; Angie Williams, Paul Mark Wadleigh, and Virpi Ylänne, "Images of Older People in UK Magazine Advertising: Toward a Typology," *International Journal of Aging and Human Development* 71, no. 2 (2010): 83–114.

25. Lynda Lee Kaid and Jane Garner, "The Portrayal of Older Adults in Political Advertising," in *Handbook of Communication and Aging Research*, edited by Jon F. Nussbaum and Justine Coupland (Mahwah, NJ: Erlbaum, 2004), 407–22, on 411.

26. Nancy Signorielli, "Aging on Television: Messages Relating to Gender, Race, and Occupation in Prime-Time," *Journal of Broadcasting & Electronic Media* 48, no. 2 (June 2004): 279–301, on 292–93.

27. Tom Robinson, Mark Popovich, Robert Gustafson, and Cliff Fraser, "Older Adults' Perceptions of Offensive Senior Stereotypes in Magazine Advertisements: Results of a Q Method Analysis," *Educational Gerontology* 29, no. 6 (June 2003): 503–19, on 516.

28. Williams et al., "Images of Older," 513–14.

29. Harwood, "'Sharp!'" 131.

30. Jake Harwood and Howard Giles, "'Don't Make Me Laugh': Age Representations in a Humorous Context," *Discourse & Society* 3, no. 4 (October 1992): 403–36, on 420–26.

31. Harwood, *Understanding Communication and Aging*, 149–76.

32. Hummert et al., "Stereotypes of the Elderly," 240.

33. Matthew R. Turner, "Black Sheriffs and Villains in White Hats: The Image of the Hero in Western Parodies," *American, British, and Canadian Studies* 17 (December 2011): 48–66, on 48.

34. Ibid., 50.

35. Fred Erisman, "Clint Eastwood's Western Films and the Evolving Mythic Hero," *Hungarian Journal of English and American Studies* 6, no. 2 (Fall 2000): 129–43; Armando J. Prats, "Back from the Sunset: The Western, the Eastwood Hero, and *Unforgiven*," *Journal of Film and Video* 47, no. 1/3 (Spring–Fall 1995): 106–23.

36. Turner, "Black Sheriffs," 64.

37. Kelly Jensen, "'Back in My Day, Son': Dialogical Constructions of the Cowboy Code of Justice," *Journal of Popular Culture* 42, no. 1 (February 2009): 90–102, on 94.

38. Ibid., 92.

39. Elliott West, "Good Guys, Bad Guys: The Movie Western and the Popular Mind," *Film & History* 5, no. 4 (December 1975): 1–12, on 4.

40. Ibid.

41. Erisman, "Clint Eastwood's Western Films;" Richard McGhee, "John Wayne: Hero with a Thousand Faces," *Literature Film Quarterly* 16, no. 1 (1988): 10–20.

42. Jon Hendricks, "Learning to Act Old: Heroes, Villains or Old Fools," *Journal of Aging Studies* 6, no. 1 (1992): 1–11, on 7.

43. Tom Robinson et al., "Older Characters in Disney."

44. Hummert et al., "Stereotypes of the Elderly."

45. Albert Bandura, "Social Cognitive Theory of Mass Communication," in *Media Effects: Advances in Theory and Research*, edited by Jennings Bryant and Dolf Zillmann (Mahwah, NJ: Erlbaum, 2002), 121–53.

Chapter Three

AAADRRIAAN! I'll Be Baaaaaack!

Schwarzenegger and Stallone as Aging Action Heroes

Norma Jones

As the population of the United States ages, some portrayals of older Americans in popular culture are becoming more multidimensional. This provides an opportunity to explore aging, broadly, as older male and female actors are taking more leading roles in films and collaborating in ensemble movies. Movie stars, as Richard Dyer notes, are important because they "are embodiments of social categories in which people are placed and through which they have to make sense of their lives, and indeed through which we make our lives—categories of class, gender, ethnicity, religion, sexual orientation."[1] Within this framework, age could be considered a social category, and aging stars, with their vigorous performances in nontraditional roles, are redefining what it means to be old for a graying population of Americans and American moviegoers.

Recently, we are seeing that film roles played by aging stars are different from those in the past decades. By this I mean that we are not simply seeing more aging stars in traditional roles, including the wise sage, the eccentric but loving grandparent, the gruff military commanding officer, and the peculiar old man or old woman rattling around in a huge but rundown estate. Instead, and in addition to more of these traditional parts in films, we are also seeing aging stars take on some unexpected portrayals. Aging actors are taking on roles as vicious criminals (Paul Newman in *Road to Perdition*, 2002), steely business owners (Helen Mirren in *The Hundred-Foot Journey*, 2014), mutant masterminds (Patrick Stewart and Ian McKellen in the *X-Men* films, 2000–2014), zombie-apocalypse-preventing United Nations investigators (Brad Pitt in *World War Z*, 2013), and the subject of this essay: ass-kicking action heroes. However, unlike some aging actors (Clint Eastwood,

Tommy Lee Jones, Donald Sutherland, and James Garner *in Space Cowboys*, 2000; Bruce Willis, John Malkovich, Morgan Freeman, and Helen Mirren in the *RED* franchise; Al Pacino, Christopher Walken, and Alan Arkin in *Stand Up Guy,* 2012), whose on-screen roles are aging with them, two 1980s action stars, Arnold Schwarzenegger (1947–) and Sylvester Stallone (1946–), are remerging and, more importantly, being accepted by audiences in roles as action heroes again. In other words, Schwarzenegger and Stallone are back on screen playing the same type of action hero roles that made them famous thirty years earlier. In fact, in the early trailer for *Terminator Genisys* (2015), it is suggested that Schwarzenegger, as the gray-haired cyborg assassin, has traveled back in time to destroy a younger version of himself (and is still protecting Sarah Connor as the same Terminator). He is still as tough and still as strong. Based on the short trailer, the only difference is in appearance because he has a full head of gray hair (see Figure 3.1). This is especially important because off screen and in other movies, Schwarzenegger's hair is graying or almost completely dark.

As aging action stars, Schwarzenegger and Stallone are changing what it means to Americans to be old. With this in mind, I profile the two aging action stars and describe the four films (*The Expendables* franchise, 2010–2014; and *Escape Plan*, 2013) in which they appeared together. In these films we see the aging film stars portraying action heroes who are stronger and smarter, and thus defying some aging conventions. While these

Figure 3.1.   Gray haired but still the Terminator, Schwarzenegger is jumping out of a helicopter. Taken from the trailer for *Terminator: Genisys*, directed by Alan Taylor, 2015.

portrayals may have some negative influences on real aging, I conclude with why I feel that their on-screen portrayals also have positive considerations for off-screen aging.

Action Stars as Action Heroes in Action Films

Building on a history of silent films, Westerns, adventure films, and even noir, "action films were about men who were larger than life, who could do things ordinary men could not."[2] From the genre's roots, the leading stars in these films have been intertwined with the sense of American maleness and American identity.[3] In other words, the images on the silver screen reflected and influenced what it meant to be an American and a man in America. For example, in Westerns, John Wayne (1907–1979) and Gary Cooper (1901–1961) "personified a victorious, postwar America as strong and self-assured, as American audiences wanted to see themselves."[4] These laconic men-of-action roles persisted in the 1950s, but the stars who played them— Burt Lancaster (1913–1994) and Glenn Ford (1916–2006), for example— were joined by more emotionally complex film heroes such as Van Heflin (1910–1971) and William Holden (1918–1981). In the 1960s, Sean Connery took over the man-of-action mantle in his James Bond appearances, and in his roles he served as a counterpoint to the brooding, antiheroic loners portrayed by Clint Eastwood (1930–) and Steve McQueen (1930–1980).

The 1980s, and into the early 1990s, were the golden age of the Hollywood action films. During this decade, we saw the launch of the long-running *Rambo* (1982–2008, *Rambo: Last Blood* is scheduled for 2015), *Terminator* (1984–2009, *Terminator: Genisys* is scheduled for 2015), and *Conan* (1982–2011, *The Legend of Conan* is rumored for 2016) film franchises. While action heroes were also portrayed by conventional-looking actors such as Chuck Norris (1940–), Harrison Ford (1942–), Kurt Russell (1951–), Bruce Willis (1955–), and Mel Gibson (1956–), it was during this golden age that the action star, as the on-screen action hero, took one of his most recognizable forms: the large body-building mesomorph. The extremely large rippling and sinewy muscles of Schwarzenegger and Stallone, along with Dolph Lundgren (1957–) and Jean-Claude Van Damme (1960–), looked different from their lankier 1980s counterparts. The Terminator, Conan, and John Rambo used their brute strength to annihilate the bad guys whereas Henry "Indiana" Jones and John McClane used a more comedic approach (perhaps wisecracks that were visible manifestations of their use of intelligence) to being action heroes. Even though several stars shared the action hero mantle, Stallone and Schwarzenegger were especially dominant in this era. In fact, entertainment reporter Gabe Toro writes that, in retrospect, Stallone and Schwarzenegger "co-owned the eighties."[5]

HOLLYWOOD STARS AND AUDIENCES

When Hollywood's leading stars become unpopular at the box office, they can be replaced with newcomers extremely quickly. After this happens, many former stars fade into obscurity and languish in low-budget independent films or straight-to-video movies. Take for example, the Julliard-trained actor Val Kilmer (1959–). He played Iceman, chief antagonist to Tom Cruise's underdog hero, Maverick, in *Top Gun* (1986); became Jim Morrison in *the Doors* (1991); and even took a turn as the iconic Caped Crusader in *Batman Forever* (1995). Entertainment reporter Bob Calhoun writes, "There was a time when Val Kilmer was the Lizard King, and he could do anything. He could dance with dead Indians, take a leak in front of Billy Idol, and try to set Meg Ryan on fire while Oliver Stone could only look on in awe from the director's chair."[6] Now, Calhoun adds, "Kilmer is mired in purgatory of straight-to-DVD action flicks"[7] while his Batman replacements, George Clooney (1961–) and Christian Bale (1974–), still headline Hollywood blockbusters.

However, a new generation of younger actors has not replaced aging action film stars. Instead of fading away, *New York Post* entertainment columnist Reed Tucker states that "there is a precedent for veteran actors punching and kicking their way into old age, of course. . . . What's unusual is just how many aging action stars there are—and how few younger actors are waiting in the wings."[8] Tucker adds that these aging action heroes are making a resurgence partly because "movie-audience demographics are changing, with more older folks heading to the theater" and "the number of moviegoers ages 40 to 60+ who went to the theater once a month or more jumped from 10.5 million to 13.7 million."[9]

In fact, *Forbes* entertainment online contributor Scott Mendelson blames poor audience targeting as the reason that the third installment in the *Expendables* franchise did not do as well at the box office when compared to the previous two films.[10] Mendelson argues the decision to try and chase a wider audience by editing the film to meet the criteria of a PG-13 rating (the previous two *Expendables* films were rated R) hurt box office numbers more than the fact that the film was leaked and downloaded 2.2 million times, illegally, before its theater premiere. In an interview with CraveOnline, Stallone, the franchise's writer and star, admitted, "I believe it was a horrible miscalculation on everyone's part in trying to reach a wider audience."[11] In other words, the primary audiences for these aging action heroes are the graying audiences who watched them in the 1980s, and are responding to them now doing essentially the same kinds of roles in the same kinds of ways thirty years later. Perhaps these audiences are allowing and accepting Stallone and Schwarzenegger, and themselves, as older but also smarter, faster, stronger, and defying aging pigeonholes.

Thirty years after the golden age of the action film, Tucker writes, "The biggest names in action movies today are virtually identical to the 1980s."[12] Mendelson agrees and adds that Hollywood has not replaced the action stars of the 1980s.[13] He writes (in 2013), "67-year-old Stallone and 66-year-old Schwarzenegger, twenty years removed from their peak popularity, are still considered prime action hero material because no one ever stepped up to replace them."[14] So instead of fading into celluloid history, Stallone and Schwarzenegger have re-emerged as action stars and their action films are once again topping box offices. In fact, Tucker suggests that newcomers such as Taylor Lautner who are vying to take over the mantle of action heroes should "grab a juice box and take a hike."[15] With this in mind, I am interested in exploring some prevalent themes in Stallone and Schwarzenegger's recent action films because they are appearing together as two action stars who are working and (not) aging on screen. But first, let me provide some background about Stallone and Schwarzenegger.

ABOUT SYLVESTER STALLONE AND ARNOLD SCHWARZENEGGER

As two aging action stars, Stallone and Schwarzenegger both achieved the American dream and Hollywood stardom, but then each took different routes to reclaiming the action hero status. Sylvester Gardenzio Stallone was born on July 6, 1946, in New York City.[16] As a child, he spent time in foster care and struggled through school. He attended college in Miami. Later, he followed his passion for acting in New York and Hollywood. Stallone also worked odd jobs in and out of film to make ends meet. During this time, he also took an interest in script writing, and from there, the "prize fighter Rocky Balboa was born and given life in a script Stallone wrote in longhand. Several producers offered to buy the screenplay, wanting to cast a name star in the title role, which Stallone insisted on playing himself. Although his bank balance was barely $100, Stallone held fast."[17] Producers Irwin Winkler and Robert Chartoff finally gave Stallone the chance to star, and *Rocky* was released in 1976.[18] The film won three Academy Awards, including Best Picture, and catapulted Stallone to Hollywood stardom. With the release of *The Expendables* (2010), Stallone is "the only actor to open a number one film across five decades."[19]

A year younger than Stallone, Arnold Alois Schwarzenegger was born on July 30, 1947, in Thal, Austria.[20] In 1968, bodybuilding legend Joe Weider invited Schwarzenegger to the United States. From there, the young bodybuilder won five Mr. Universe and seven Mr. Olympia titles between 1968 and 1980.[21] In fact, he still holds the world record as the youngest person (23) to win a Mr. Universe title. In addition to his bodybuilding career,

Schwarzenegger also pursued a career in acting with early appearances in some films and television shows (*Hercules in New York*, 1969, and credited as Arnold Strong; *Happy Anniversary and Goodbye*, 1974; *Stay Hungry*, 1976; *The Streets of San Francisco*, 1977; the docudrama *Pumping Iron*, 1977; *Scavenger Hunt*, 1979; *The Jayne Mansfield Story*, 1980). His breakthrough came from his role in the Oliver Stone–penned adaption of *Conan the Barbarian* (1982). *Conan the Destroyer* (1984) quickly followed, as did his first appearance in perhaps his most recognized role, the title character in the *Terminator* film series.

In addition to being a bodybuilding champion, successful entrepreneur (he was a millionaire in his twenties, even before entering Hollywood), and action film star, Schwarzenegger also had a very active political career. Two years later after the release of *The Terminator* (1984), Schwarzenegger married Maria Shriver and, through that marriage. became part of one of the most politically influential families in the United States. Shriver is the daughter of Sargent Shriver and Eunice Kennedy Shriver. This also means that she is the niece of President John F. Kennedy as well as Senators Robert and Edward Kennedy. In 1990, Schwarzenegger received his first official government appointment, from President George H. W. Bush, as the chairman of the President's Council on Fitness, Sports, and Nutrition.[22]

As two actors that shared the film action hero throne, Stallone and Schwarzenegger also shared a few off-screen characteristics. Both had notable issues with their spoken lines. Stallone suffered partial facial paralysis at birth, and even after over four decades of living in the United States, Schwarzenegger maintains a heavy Austrian accent. Off screen, both men are characterized as achievers of the American Dream. Stallone came from a humble background, followed his passion for acting and writing, held strong against selling his *Rocky* script, and is now one of the most successful actor/writer/producers in Hollywood. Schwarzenegger started bodybuilding in the basement of his parents' Austrian home and then followed his passion to the United States to become a world-renowned bodybuilder, Hollywood movie star, and holder of both appointed and elected government positions.

AFTER THE GOLDEN AGE

Toward the end of the golden age of action films and into the twenty-first century, Stallone seemed to be destined for celluloid obscurity. He had a string of box office flops such as *Assassins* (1995), *Get Carter* (2000), *Driven* (2001), *Eye See You* (2002), *Avenging Angelo* (2002), and *Shade* (2003). He then engineered his comeback by aging with his iconic roles in *Rocky Balboa* (2006) and *Rambo* (2008). Meanwhile, Schwarzenegger was taking his turn in politics. After some lukewarm films (*The 6th Day* [2000] and

Collateral Damage [2002]) Schwarzenegger won the 2003 California recall election and became the governor of that state. He won re-election in 2006 and served as California's "Governator" until 2010. During his time as governor, Schwarzenegger's film appearances included real cameos (*Around the World in 80 Days* [2004] and *the Kid and I* [2005]) as well as a digital cameo in *Terminator Salvation* (2009).

Other golden-age era action stars took on-screen characters that aged with them (Ford and Russell), languished in low-budget indies and direct-to-video (Lundgren and Van Damme), or disappeared from films altogether (Norris). The different post–golden age career trajectories might have resulted from the previously mentioned trend in Hollywood, in which newcomers are quick to fill voids left open by stars underperforming at the box office. So, during this time, younger actors were being ushered in to try and take over the action hero mantle. For example, part of the *Mummy* franchise was split off as a vehicle for Dwayne "The Rock" Johnson in *The Scorpion King* (2002). Another wrestler, John Cena, was also given a shot at that top spot, with films such as *The Marine* (2006). However, these newcomers did not take the action hero mantles away from Stallone and Schwarzenegger. Instead, both men are reclaiming their action hero mantles because they are playing the same roles they did thirty years ago.

While Schwarzenegger and Stallone dominated many 1980s and early 1990s action films, they did not appear on screen together during this golden age.[23] As action stars, they were characterized by their rivalry and competitiveness. In a recent *Tonight Show* appearance, Stallone told Jimmy Fallon, "We were very competitive, yeah, I think hate is a good word. . . . I really respect this guy. I think he is brilliant, what he has done, what he has accomplished. He's had three different careers. But, I wanted to strangle him."[24] Their competitiveness played out on movie screens in the 1980s and into the 1990s. As Fallon asked Stallone, "You would do *Rambo*, and then he would do . . . " without missing a beat, Stallone jumped in and said, "*Commando*."[25] So, it could be argued that their competitiveness created, in part, the golden age of action films because the two constantly tried to outperform each other. In fact, Fallon characterized their past rivalry as similar to that of the Rolling Stones and the Beatles, because the two bands kept releasing better and better albums to try and top each other.[26] As such, fans and moviegoers could be characterized as ecstatic when Stallone and Schwarzenegger finally shared a screen.

ABOUT THE *EXPENDABLES* FRANCHISE AND *ESCAPE PLAN*

In the *Expendables* franchise, Barney Ross (Stallone) leads a team of elite mercenaries in dangerous international missions that include saving hostages from Somalian pirates, assassinating dangerous dictators, rescuing kidnapped billionaires, as well as retrieving weapons of mass destruction from terrorists and arms dealers.[27] In the first *Expendables*, Ross describes his team: "We are the shadows and the smoke in your eyes. We are the ghosts that hide in the night."[28] Across the three films, the Expendables mercenary team is made up of close-combat fighter and second-in-command Lee Christmas (Jason Statham, 1967–), martial artist Yin Yang (Jet Li, 1963–), dangerous but mentally unbalanced chemical engineer Gunner Jensen (Dolph Lundgren, 1957–), demolitions and grappling expert Toll Road (Randy Couture, 1963–), strongman and heavy weapons specialist Hale Caesar (Terry Crews, 1968–), young sniper Billy the Kid (Liam Hemsworth, 1990–), former soldier Galgo (Antonio Banderas, 1960–), the agile assassin Doc (Wesley Snipes, 1962–), and former Navy SEAL Smilee (Kellan Lutz, 1985–).

The Expendables fight against other mercenaries and archvillains such as James Monroe (Eric Roberts, 1956–), Jean Vilain (Jean-Claude Van Damme, 1960–), and Conrad Stonebanks (Mel Gibson, 1956–). The team takes assignments from government spies such as Church (Bruce Willis, 1955–) and Drummer (Harrison Ford, 1942–), and gets help from friendly mercenaries such as Trench (Schwarzenegger), Booker (Chuck Norris, 1940–), and Bonaparte (Kelsey Grammer, 1955–). When the first *Expendables* film was released in 2010, it marked the first time Stallone and Schwarzenegger appeared in a film together. Schwarzenegger was not credited in the film, but had bigger roles in subsequent *Expendables* movies.

In 2013, Schwarzenegger and Stallone headlined a film for the first time in *Escape Plan*. In the film, Ray Breslin (Stallone) is a structural security expert and a co-owner in B & C (Breslin & Clark) Security. His job is to help improve prison security by going undercover as a prisoner and then escaping from the correctional facilities. His business partner, Lester Clark (Vincent D'Onofrio, 1959–), describes Breslin to a warden: "Over the years, Ray has broken out of fourteen of these institutions. Some people have a talent to paint, some to sing. . . . Ray Breslin, he possesses a unique set of skills. He is able to break out of any prison designed by man."[29] In fact, Breslin's book, *Compromising Correctional Institution Security*, is described as "the gold standard in the field."[30] At B & C, Breslin is assisted by Abigail (Amy Ryan, 1968–) and Hush (Curtis "50 Cent" Jackson, 1975–).

A lawyer working for the Central Intelligence Agency (CIA), Jessica Meyer (Caitriona Balfe, 1979–) asks B & C to help test a prototype prison called the Tomb. The Tomb is built because, as Meyer describes, "The Agency is looking for alternate situations for incarcerating the sort of people who commit acts so despicable they're best . . . well, how can I put it . . . disappeared. We are currently testing a prototype to deal with people no government wants on their books."[31] At Clark's urging, Breslin, Abigail, and Hush grudgingly take the assignment. After he is taken to the prototype prison, he meets Warden Willard Hobbs (Jim Caviezel, 1968–) and his lead guard, Drake (Vinnie Jones, 1956–). Breslin soon realizes that Hobbs knows his true identity and has built the prison based on his book, *Compromising Correctional Institution Security*. To stay out of solitary confinement, Breslin strikes a deal with Hobbs. He is to get information concerning the where-abouts of international financier Victor Manheim from fellow inmate Emil Rottmayer. However, instead of helping Hobbs find Manheim, Breslin works with Rottmayer to outwit the younger warden and, together, they break out of the Tomb.

AGING ACTION STARS IN THE *EXPENDABLES* FRANCHISE AND *ESCAPE PLAN*

As the two aging action stars have remerged as on-screen action heroes, they are changing what it means to be an older American. They are showing Americans that they can be physically stronger and mentally smarter.

Physically Stronger

In both the *Expendables* series and *Escape Plan*, the characters that Stallone and Schwarzenegger portray are physically stronger when compared to many of the younger men around them. In all three of the *Expendables* films, Stallone is at least a decade older than the actors playing his mercenary teammates. Lundgren is closest in age to Stallone (eleven years younger), and Hemsworth is the youngest (forty-four years younger). However, despite these two-digit age differences, the aging action star portrays a man who not only keeps up with his teammates, but also leads the team. Also in the first *Expendables*, Ross fights in a field, with Christmas alongside, against much younger soldiers. In this scene, he shoots five soldiers (two of the shots fired while he was upside down), throws a knife into another soldier, and is physi-cally strong enough to break the remaining soldier's neck. Also, Stallone is the only fighter strong enough to fight, and ultimately kill, the archvillain in the climactic scenes of the second and third films of the franchise. The younger teammates do not play roles in these final fights. In other words, he is the strongest fighter in the mercenary group despite his greater age.

Next, as part of planning their escape from the Tomb, Rottmayer starts a fight with fellow inmate Javed (Faran Tahir, 1963–). Schwarzenegger is sixteen years older than Tahir, but in his role as Rottmayer, the older prisoner is portrayed as successfully pinning down the younger one while also fight-ing a second inmate closer to Javed's age. So, Schwarzenegger, in his late sixties, is portrayed as physically stronger as his character is fighting and besting two men barely in their fifties. Also, during a staged prison brawl, Rottmayer and Breslin dodge machine gun fire and tear gas grenades, easily overpower numerous inmates as well as armed and armored prison guards, and then climb up several stories worth of steel trusses. As men in their late sixties, they are portrayed as just as fit, nimble, strong, and fast as they were in their thirties.

Finally, before Breslin can escape the Tomb, he has to fight the lead prison guard, Drake. As actors, Stallone (sixty-seven at the time of film's release) is almost twenty years older than Jones (forty-eight). However, in the film, the two fight almost as equals. Breslin easily breaks out of two chokeholds, trades several hard punches with Drake, and ultimately kills the guard by overpowering him and then shoving him down a flight of stairs. In the film, being almost seventy is not a limitation in an all-out physical brawl. Their advanced ages are not physical handicaps. Instead, as actors, Stallone and Schwarzenegger portray, in these films, characters who are physically stronger than their younger counterparts. By doing so, they are breaking conventions and changing assumptions associated with aging. However, they do not stop at the physical level because they also play roles in which they are mentally superior to younger characters.

Smarter

The characters that Schwarzenegger and Stallone portray are smarter, in many cases, when compared to their younger counterparts. In an exchange between Breslin and Rottmayer, we see Breslin's intellect at work while formulating the pair's escape from the Tomb:

Rottmayer: Let's say you're right. How do we cut metal?

Breslin: We don't cut, we don't cut at all. This place is subterranean. There's moisture in the air. Whoever built this place should have used aluminum rivets to hold those panels down, but they used steel. Steel rusts over time. We apply that, we'll concentrate the heat to those rivets and they'll expand and snap right the f*ck off.

Rottmayer: Concentrated heat?

Breslin: Yeah, from the piece of metal you gave me. You expose a tooth-paste-polished piece of metal to sunlight.

Rottmayer: Or the lamps in the box [isolation area cells that punish the prisoners by caging them in a small wire box, and then shining an extremely bright and hot light on them].

Breslin: Right, at a hundred degrees centigrade, steel expands .03 cubic centimeters and those rivets are gonna come right off . . .

Rottmayer [stares and laughs at Breslin]: You don't look that smart.[32]

So, Stallone, as Breslin, is portrayed as being much smarter than the builders of the Tomb despite the fact that they used his book (and in effect, his blueprints) to build the prototype prison. In a more specific comparison, Breslin is much cleverer than the much-younger Hush. Hush is supposed to be brilliant, and in the film, he is described as a freakishly gifted techno-thug. Towards the beginning of the film Breslin walks into the B & C office, and we see that he has been testing Hush, long term:

Breslin [walks into Hush's office and asks]: What do you got for me?

Hush [shows Breslin an intricate 3D puzzle on his computer screen]: Check it out.

Breslin: That's good. Very smart. Did you do this all by yourself? I'm impressed. Genius.

[Hush smiles in response to Breslin's praise, but the older man clicks on a few buttons and easily solves the puzzle]

Breslin: You're smart, but . . . sorry, not smart enough.

[Hush shakes his head in disbelief]

Breslin [encouraging]: Don't be bitter.

So, in this scene, we see that Hush has been and is continuing to try and impress his intellectual superior, the older Breslin. This theme of being older and smarter is also echoed throughout the prison break in *Escape Plan* as Breslin and Rottmayer outsmart the younger Hobbs despite the warden's overwhelming advantage (armed guards and state-of-the-art prison surveillance technology). Also, Rottmayer fooled both Breslin and Hobbs, as he was actually Mannheim. He manipulates the entire situation from inside the Tomb to help Breslin escape.

In the *Expendables* series, Stallone is the strategist of his mercenary team. He plans their attacks, and in doing so, he outsmarts Somalian pirates, Nepalese militant kidnappers, as well as Denzali prison guards and armored prison transport. So, instead of old age being a mental handicap, the two action heroes are portrayed as smarter than much-younger men. In fact old age is not at all detrimental; as older men, they are smarter *and* stronger than younger ones. In other words, they are defying aging.

DEFYING AGING

In the four films, the characters played by Stallone and Schwarzenegger seemingly defy their aging process. This is exemplified primarily in on-screen fighting sequences that are virtually identical to those that could have taken place thirty years earlier. For example, shortly after Breslin and Rottmayer meet in *Escape Plan*, they stage a fight that so that the security expert can scope out different areas of the Tomb. As they trade punches and jabs, Rottmayer sucker punches Breslin in the face, and Breslin falls to the ground. He gets up and delivers a roundhouse to Rottmayer's jaw. Rottmayer laughs off the punch and tells Breslin: "You hit like a vegetarian."

Breslin: Do I?

Rottmayer [shoves Breslin]: You can do better than that. Come on. Let's see it.

Breslin [delivering a second roundhouse punch to Rottmayer's stomach]: Try this.

Breslin [following up with a hook to Rottmayer's face before he can recover]: Hurt?

Rottmayer [winded]: That was good.

Breslin [throwing another left hook]: Look what's coming!

Rottmayer responds with a series of uppercuts and then physically picks up Breslin and throws him in a delayed vertical suplex. In other words, this screen fight shows a man in his late sixties easily picking up another man, weighing roughly 180 pounds, then throwing him overhead (see Figure 3.2), and the two land on their backs without any serious injuries.[33] This throw is difficult and even harder when factoring in age. While this physical feat is possible at his age, my point is that this fighting move is very similar to, if not exactly the same as, other fight scenes from action films thirty years earlier. So, their on-screen fighting abilities have changed and aged with them.

The fights between Ross and the archvillains in the second and third installments of *The Expendables* could also have been lifted from 1980s action films. For example, in *Expendables 2*, Ross and Vilain (Van Damme) trade punches, kicks, slams, and throws like they might have in the 1980s.[34] We also see this same type of sequence in the third *Expendables*, as Ross fights Stonebanks in the film's climax. As aging action stars, Stallone and

Figure 3.2. Rottmayer (Schwarzenegger) throws Breslin (Stallone) in a standing vertical suplex. Taken from *Escape Plan*, directed by Mikael Håfström, 2013.

Schwarzenegger portray characters who defy their age because they are playing roles that are the same as the ones they played thirty years ago.

ON-SCREEN ACTION HEROES AND REAL OFF-SCREEN AGING

While changing the understandings and perceptions of aging, the on-screen portrayals offered by Stallone and Schwarzenegger may suggest both positive and negative considerations. First, the portrayals are beyond unrealistic. As mentioned above, the actors are not fighting like typical men in their late sixties. Instead, they are rehashing the same fight sequences from when they were much younger. These unrealistic sequences are possible through the help of much-younger stuntmen. For example, in *Escape Plan* and the *Expendables* films, multiple stunt doubles are listed for Stallone. Also, one of his stunt doubles was born in 1976.[35] This means that to achieve some of his age-defying on-screen moves, Stallone had to use a stunt double who is thirty years younger and was born the same year *Rocky* was released. This is especially problematic if aging Americans measure their own physical prowess by comparing themselves to Stallone.

Additionally, as aging stars, Schwarzenegger and Stallone have to film differently than they did in the 1980s. In Tucker's article on on-screen aging action heroes, Schwarzenegger notes that the aging actors received daily cortisone shots because, as Stallone adds, their bodies are like machines so, the parts wear out.[36] Despite that reality, both stars look incredibly fit in their late sixties. In fact, three decades later, Stallone appears to be larger and more muscular than he was as the younger John Rambo and Rocky Balboa. But, as trainer Harley Pasternak points out, hormone and testosterone levels drop in aging bodies, so, "I doubt that a lot of these men would look the way they do without a pharmaceutical assist."[37] One such assist is human growth hormones (HGH).

Elizabeth Weise, in *USA Today*, reports that Stallone "has stated publicly that he took human growth hormone and testosterone, substances that supposedly promote a lean, muscular body."[38] However, the hormone is dangerous because while it may help the aging actors appear younger externally, HGH may also be extremely harmful internally. WebMD lists possible side effects of HGH as including an "increased risk of diabetes" and contributing to "the growth of cancerous tumors."[39] Weise adds that researchers have established that HGH "can cause or worsen diabetes, arthritis, heart disease and possibly cancer."[40] So, by turning to HGH, some action stars such as Stallone could actually be harming themselves over the long term in an effort to maintain a younger outward appearance. This suggests dangerous pharmaceutical measures for older Americans that try to defy aging. So, instead of healthy aging, these portrayals might be harmful by setting unrealistic and unattainable expectations by means of dangerous pseudo-medical options. However, I also feel that despite these negative considerations, the two aging action stars and the roles they are playing may also have some positives with respect to real aging.

In *Escape Plan*, Hobbs taunts Breslin and Rottmayer with what might be considered a reflection of the real power that younger individuals have over aging ones in our society. Hobbs tells the older men, "You can play your games all day, Mr. Breslin, but I'm still in control. Whatever you do, I have the power. I own your ass."[41] By defeating Hobbs, the older prisoners disrupt that ageist power dynamic. Off screen, this type of portrayal might be useful in dispelling some of the negative perceptions of real aging. Also, as both action stars play roles that portray older men as smarter and stronger than younger ones, Stallone and Schwarzenegger might also be, as Richard Dyer claims, challenging some norms and ideologies surrounding aging.[42] In other words, instead of succumbing to ageist power exerted by the young, they are fighting and defeating that power that attempts to constrain them. Thus, the two aging action stars might be creating a space in popular culture that allows some negative norms associated with aging to not only be disrupted but also challenged, and perhaps even defeated.

Most importantly, these films and portrayals may also encourage discussion of healthy real-world aging that might be helpful in removing some of the social limitations of old age, which could constrain these men from continuing to do what they do best. For example, outside of the films, Van

Damme explains, "You have to keep on going. It's what we have inside of us."[43] In other words, instead of being forced to take on drastically inferior roles (as stereotyped aging characters or in extremely low-budget indies and direct-to-video productions) or even stop their careers altogether, these older stars might be allowed to continue making movies. As such, I feel that the best expression of this constraint is in the third *Expendables* installment. In the film, Ross is recruiting young and hungry fighters (such as Smilee, as portrayed by the twenty-nine-year-old Lutz) for his new mercenary team. During his scouting trip with Bonaparte, a former soldier, Galgo (played by fifty-four-year-old Banderas), lies about his age for a chance to fight with Ross:

Bonaparte: Galgo! You sent me another fake resume?

Galgo: Eh, Mr. Ross, I can do what you need, whatever you need. I am healthier than I look, stronger than I look, faster than I look. Actually, faster than anybody I know.

Bonaparte [looking at the fake resume, questions Galgo]: You were born in 1984?

Galgo: Of course not! But, I feel like I was born in '84.[44]

Ross and Bonaparte try to leave, but Galgo begs: "Mr. Ross, Mr. Ross. Please. You see, it's like I have discovered the Fountain of Youth. . . . Mr. Ross, age is just a state of mind. You know, you're only old when you surrender. When you give up, and I haven't." And as Ross and Bonaparte walk away, Galgo yells: "I need a job! All I know what to do is killing people! And I do that very well!"[45]

In conclusion, I hope that despite some very real negative consequences associated with their on-screen heroic portrayals, Schwarzenegger and Stallone, as aging heroes and action stars, are challenging and dispelling what it means to be an older American. By changing the meaning of aging on screen, the two once-and-current action stars could very well be encouraging healthy and empowered off-screen aging.

NOTES

    1. Richard Dyer, *Heavenly Bodies: Film Stars and Society*, 2nd ed. (New York: Routledge, 2004), 16.
    2. Barna William Donovan, *Blood, Guns, and Testosterone: Action Films, Audiences, and a Thirst for Violence* (Lanham, MD: Scarecrow, 2010), x.
    3. Ibid.; Tim Edensor, *National Identity, Popular Culture and Everyday Life* (New York: Berg, 2002), 139.
    4. Donovan, *Blood, Guns, and Testosterone*, xi.

5. Gabe Toro, "Sylvester Stallone Blames His Movie Bombs on Arnold Schwarzenegger," CinemaBlend, August 15, 2014, http://www.cinemablend.com/new/Sylvester-Stallone-Blames-His-Movie-Bombs-Arnold-Schwarzenegger-66790.html (accessed October 1, 2014). Authors (including Donovan's *Blood, Guns, and Testosterone*; Mark Gallagher's *Action Figures: Men, Action Films, and Contemporary Adventure Narratives*; and Yvonne Tasker's *Spectacular Bodies: Gender, Genre and the Action Cinema*) have focused on the other aspects of action heroes and action, including conceptions of the male body, masculinity, violence, and spectacle. I am bracketing them for the purposes of this chapter.

6. Bob Calhoun, "Val Kilmer's Dramatic Decline," *Salon*, April 30, 2011, http://www.salon.com/2011/04/30/blood_out_review/ (accessed October 1, 2014).

7. Ibid.

8. Reed Tucker, "Hollywood Loves Its Aging Acting Heroes," *New York Post*, February 16, 2014. http://nypost.com/2014/02/16/ready-aim-retired/ (accessed March 10, 2015).

9. Ibid.

10. Scott Mendelson, "PG-13, Not Piracy, Killed 'Expendables 3,'" *Forbes*, August 18, 2014, http://www.forbes.com/sites/scottmendelson/2014/08/18/pg-13-not-piracy-killed-expendables-3/ (accessed October 1, 2014).

11. Fred Topel, "Interview: Sylvester Stallone Promises R-Rated 'Expendables 4,'" Crave-Online, November 23, 2014, http://www.craveonline.com/film/interviews/792031-interview-sylvester-stallone-promises-r-rated-expendables-4 (accessed November 25, 2014).

12. Tucker, "Hollywood Loves Its Aging Action Heroes."

13. Scott Mendelson, "Why Schwarzenegger, Stallone Aren't Movie Stars Anymore," *Forbes*, October 22, 2013, http://www.forbes.com/sites/scottmendelson/2013/10/22/why-schwarzenegger-stallone-arent-movie-stars-anymore/ (accessed October 1, 2014).

14. Ibid.

15. Ibid.

16. "Sylvester Stallone," Bio, http://www.biography.com/people/sylvester-stallone-9491745#synopsis (accessed October 1, 2014).

17. "Bio," SylvesterStallone.com, http://www.sylvesterstallone.com/bio/ (accessed October 1, 2014).

18. I did not include the *Rocky* franchise as part of the action film genre because they are considered to be boxing or sport movies, and the first two movies predate the 1980s.

19. "Bio," SylvesterStallone.com.

20. "Bio," Schwarzenegger.com, http://www.schwarzenegger.com/bio (accessed October 1, 2014).

21. Ibid.

22. Ibid.

23. However, they took a few shots at each other in films such as *Twins* (1988), *Tango & Cash* (1989), *Last Action Hero* (1993), *Demolition Man* (1993), and *True Lies* (1994).

24. *The Tonight Show with Jimmy Fallon*, "Sylvester Stallone," season 1, episode 108, Television series, National Broadcasting Company (NBC), August 14, 2014.

25. Ibid. Both movies were released in 1985.

26. Ibid.

27. *The Expendables*, directed by Sylvester Stallone (2010; Santa Monica, CA: Summit Entertainment, 2010), DVD; *The Expendables 2*, directed by Simon West (2012; Santa Monica, CA: Summit Entertainment, 2012), DVD; and *The Expendables 3*, directed by Patrick Hill (2014; Santa Monica, CA: Summit Entertainment, 2014), DVD.

28. *The Expendables*.

29. *Escape Plan*, directed by Mikael Håfström (2013; Universal City, CA: Summit Entertainment, 2014), DVD.

30. Ibid.

31. Ibid.

32. Ibid.

33. On his website, Stallone notes that he weighed about 175 pounds for earlier films, so his actual weight is a rough estimate on my part.

34. In the part of Vilain, Van Damme even throws in the signature flying 360-degree spinning split hook kick that was first popularized in *Bloodsport* (1988).

35. Stanimir Stamatov was credited as Stallone's stunt double in *The Expendables* and *The Expendables 2*. According to his page on the Stunt Factory site (http://stuntfactory.eu/stany), Stamatov was born in 1976.

36. Tucker, "Hollywood Loves Its Aging Acting Heroes."

37. Ibid.

38. Elizabeth Weise, "Stallone Puts Muscle behind HGH; Raises Alarms," *USAToday*, February 6, 2008, http://usatoday30.usatoday.com/news/health/2008-02-05-human-growth-hormone_N.htm (accessed October 1, 2014).

39. "Human Growth Hormone (HGH)," WebMD, http://www.webmd.com/fitness-exercise/human-growth-hormone-hgh?page=2 (accessed October 1, 2014).

40. Weise, "Stallone Puts Muscle."

41. *Escape Plan.*

42. Richard Dyer, *Stars* (London: British Film Institute, 2004).

43. Tucker, "Hollywood Loves Its Aging Action Heroes."

44. *The Expendables 3.*

45. Ibid.

Chapter Four

Under the Wide and Starry Sky

Hollywood and Aging Astronauts, 1996–2000

A. Bowdoin Van Riper

Robert Heinlein's science fiction story "Requiem" (1940) begins with the epitaph that Robert Louis Stevenson composed for his tombstone, erected on a hilltop in Samoa:

> Under the wide and starry sky
> Dig the grave and let me lie
> Glad did I live and gladly die
> And I laid me down with a will!

Those lines, the story declares, "appear in another place—scrawled on a shipping tag torn from a compressed-air container, and pinned to the ground with a knife."[1] The "other place" is the surface of the Moon, where D. D. Harriman—the elderly hero of the story—has paid two down-on-their-luck rocket pilots to bring him, even though he knows that the rigors of the flight may well kill him. Harriman, a swashbuckling capitalist in the tradition of Rockefeller and Carnegie,[2] financed the first lunar landing and inaugurated the colonization of the solar system, only to be barred—on medical and legal grounds—from going to the Moon himself. Unwilling to bring his people to that Promised Land without setting foot there himself, he liquidates his private fortune and begins plotting the last great adventure of his life.

Harriman's advanced years made him a relative rarity among fictional space travelers of the "Golden Age" of science fiction. The exploration of space—even when authors hand-waved its physical rigors away with references to quasi-magical technologies—remained a young person's game. Older men might send the vigorous young heroes out into the void (like the Port Admiral in E. E. Smith's *Galactic Patrol*), or even ride along as a passenger

49

on someone else's adventure (like Doctor Zarkov in the *Flash Gordon* serials of the 1930s, or Professor Newton in the 1950s television series *Rocky Jones, Space Ranger*), but they were rarely the explorer, and never the hero of the story. Once real-world astronauts began to enter the public's consciousness in the late 1950s, aging astronauts became even scarcer in print science fiction, and virtually disappeared from film and television screens. They remained in eclipse for nearly forty years until, on the brink of the millennium, they reappeared in force.

Five of the six space travel blockbusters produced in Hollywood at the turn of the millennium feature aging, or even elderly, space travelers played by A-list Hollywood actors, such as Clint Eastwood, or established European stars, like Terence Stamp. Two of them—the eccentric billionaire in *Contact* (1997) and the flight director in *Mission to Mars* (2000)—"merely" live and work aboard space stations, functioning in low Earth orbit as they might have in London or Houston. The others, however, board spacecraft alongside much younger men and women and—in *Deep Impact* (1998), *Red Planet* (2000), and *Space Cowboys* (2000)—venture into the unknown, redefining Hollywood's image of aging astronauts along the way.

The aging astronauts in these turn-of-the-millennium films are not (like their pre-1960 counterparts) distant authority figures or passenger-advisors who watch the action from the sidelines. They are explorers and adventurers, partners with their younger crewmates, but set apart from them by their different skill sets, different experiences, and different attitudes toward the possibility of dying. This essay is a profile of those astronauts—Bud Chantillas of *Red Planet*, Spurgeon Tanner of *Deep Impact*, Frank Corvin and "Hawk" Hawkins of *Space Cowboys*—as they set out to make one last "giant leap" into the unknown.

THE HEIRS OF JOHN GLENN

The heroes of the first era of manned spaceflight, which began with Yuri Gagarin's single orbit of the Earth in April 1961 and concluded with Apollo 17's departure from the Moon in December 1972, were men of a certain age. Born ten to fifteen years after the end of the First World War, they were in their mid- to late thirties when they climbed aboard the towering, thundering rockets of the era for their trips to Earth orbit and beyond. Alan Shepard was thirty-seven when he became the first American in space, Buzz Aldrin thirty-six when he space-walked on Gemini XII, and Neil Armstrong thirty-eight when he took his "one small step" onto the lunar dust. John Glenn was considered "old" by National Aeronautics and Space Administration (NASA) standards when, at forty-one, he became the first American to orbit the Earth. The nine Apollo missions that orbited or landed on the Moon were commanded by astronauts whose average age was a few months past forty.[3]

The fictional astronauts who populated American movie and television screens in the 1960s and 1970s fit the same mold.[4] Lee Stegler of *Countdown* (1968), Frank Poole and Dave Bowman of *2001: A Space Odyssey* (1968), and all four astronauts in *Marooned* (1969) could have stepped out of a NASA publicity photo. Dr. John Robinson of *Lost in Space* (1965–1969)— despite being a world-famous scientist and the father of an adult daughter— is no older in the first season of the series than Glenn was on his Project Mercury flight.[5] *Star Trek* (1966–1969), though set in a twenty-third-century world with social norms different from our own, takes place aboard a starship where a thirty-four-year-old captain, forty-year-old doctor, and forty-five-year-old chief engineer oversee a crew whose ages seem to cluster between twenty-eight and thirty-two.[6] Conspicuously older and younger space travelers, present though not common in the popular culture of the 1950s, disappeared in the 1960s as reality and imagination converged.

Professional and popular discourse alike framed space as a tough, demanding environment that could only be endured by vigorous and healthy men in peak physical condition. Astronauts were expected to possess what Tom Wolfe, writing of the Project Mercury astronauts, would later call the "Right Stuff": the quality that allowed a man to

> go up in a hurtling piece of machinery and put his hide on the line and then have the moxie, the reflexes, the coolness to pull it back in the last yawning moment—and then to go up again *the next day*, and the next day, and every next day, even if the series should prove to be infinite.[7]

The young (too brash, too unfocused) and the old (too slow, too cautious) were thus excluded.

The professional reality of space exploration began to change, in 1981, with the first test flights of the space shuttle. NASA's vision of the shuttle as a "space truck" that would launch satellites and act as a platform for scientific research meant that all of its missions would be variations on the theme of a low-Earth-orbit-and-back trip, rather than an ever-escalating series of leaps into the unknown.[8] Surprises would be less frequent, emergencies less dire (if only because home was closer), and the physical demands of flight less taxing. The creation and use of the shuttle enabled NASA astronauts to extend their flight careers throughout their forties and even into their fifties.[9] John Young, who had been "old" when he commanded Apollo 16 at forty-two, commanded the first orbital test flight of the shuttle at fifty-one, and a second flight at fifty-three. Vance Brand, another Apollo-era veteran, commanded three shuttle flights, all while he was in his fifties, and the last when he was fifty-nine. Dr. Story Musgrave, the most spectacular example of

NASA's new openness to older space travelers, flew on the first of his record six shuttle missions when he was forty-seven, and the last when he was sixty-one. A few months after his fifty-first birthday, he performed three space-walks in five days during a mission to repair the Hubble Space Telescope.

Despite these real-world models, film and television portrayals of older astronauts were—with the notable exception of Captain Jean-Luc Picard on *Star Trek: The Next Generation*—all but nonexistent in the 1980s and early to mid-1990s. The aging astronauts played by Jack Nicholson in *Terms of Endearment* (1984), Martin Sheen in *Beyond the Stars* (1989), and Barry Corbin in the television series *Northern Exposure* (1990–1995) were thoroughly and comfortably grounded, their adventuring days long behind them. The trend was reinforced by a flurry of Apollo-themed documentaries commemorating the twentieth (1989) and twenty-fifth (1994) anniversaries of the first lunar landing, which featured graying, balding Apollo-era vete-rans as commentators. The dichotomy, in popular culture at least, was clear: Young men flew, and old men (their flying days behind them) watched from the ground and contemplated what it meant.[10]

The tipping point in Hollywood's portrayals of older astronauts as heroes came in 1995, the year that the space shuttle *Discovery* rocketed into orbit with a crew of—as the NASA official announcing the launch put it—"six astronauts and one American legend." John Glenn's return to space at the age of seventy-seven did far more for NASA's public image than it did for the medical research that was the official justification for his presence. It did nearly as much, however, for the visibility of aging cinematic astronauts, who saved the world several times over in the five years that followed Glenn's second trip to orbit.

BUD CHANTILAS TAKES THE LONG VIEW

Red Planet was the second of the two Mars-themed films released in 2000. Like its more successful (and more critically admired) competitor, *Mission to Mars*, it is a "space travel procedural"[11] that borrows its dramatic structure from the central section of *2001: A Space Odyssey*. It unfolds as a series of vignettes about technological problems, imbedded in a larger story about a scientific problem (which may actually be an existential problem). *Red Plan-et* establishes the larger dimensions of its fictional mission with an opening voice-over by its commander, Kate Bowman (Carrie-Anne Moss): Earth is dying, choked by the waste products of industrial civilization, and human-kind—in a desperate bid to create a new home—is attempting to seed Mars with genetically engineered algae that will create a breathable atmosphere. In the same narration, Bowman introduces Dr. Bud Chantilas[12] (Terence

Stamp): the mission's chief scientist and the character most concerned with those larger dimensions.

Bowman's voice-over, clearly intended as an entry in her personal log, describes Chantilas as "the soul of the crew." The word choice—"soul," rather than "heart"—is significant. Chantilas is old enough to be the grandfather of any of the other five crew members, but he is not a "grandfatherly" figure. The typical Hollywood "grandfather" character—whether played by Guy Kibbee in *Captain January* (1936), Walter Brennan in *The Real McCoys* (1957–1963), or Peter Falk in *The Princess Bride* (1987)—is warm and caring beneath his gruff exterior. Chantilas's seriousness, in contrast, goes all the way to the bone, and his relationship with Gallagher (Val Kilmer)—the film's everyman figure—is close, but not familial. Chantilas treats the younger man as a stern *sensei* might treat a gifted but undisciplined student: with affection tempered by a deep and abiding sense of exasperation.

Chantilas is framed, in scenes of shipboard life scattered through the first third of the film, as the only "grown-up" aboard the *Mars-1*. His five shipmates brew moonshine in the ship's lab, daydream about sex, and jokingly discuss leaving humankind to its fate and setting themselves up as sole rulers of Mars. Chantilas stands apart from such frivolity: physically absent or, when present, detached and disinterested. Conspicuously older than his shipmates—more conscious, perhaps, of death—he alone seems to feel the gravity of their task, and to truly appreciate what is at stake. He alone seems conscious that failure will bring not just their own individual ends, but the end of humankind itself.

Alone among his shipmates, Chantilas focuses on the big picture and the long view. The others focus on *how*; Chantilas is interested in *why*. If humankind allows itself to go extinct, he asks Gallagher early in the film, "then what was the point of anything? Art, beauty—all gone—the Greeks, the Constitution, people dying for freedom, ideas. None of it meant anything? What about religion? Do we give up on God, too?" Gallagher, a systems engineer by training and an intuitive gadgeteer-genius by temperament, is bemused to suddenly be in such unexpectedly deep philosophical waters. Did you, he asks Chantilas with a raised eyebrow, "give up on" science in favor of religion? Not at all, the older man explains: he turned to philosophy after realizing that "science couldn't answer any of the really interesting questions." He retains a childlike sense of wonder, and an awareness of nature's near-infinite diversity and its ability to startle even the most experienced observer. "Who knows," he says wryly, "I may pick up a rock and it'll say underneath 'Made by God.' The universe is full of surprises."

Chantilas's interest in big questions, openness to the unexpected, and weaving of God and faith into discussions of science align him with the popular image of Albert Einstein: the scientist as gentle mystic. His relationship with Gallagher establishes him as a twenty-first-century Yoda: a stern elder/teacher who understands the world in ways his young colleagues can barely comprehend. Both roles position him as the principal source of wisdom and insight in the story, and the last act of the film—which plays out long after Chantilas himself is dead—reinforces the idea.

Mars proves, against all logic and in defiance of scientists' expectations, to have acquired a thin-but-breathable atmosphere. The algae shipped from Earth as part of the terraforming process has provided food for a species of Martian insects, causing them to multiply and cover the surface. Devouring the algae and excreting oxygen, the insects have transformed Mars more comprehensively than the algae itself ever could have. Better yet, as geneticist Quinn Burchenal (Tom Sizemore) tells Gallagher, they might provide the key to cleaning up Earth's poisoned atmosphere, making the transformation of Mars into a new home for mankind unnecessary. Nature is, as Chantilas explained to Gallagher before the landing, full of surprises . . . the essential thing is to remain open to them.

The final scenes of *Red Planet* show Bowman and Gallagher, the only survivors of the mission, beginning the return journey to Earth aboard *Mars-1*. The Martian insects—Earth's unlikely saviors—travel with them, but so (in spirit) does Chantilas. "God works in mysterious ways," Gallagher observes, referring both to the bugs and to reports that he is being hailed as a hero on Earth. He contemplates the golf-ball-sized Martian rock that Chantilas studied as he died, wondering if the elder scientist discerned evidence of God's presence in it. Bowman, too, is thinking of him. "Maybe Chantilas was right," she muses in a voice-over from her personal log, "maybe it's not just the science. I sure don't know." The pair return home uncertain, questioning, and contemplative, having absorbed—whether they realize it or not—the lessons that "the soul of the crew" tried so hard to teach them.

"FISH" TANNER SAVES THE WORLD

Deep Impact—like *Armageddon,* with which it shared the summer of 1998—is a film about the impending end of the world and the team of astronauts recruited to save it. Five of the spacefaring heroes are variations on a familiar theme: young, fit, bright-eyed, and intense. The sixth member of the crew stands, in every scene prior to liftoff, conspicuously to one side of the group, observing but not participating. He is older—easily old enough to be their father—with thinning hair, a wrinkled face, and the hint of a paunch straining the front of his sport shirt. He listens more than he talks, and speaks in unhurried sentences shaded by a soft southern accent. He is Captain Spurgeon "Fish"[13] Tanner (Robert Duvall): naval aviator, test pilot, Apollo astronaut, and—in the context of the film—a living legend from NASA's heroic age, twenty-five years gone by.

The tension between Tanner and the younger astronauts is palpable. Sizing up his crewmates in conversation with a fellow Apollo-era veteran, he acknowledges that "they've been trained in ways *I'll* never understand," and "they're smarter and in better shape than we ever were in the old days." What worries him is not their skills, but their ability to cope with the unexpected. Contemplating their mission—landing an untested spaceship on the surface of a speeding comet and pushing it off course with carefully placed nuclear bombs—he concludes: "I guess I'd be a lot happier about this whole thing if I thought that any of 'em were as scared as I am." The younger astronauts, discussing Tanner among themselves, profess pro forma respect for his past accomplishments, but dismiss him as a man whose time has passed. Take former NFL star Frank Gifford, one declares: "He was a great player in his time, but if he played now he'd get his ass *busted.*" They see Tanner's presence on the mission as a matter of public relations: a product of the space agency's desire for a "familiar face" among the crew. The events of the mission, however, consistently prove Tanner right and the younger astronauts wrong. He has knowledge and experience that they lack, without which the mission has little hope of success and humankind little hope of survival.

NASA assigns Tanner to the crew because he is, by virtue of his age, the only astronaut still in active service who has landed a spacecraft on the surface of another world. Confident of their own skills, the younger astronauts are unimpressed. Landing on the immense, geologically stable Moon is, they argue, nothing like landing on a comet that spins on its axis once every fourteen hours and unpredictably spews geysers of steam from its fissured surface as it approaches the Sun. "You haven't trained for this," they tell Tanner bluntly, but they have—practicing the mission hundreds of times in computerized simulations. The older man responds with a shake of his head. "It's not a video game, son," he tells mission commander Oren Monash, "it really isn't." Later, as he prepares to fly the *Messiah* through the comet's unstable "coma" of rock, dust, and gas and land on its nucleus, he asserts his expertise in more specific terms, comparing himself to the Mississippi River pilots of Mark Twain's era, who mastered only one stretch of the vast river, but knew that segment intimately. "For the next few hours," he declares over the intercom as he takes control from the onboard computer, "this is *my* ship." Tanner, like his real-world counterparts John Young and Vance Brand, is a veteran of NASA's heroic Project Apollo years, still flying in the space shuttle era. He has skills and experiences that the younger astronauts, as products of the shuttle era, never had the opportunity to develop because they trained for a different kind of mission.

The landing is flawless, but the events that follow—as the crew of the *Messiah* unload and place the nuclear bombs—establish the value of Tanner's age and experience. As direct sunlight strikes the portion of the comet where the rest of the crew is working, it unleashes one gas geyser after another. The young astronauts become increasingly agitated, with their voices rising and words tumbling over one another as they try to hurry through the prescribed flight plan. Fish, in contrast, remains calm and soft-spoken as he improvises a solution: severing the tethers holding *Messiah* to the comet, and delicately skimming the ship over its jagged surface to rescue the landing party, stopping only when his fuel supply is nearly gone.[14] Displaying the nonchalance for which the early astronauts were famous, he quips: "Thought I'd better come pick you kids up after school." Tanner's experience does not, however, manifest itself as merely bravado. When a gas jet hurls one of the crew off the comet and into space, it is Tanner who makes—and, with a stern fatherly voice, enforces—the hard call to "let him go."

The crew's final act, which destroys the comet and saves humankind from extinction, is Tanner's idea, and the ultimate expression of his ability—honed in the go-for-broke days of Project Apollo—to solve complex operational problems on the fly. The detonation of the nuclear bombs has blasted a two-mile-deep hole in the comet, but failed to deflect it from its trajectory. The younger members of the crew—having come to the end of the mission plan they had practiced and trained for—are stymied, but Fish is undaunted. As the others mentally prepare for the end of the world, he begins to formulate one last, epic improvisation: dive the *Messiah* to the bottom of the crater that the bombs made, then detonate the four remaining bombs in her hold, along with her nuclear engines. The resulting explosion, he explains to his crewmates, should be enough to shatter the comet into fragments small enough to burn up in Earth's atmosphere.

It is a measure of the generational gulf between Tanner and the rest of the crew that the younger astronauts do not, at first, recognize the core of the plan: The deliberate sacrifice of the *Messiah* and her crew to give humankind not a certain reprieve but "a chance." Fish himself, meanwhile, has already come to terms with what his plan involves; indeed, he has come to terms with it decades before. The possibility of dying in space—that an astronaut, a crew, or a ship might not return safely to Earth—was once woven into the way that NASA did business.[15] Tanner, as the last active veteran of that era, remembers when.

PRESENT AT THE CREATION: FRANK CORVIN AND SPACE BEFORE NASA

From the late 1940s to the early 1960s, Air Force test pilots pushed experimental jet- and rocket-powered aircraft ever faster and ever higher in the skies over the California desert.[16] The research program served the Air Force's need for data about high-speed, high-altitude flight (vital in an era when atomic weapons were carried by jet bombers, and air defense was built around jet fighters), but it also served as a stepping-stone toward outer space. It seemed natural that the high-performance aircraft of the 1950s would, in a technological generation or two, give rise to "space planes" capable of operating both in Earth's atmosphere and in the vacuum beyond.[17] The dream of a seamless transition from atmospheric flight to spaceflight ran off the rails in October 1957, when *Sputnik I* rocketed into orbit atop a massive R-7 rocket. Intercontinental ballistic missiles (of which the R-7 was an early example) rendered "next-generation" bombers irrelevant, and—as the "space race" inaugurated by *Sputnik* heated up—modified versions of them provided a ready solution to the problem of launching payloads into space. Research on space planes (such as NASA's X-15 and the Air Force's X-20 Dyna-Soar) continued into the early 1960s, but this became a technological dead-end . . . a road not taken.[18]

Released in 2000, *Space Cowboys* is the story of four men who, as young Air Force officers, worked on a (fictional) space plane program named Project Daedalus, only to see their dreams of spaceflight crumble when NASA's rocket-boosted "capsules" replaced the Air Force's rocket-powered aircraft as America's preferred road to space. Forty years later, however, NASA officials approach the leader of the group, Frank Corvin (Clint Eastwood), to ask for his help. IKON, an aging Soviet satellite, a relic of the Cold War, is on the verge of falling into Earth's atmosphere; unless it can be boosted into a higher orbit, it will break up on reentry, and the falling wreckage will wreak havoc on Earth. Informed that only he has the knowledge needed to repair the satellite, Corvin agrees to help, but insists that he and his Project Daedalus teammates, now in their seventies and long retired from the Air Force, go into space and do the work themselves.

Space Cowboys is, in one sense, the "Fish" Tanner subplot from *Deep Impact*, scored for four voices instead of one. Corvin and his buddies— "Hawk" Hawkins (Tommy Lee Jones), "Tank" Sullivan (James Garner), and Jerry O'Neill (Donald Sutherland)—are, like Tanner, spacefaring versions of Lewis Carroll's comic figure Father William: old men who show doubting younger men (as in *Deep Impact*, the shuttle crew) that they are still formidable. The younger astronauts are, as in the earlier film, highly intelligent and superbly trained, but—having come of age in an era when spaceflights never ventured into unknown territory—they lack the ability to innovate in a crisis. When it becomes clear that IKON is not simply a satellite but a secret Cold War–era weapons platform, programmed to launch its six nuclear missiles at American targets if it falls below a certain altitude, the NASA astronauts aboard *Daedalus* find themselves without a plan and in over their heads. When mission commander Ethan Glance (Loren Dean) attempts to deal with the situation, acting on secret orders from NASA administrator Bob Gerson

(James Cromwell), he accelerates the decay of IKON's orbit, damages the shuttle, and badly injures himself and another astronaut.

The four old-timers, in contrast, are in their element. Holdovers from an age when test pilots and astronauts routinely "pushed the envelope"—reaching for speeds, altitudes, and destinations never attained before—they face emergencies, and devise solutions, without waiting for advice from the ground. They know, by virtue of their age, things the younger astronauts never had reason to learn. Corvin is intimately familiar with IKON's circuitry because its design is based on one that he—in his post–Air Force career as an electrical engineer—created for NASA's *Skylab* space station, and that the KGB subsequently stole. Having flown high-performance experimental aircraft in the 1950s, before the era of computer-assisted controls and guidance systems, he is at home in the damaged shuttle, and able to bring it home to a safe landing at the Kennedy Space Center.

Hawkins, who also flew in Project Daedalus, has the same pre–computer era skills and experience, and a natural "touch" on the controls that exceeds even Corvin's. Knowing this, and knowing (from a pre-mission physical) that he has terminal cancer, he volunteers for the most audacious act of heroism in the film. He climbs aboard IKON and, using controls jury-rigged by Corvin, utilizes the rocket motors of its nuclear missiles to "fly" it out of orbit and into deep space—thereby hastening his own death by eight months, but ensuring that the infernal Cold War relic will never again endanger Earth. He declares, in his parting words to his old friend, that he intends to aim for the Moon: the destination that, in their long-ago Project Daedalus days, they had both hoped to reach. The film ends with a wordless pan across the lunar surface confirming that, against all odds, he made it.

The knowledge that enables the aging astronaut-heroes of *Space Cowboys* to save the shuttle, its crew, and untold millions of lives on Earth is not, however, solely technical. The quartet's experience with the space program is older than Apollo, Gemini, or Mercury—older even than NASA itself. The younger astronauts on the shuttle know Gerson only as a revered and respected senior administrator with decades of service to NASA, and Glance is willing to follow his off-the-record orders, with disastrous results. The four old-timers, in contrast, knew Gerson when he was the Air Force colonel in charge of Project Daedalus, who terminated the program (and derailed their dreams of reaching the Moon) in order to serve his own career ambitions. They treat him warily, aware of his self-serving nature and history of duplicity, and are not surprised to find that he has lied to them. On a deeper level—as veterans of the days before détente, when the Cold War ran hot—they also know that governments lie to each other, lie to their people, and lie to those who wear their uniform. Confronted with the knowledge that Gerson (and, implicitly, NASA) has kept vital information from them, they are appalled—but not surprised.

CONCLUSION: THE UNDISCOVERED COUNTRY

All three films discussed here end with an aging astronaut-hero dying in space, each having sacrificed himself to ensure the success of the mission. All three make the sacrifice willingly and without regret, certain—like countless fictional space travelers before them—that "the needs of the many outweigh the needs of the few . . . or the one."[19] All three, however, also find personal meaning and individual satisfaction in the deaths they choose for themselves.

Chantilas, in his last moments of life, says to Gallagher: "Hey . . . I got to see Mars." The words are simple, the sentiment behind them profound. As a scientist, he can imagine no greater satisfaction than being among the first to set eyes on a brand-new world, full of untold wonders and surprises waiting to be explored. As a passionate believer in the ability of humankind to achieve extraordinary things, he can imagine no greater satisfaction than being part of the greatest human adventure of all. Like the astronaut in Theodore Sturgeon's short story "The Man Who Lost the Sea" (1959), he finds that the pain of dying on Mars pales beside the sheer wonder of *being* on Mars.

Hawkins, like Harriman in "Requiem," achieves the great, unfulfilled ambition of his life as he is in the process of dying. He sets out for the Moon, knowing he will never return, and dies there with a smile on his face. The final image in the film shows him on the lunar surface, propped in a sitting position amid the wreckage of IKON, with the full Earth reflected in the visor of his spacesuit.[20] His face is turned back toward the Earth, but the song playing on the soundtrack—"Fly Me to the Moon," a pop standard that became an unofficial anthem for Project Apollo after Frank Sinatra recorded it in 1964—suggests that his thoughts are elsewhere. The song treats the Moon not as a final destination, but merely as the first step on an open-ended journey to Mars, Jupiter, and beyond. As the singer wistfully contemplates "playing among the stars," the audience is invited to wonder if Hawk, in his imagination, is doing just that.

Tanner's last words, spoken softly in the last moment before the *Messiah* and her crew are vaporized in the heart of the comet, are deceptively simple: "Mary, I'm coming home." Yet, like the song in *Space Cowboys*, they imply a great deal. The words reflect Tanner's faith—the Christian belief that one who dies is "called home" by God—but also his conviction (alluded to earlier in the film) that "home" existed whenever and wherever he and Mary were together. It also evokes an image nearly as old as aviation itself: the dying pilot whose machine disappears into the clouds or among the stars, and who is raised directly into heaven without ever again touching the Earth.[21]

For Chantilas and Hawkins, death is final: an end to their last great voyage, and to all voyaging. For Tanner, death is the beginning of one more voyage into "that undiscovered country" where his God, and his beloved, wait to receive him. All three, however, die fulfilled. They are explorers, and they died exploring—using the last moments of their life to crest one last range of hills and see what lay beyond. The words on Stevenson's marker in Samoa—the ones that also mark D. D. Harriman's makeshift grave in the lunar dust—would serve equally well for any of them:

> This be the verse that you grave for me:
> Here he lies where he longed to be,
> Home is the sailor, home from the sea,
> And the hunter home from the hill.

NOTES

1. Robert A. Heinlein, "Requiem," in *The Past Through Tomorrow: Future History Stories* (1967; New York: Berkeley, 1986), 245.

2. Harriman's name is likely an allusion to railroad baron E. H. Harriman (1848–1909).

3. If not for Alan Shepard, who commanded Apollo 14 when he was forty-seven, the average age would be thirty-nine.

4. The broader history of astronauts in space age popular culture is surveyed in Matthew H. Hersch, "Return of the Lost Spaceman: America's Astronauts in Popular Culture, 1959–2006," *Journal of Popular Culture* 44, no. 1 (2011): 73–92.

5. The ages of Robinson's two younger children are given in the pilot as nine (Will) and thirteen (Penny); the age of the eldest (Judy) is not specified, but she appears to be eighteen or nineteen, and is treated as an emancipated adult, free to choose whether to join her parents and siblings in space.

6. Kirk's age is from Stephen E. Whitfield, *The Making of Star Trek* (New York: Ballantine, 1968), 215. Both the first and second pilots for the series featured ship's doctors a generation older than the captain; McCoy was originally conceived in similar terms, but quickly emerged as a slightly older friend rather than a father figure.

7. Tom Wolfe, *The Right Stuff* (New York: Farrar, Straus, and Giroux, 1979), 24.

8. David Hitt and Heather R. Smith, *Bold They Rise: The Space Shuttle Early Years* (Lincoln: University of Nebraska Press, 2014), 22–24.

9. On the changes in the astronaut corps brought about by the shuttle, see Hitt and Smith, *Bold They Rise*, 54–74; Joseph D. Atkinson and Jay M. Shafritz, *The Real Stuff: A History of NASA's Astronaut Recruitment Program* (New York: Praeger, 1985), 133–79; and Henry S. F. Cooper, *Before Liftoff: The Making of a Shuttle Crew* (Baltimore, MD: Johns Hopkins University Press), 18–33.

10. A similar pattern is evident in written science fiction, with Arthur C. Clarke's short story "The Call of the Stars" (1957) and Michael P. Kube-McDowell's novel *The Quiet Pools* (1990) just two examples among many.

11. Science fiction's analog to the "police procedural" subgenre of detective stories, space travel procedurals place as much (or more) dramatic emphasis on the journey as on the destination. *Destination Moon* (1950) is an early example, *Gravity* (2013) a recent one.

12. His first name is given in the script, but never actually spoken on screen.

13. "Spurgeon . . . Sturgeon . . . Fish," Tanner says at one point, explaining his nickname to one of the younger astronauts. "It took about five minutes my first day at the Naval Academy."

14. The scene echoes, almost certainly by design, Neil Armstrong's maneuvering of *Eagle* away from a dangerous boulder field during the Apollo 11 landing, and his eventual touchdown with only forty seconds' worth of fuel left in the tanks.

15. See, for example, William Safire, "In the Event of Moon Disaster" [memo to H. R. Haldeman], July 18, 1969. http://www.archives.gov/presidential-libraries/events/centennials/nixon/images/exhibit/rn100-6-1-2.pdf (accessed November 6, 2014).

16. Richard P. Hallion, *Designers and Test Pilots* (Alexandria, VA: Time-Life Books, 1983), 106–48, is a useful overview. First-person accounts include Chuck Yeager et. al., *The Quest for Mach 1: A First Person Account of Breaking the Sound Barrier* (New York: Penguin Studio, 1997); William Bridgeman and Jacqueline Hazard, *The Lonely Sky* (New York: Holt, 1955); and A. Scott Crossfield and Clay Blair, Jr., *Always Another Dawn* (New York: World Publishing, 1960).

17. On the history of the dream, see A. Bowdoin Van Riper, *Imagining Flight: Aviation and the Popular Imagination* (College Station: Texas A&M University Press, 2003), 131–51.

18. On the reality of winged space planes, see Michelle Evans, *The X-15 Rocket Plane: Flying the First Wings into Space* (Lincoln: University of Nebraska Press, 2013); and Andrew J. Butrica, *Single Stage to Orbit: Politics, Space Technology, and the Quest for Reusable Rocketry* (Baltimore, MD: Johns Hopkins University Press, 2003).

19. These specific words are spoken by Spock as he dies of radiation poisoning in *Star Trek II: The Wrath of Khan* (1982), but the sentiment is present in science fiction films as diverse as *Destination Moon* (1950), *Marooned* (1969), *Star Wars* (1977), *Armageddon* (1998), and *Mission to Mars* (2000).

20. It bears a striking similarity to the illustration used with the original magazine publication of "Requiem" (*Astounding Stories,* January 1940, 81).

21. The image goes back at least to World War I, and figured prominently in the public grieving for the seven astronauts killed in the *Columbia* disaster. See Van Riper, *Imagining Flight*, 123–26; and A. Bowdoin Van Riper, ". . . And Touched the Face of God: Memorializing Disaster in the U.S. Space Program," in *We Are What We Remember*, edited by Jeffrey Lee Meriwether and Laura Mattoon D'Amore (Newcastle upon Tyne, UK: Cambridge Scholars Publishing, 2013), 102–6.

II

Diversity Concerns:
Sexuality, Race, and Gender

Chapter Five

Queering Aging?

Representations of Liberace's Intimate Life in HBO's
Behind the Candelabra

Gust A. Yep, Ryan Lescure, and Jace Allen

> Queering [generally refers] to an active process of making an unquestioned
> and taken-for-granted idea or social relation into an unfamiliar or strange one
> to unpack its underlying power relations and to offer possibilities of resistance
> and other ways of thinking, doing, living, and loving.
>
> —Gust Yep[1]

> [Age and aging are] far more social than chronological.
>
> —Cheryl Laz[2]

By 2030, in the United States alone, between two to six million lesbian, gay,
and bisexual (LGB) adults will be over the age of sixty-five.[3] Even members
of this group who enjoy racial, class, and bodily privileges—for example,
white and middle- to upper-class people with able bodies—are likely to
encounter cultural prejudices. Since their age (older adults) and sexuality
(LGB) are not considered "normal" in U.S. society, these individuals are
likely to experience prejudice as they circulate in the social world. Jim Whaler and Sarah Gabbay, for example, note that older gay men experience "accelerated aging," that is, a devaluation by self and others for not appearing
youthful in a subcultural—and cultural—context of youthism in the United
States.[4] In addition, researchers have documented different needs,[5] stereotypes,[6] and narratives of their sexual bodies[7] in the LGB aging population. In
spite of their uniqueness as a group and the critical need to develop a greater

understanding of aging in this population,[8] research on older sexual minority individuals in the United States has been limited.[9] To partially address this need and recognizing that "for the aging person, [media representations] provide not a mirror of the present, but one of possibilities,"[10] we examine how gay male aging is represented in HBO's highly acclaimed film, *Behind the Candelabra*.[11] To do so, our chapter is divided into five sections. We start with an overview and synopsis of *Behind the Candelabra*, our cultural artifact, before we present queer theory, the perspective for our analysis. We then discuss current representations of aging before we examine the film's portrayal of Liberace, who was a larger-than-life entertainer, an older American gay male, and ultimately a tragic hero. We conclude by exploring the implications of our analysis for further examination of aging in sexual minority populations and for consumption of representations of aging gay male images in popular media.

BEHIND THE CANDELABRA: A BRIEF OVERVIEW

Premiering in May 2013, *Behind the Candelabra* centers on the volatile six-year love affair between the notoriously flamboyant, widely known, and aging closeted gay entertainer Liberace (portrayed by Michael Douglas) and the much-younger Scott Thorson (portrayed by Matt Damon). The film was released to massive critical acclaim, ultimately winning nineteen of the thirty-five awards it was nominated for, including two Golden Globes for Best Mini-Series or Motion Picture Made for Television, and Best Performance by an Actor in a Mini-Series (Douglas). The film begins in 1977 with Thorson attending a Liberace performance with a mutual friend who later introduces the two backstage. Liberace is clearly drawn to the young, attractive Thorson. Through a series of events, Liberace invites Thorson to his palatial Las Vegas home, where Thorson, who has a veterinary background, notices that one of Liberace's dogs is suffering from a treatable form of temporary blindness. After he treats the dog, Liberace insists that Thorson be his "assistant," which, in addition to its obvious romantic and sexual subtext, involves living with and working for Liberace. Predictably, shortly after Thorson moves in with Liberace, they become lovers. Their romance begins without issue, but Liberace soon starts controlling the increasingly isolated Thorson by doing things such as managing his weight and mandating unnecessary plastic surgery. As their relationship deteriorates, Thorson develops a drug addiction, while Liberace pursues even younger men. When Liberace finds a new, younger paramour, Thorson is left with nothing, yet he still loves and cares for Liberace.

A QUEER PERSPECTIVE

Throughout this essay, we use "queering aging" in two senses. First, we seek to deconstruct and analyze aging as a social construction with an emphasis on gay men in the United States. Second, we seek to recover and highlight the sexuality of aging adults as they function within, through, and against social and cultural assumptions of the absence of sexuality in their lives. Before we discuss this more specifically in relation to *Behind the Candelabra*, we first contextualize our use of the term "queer."

According to Annamarie Jagose, queer originally meant, at best, slang for homosexual, and at worst, a homophobic slur.[12] In recent years, queer has been resignified and reappropriated within popular culture and academia as a framework for highlighting and deconstructing the violence of normativity.[13] In its resignified sense, queer is often used in two broad ways: as an umbrella term for self-identified individuals of various culturally non-normative sexualities, and as an emergent and fluid theoretical model.[14] This resignification is highly political. It highlights the ways that power and dominant cultural ideologies are constructed and maintained through communication, and provides a theoretical model through which these ideologies can be questioned and altered. As a theoretical model, queer theory is often concerned with deconstructing heteronormativity, which refers to the assumption that a specific expression of heterosexuality is the "normal" form of human sexuality and that all other expressions are deviant.[15] Queer theory does not define itself solely in relation to heteronormativity or even sexuality, however. As David Halperin explains, "queer is by definition whatever is at odds with the normal, the legitimate, the dominant."[16]

While queer theory is notoriously difficult to define, as open-endedness and fluidity are among its key commitments,[17] studies employing a queer theoretical framework tend to share similar characteristics. This generally includes a concern with interrogating, deconstructing, and reconfiguring the power relations that are written into socially constructed normativities—that is, what a culture accepts as normal and taken-for-granted at a specific historical moment (e.g., marrying for love; display of younger and fit bodies but not older ones in mass media). Indeed, queer signifies non-normativity and provides "another view, another discursive horizon, and another perspective from which social relations can be analyzed and examined."[18] By looking at what is considered non-normative—that is, what a culture considers strange or abnormal—we can understand how the normal is always already constructed and dependent on the abnormal. For example, the normality of heterosexuality as a cultural given in society is utterly dependent on the construction of deviance and abnormality associated with other forms of sexuality, such as homosexuality. Queer theory allows us to examine this relationship (e.g., heterosexuality-homosexuality; adults-older adults) and unpack its underlying power relations (i.e., who benefits from such constructions, and who is stigmatized?). Using this lens, we turn to a discussion of the construction of aging bodies in popular culture.

REPRESENTATION OF AGING

Within the context of U.S. culture, aging bodies are perceived as being in a state of decline and are generally considered to be less desirable and valuable than youthful bodies. [19] Since bodies that are culturally perceived as attractive occupy a central position in mainstream U.S. films and television programs, the aging bodies of older adults deviate from the status quo and are therefore rendered invisible. In relation to their numbers in the U.S. population, older adults are notably underrepresented in both television and film, while younger adults are overrepresented. [20] The general lack of representation of sexuality among older adults creates a narrow range of possibilities for imagining their sexual lives, experiences, and interactions.

Since aging bodies are culturally perceived to be undesirable, they are also perceived as nonsexual. This results in the stereotypical notion that older adults themselves are nonsexual. In U.S. society, according to Thomas Walz, the sexual representations of older adults are inaccurate, unflattering, confusing, and contradictory. [21] Walz elaborates, "It is as if we suspect old people are sexual, but have a hard time imagining it, and, if it turns out they are sexual, we would prefer they were not. The thought of their being sexual is disconcerting." [22] Of course, as Walz also notes, a major exception to this idea is the fact that old men are often represented in cultural texts as "sexually driven, but also sexually inappropriate and/or sexually impotent." [23]

Like heterosexual older adults, lesbian and gay subjects also tend to be greatly underrepresented in mediated representations, though their representations occur more frequently than those of bisexual and transgender individuals. Representations of lesbian and gay subjects on television are increasing, but these representations tend to problematically maintain hierarchies of power and privilege and are often confined to subjects who are also white, young, and have a high socioeconomic status. [24] While television shows such as *Modern Family*, for example, are often heralded for merely *presenting* a lesbian or gay character, these characters tend to maintain stereotypes about lesbian and gay individuals rather than dispel them. Unsurprisingly, mediated representations of older lesbian and gay adults are even scarcer than those of heterosexual older adults. According to Michael Johnson, Jr., older gay men are rendered invisible through their extremely infrequent representation on television, and this invisibility renders their identities inconsequential. [25]

MEDIA PORTRAYAL OF LIBERACE IN
BEHIND THE CANDELABRA

In a media landscape of scarce, unflattering, and contradictory representations of older adults in the United States, how are aging gay men portrayed? Using a queer perspective to analyze the portrayal of the aging Liberace, we observe that the film simultaneously reinforces and challenges sexual and gender stereotypes of older adults, particularly those of older gay men. We discuss them next.

Aging Gay Men and Sexual Stereotypes

Older gay men are caught in a conundrum: they are generally invisible in popular media, and when they are present, they are trapped in the crossfire of contradictory cultural stereotypes. As older adults, they are assumed to be simultaneously sexually normative (i.e., heterosexual) and nonsexual. As gay men, they are simultaneously sexually non-normative and hypersexual. As Nancy Knauer accurately observes, ageism and homophobia intersect to render "a [gay] elder all but unthinkable because elders are not considered to be sexual and [gay men] are, too often, viewed as only sexual."[26] This is precisely the intersection—the asexual older adult and the hypersexual gay man—we find Liberace inhabiting in *Behind the Candelabra*. Portrayed as a hypersexual older gay man, such representation visibly challenges and reinforces dominant cultural stereotypes.

While Liberace's representation as a hypersexual older gay man was highly visible in many scenes within the film, one scene particularly stands out as a challenge to the stereotype of older adults as nonsexual. Additionally, we point out that this scene featured an expression of older gay sexuality in a way that is rarely featured in mainstream U.S. films and television programs. In this particular sex scene, we see the older gay man offering a recreational aphrodisiac (popper) to Thorson as the sweaty young man is grunting and thrusting behind Liberace. When offered the popper, Thorson shakes his head and states, "No, I don't like it." In response, Liberace states, "It makes it better." Shortly after this, Liberace is shown inhaling the popper while still having sex with Thorson. This scene challenges the stereotypical notion of older adults as nonsexual, centering Liberace as a highly sexual being concerned with further enhancing his feelings of pleasure through recreational drug use. This scene also renders visible a markedly gay expression of sexuality through explicitly depicting anal sex between two men and the use of poppers, which tends to be commonly associated with men who have sex with men.[27] The presence of this markedly gay scene and its location in a film that was released through a mainstream channel deviates from representational norms and provides a highly visible challenge to the dominant cultural notions that older adults are nonsexual and that older gay adults do not exist. However, we do not argue that it does so without problem.

While the vivid and intense sexual scenes between Liberace and Thorson challenge assumptions of lack of sexuality among older adults in contemporary U.S. culture, the content of such scenes, and the plot in general, reinforce the persistent cultural stereotype of gay men as sexually predatory.[28] This type of sexually promiscuous and predatory gay male can be seen in a number of popular cultural representations. One such example is Christian, a major protagonist on *Latter Days*, an independent film released in 2003, in which he is continually moving on to his next conquest, including seemingly straight men and Mormon missionaries. In *Behind the Candelabra*, more specifically, the portrayal of Liberace reifies popular conceptions of the hypersexual older gay man who preys on seemingly "innocent" younger men—for example, Thorson—to satisfy his unquenchable sexual appetite.

Liberace's insatiable sexuality is depicted throughout the film. In their first evening together, for example, after convincing an apprehensive Thorson to spend the night in his mansion, Liberace promised to stay on his side of the bed. The promise, however, is quickly broken when Thorson wakes up and Liberace immediately reaches for Thorson's erect penis, culminating with Liberace performing fellatio on a mildly uncomfortable looking Thorson. In another scene, we see Liberace and Thorson alternating between having sex and eating. After having sex again and trying to catch his breath, Thorson asks Liberace, "Do you mind if I ask you something? How do you stay hard for so long? I mean . . . that was the fourth time since lunch!" The scene seems to suggest that older gay men have unquenchable sexual appetites—in this case, more so than Thorson, a much younger self-identified bisexual man.

Liberace's hypersexuality, a common stereotype of gay men,[29] is depicted not only in the film's explicit sexual scenes. Indeed, it is a central theme in the plot and portrayed through his interactions with younger men, regardless of their sexual orientation. From the very beginning of the movie, Liberace's interest in younger men is clear and palpable. This ranges from showcasing his male protégé during a concert performance, his subsequent flirtation with Thorson in the presence of his current lover at the end of that same performance, to the seemingly endless string of young lovers he pursues and eventually discards. To pursue the wholesome and innocent Thorson, Liberace's predatory tendencies are revealed when he flies Thorson, in his personal airplane, to spend an evening in his mansion. With seduction in mind, Liberace invites Thorson to join him in a candlelit hot tub, with a bottle of champagne, spectacular nocturnal views, and intimate conversation, all while showering Thorson with compliments and sharing personal revelations. Although Thorson seems reluctant and uneasy with Liberace's unrelenting sexual advances, Thorson, in the end, capitulates, starts a sexual relationship with him, and they become lovers.

Aging Gay Men and Gender Stereotypes

In U.S. culture, gay men tend to be stereotypically perceived as effeminate and having more in common with heterosexual women than with heterosexual men.[30] Gay men and heterosexual women, for example, are stereotyped as having better fashion sense and emotional intelligence than heterosexual men. Gay men are also stereotypically perceived to strongly connect their physical appearance to their self-worth,[31] which generally tends to be thought of as feminine in U.S. culture. Gender stereotypes of gay men, such as these, are portrayed to reinforce the pervasiveness and invisibility of hegemonic masculinity in U.S. culture.[32] Hegemonic masculinity, according to R. W. Connell, refers to "the configuration of gender practice which embodies the currently accepted answer to the problem of the legitimacy of patriarchy, which guarantees (or is taken to guarantee) the dominant position of men and the subordination of women."[33] In other words, hegemonic masculinity is the most culturally revered form of masculinity in a particular context and at a particular point in time. The dominant cultural construction of gay men as effeminate through stereotyping blunts the efficacy of gay men's transgressions of gender norms, which advances heterosexual dominance.[34] Focusing on the portrayal of Liberace in *Behind the Candelabra*, our analysis suggests that it simultaneously reinforces and challenges gender stereotypes—such as femininity and passivity—of aging gay men.

Gay men tend to be stereotypically perceived by both men and women as more feminine than their heterosexual counterparts.[35] The stereotype of Liberace as feminine is portrayed throughout the film, but is very often found in relation to his grave concern over his physical appearance and his aging body. In one particularly notable scene, Liberace and Thorson are watching television, specifically to view Liberace's appearance on *The Tonight Show Starring Johnny Carson*. As soon as he sees himself on screen, Liberace engages in a very dramatic critique of his appearance. Sitting on the couch and anxiously leaning forward, he exclaims, "Oh my Christ! I . . . I . . . I look like my father! I look like my father in drag!" He then stands up and moves toward the television with a look on his face that blends awe and disbelief before exclaiming, "I look like my father in *Hush . . . Hush, Sweet Charlotte!*" The scene immediately cuts to Liberace meeting with his plastic surgeon, who plans to make Liberace look "as young as Scott." In response, Liberace states, "Ah, thank you. I feel so much better. I mean, that Carson show was like looking at, uh, Dorian Gray wither away in public."

In addition to concerns over his appearance, Liberace is portrayed as extremely flamboyant—and feminine. Ranging from his elaborately bejeweled stage costumes and coats, his excessive jewelry, and his collection of hairpieces to his gaudy home furnishings and ornate gold fixtures in his surroundings, Liberace is presented as the prototypical "queen," that is, a flamboyant and ostentatious older gay man. A feminine gay man is culturally expected to be sexually passive—to play the symbolic role of "woman" during sexual encounters.[36] Indeed, that is what Liberace does with Thorson and presumably other young lovers. In his intimate physical relationship with Thorson, Liberace is depicted as the one who is repeatedly penetrated, thus maintaining and reinforcing the gender stereotype of gay men as passive and, therefore, feminine.

Another quality associated with femininity is consumption, particularly as manifested and expressed through an intense interest in shopping.[37] In the film, Liberace is portrayed as a lavish and extravagant consumer. For example, he purchases fine clothing and ornate jewelry for himself and Thorson. His mansion is filled with sumptuous and opulent objects and artifacts, and his glimmering piano (along with his ostentatiously sequined outfits) on stage is always decorated with a colorful and gaudy candelabra. In addition, Liberace also loves to cook, another signifier of femininity. One particular scene seems to capture these qualities succinctly. After having sex with Thorson, Liberace tells him: "We'll go shopping tomorrow. After cooking and sex, I think shopping is the reason to get up every day."

The film, however, also challenges gender stereotypes—such as passivity (and lack of control) in interpersonal relationships. For example, Liberace is portrayed as the breadwinner and the man in control of his intimate relationships. Being a commanding father figure, breadwinning, and maintaining control over others tend to be associated with hegemonic masculinity.[38] In a scene depicting an argument between Liberace and Thorson, signaling the beginning of their relational de-escalation, Liberace says, "Oh, God! All of the sudden we're sounding like gay Lucy and Ricky" to which Thorson asks, "Why am I the Lucy?" Looking down on Thorson, Liberace replies, "Because I'm the bandleader with the nightclub act." When they eventually break up, Liberace displays his power by having Thorson forcibly removed from his mansion while he welcomes his next new and younger lover. In such portrayals, Liberace takes on qualities of hegemonic masculinity and potentially challenges the assumed femininity of gay men.

CONCLUSION AND IMPLICATIONS

Throughout this chapter, we observed that *Behind the Candelabra* simultaneously reinforces and challenges sexual and gender stereotypes of older adults. It does so through its multifaceted depiction of Liberace as a tragic, aging hero who simultaneously bucks and revels lavishly in social customs.

We noted that the film's representation of Liberace as a highly sexual older gay man both reinforces the stereotype of gay men as hypersexual and challenges the idea that older adults are asexual. Additionally, we found that the film's representation of Liberace both reinforces stereotypes of gay men as effeminate and passive, but also challenges these stereotypes by showing that he exerts a great deal of control within his interpersonal relationships. We now turn our discussion to the implications of our analysis for further examination of aging in sexual minority groups and for consumption of mediated representations of aging gay men.

Our analysis suggests several major implications for further examination of aging in sexual minority populations. First, it is necessary to analyze the mediated representations of older adult women and transgender people across sexualities. Representations of an aging body are mediated by gender; for example, women's aging bodies are likely to be viewed differently than those of men in a patriarchal culture. Second, since there is much more to an individual's identity than age and sexuality, it is necessary to analyze how cultural meanings associated with race, class, gender, sexuality, body type, nation, and religion, among other vectors of difference, intersect to influence mediated representations. By examining such intersections, we can mark and potentially disrupt stereotypes such as older gay men as a mostly white and economically secure population in the United States. Third, it is important to recognize that cultural texts often function dialectically, that is, they do not simply reinforce or challenge stereotypes but, more likely, do both simultaneously with various effects. Recognizing such dialectics can produce more nuanced and complex analysis of popular cultural products. Finally, it is important to pay more attention to the sociocultural aspects of aging. As stated earlier, aging is not a mere chronological fact; it is a social construction influenced by culture and history.

Our analysis also suggests some major implications for consuming representations of aging gay male images in popular media. First, it is important to mark the frequent mediated representations of aging gay men as white, able-bodied, middle- to upper-class U.S. citizens. As a process of highlighting and calling attention to the pervasiveness of particular media images, marking makes the taken-for-granted visible, which can open up new ways of imagining and conceiving aging sexual minority people. Second, the limited mediated representations of aging gay men can result in the production of new normativities, such as class (e.g., affluence and access to social resources) and body (e.g., fitness, grooming, and style). Such new normativities create new hierarchies—and potentially erase and pathologize those who do not or cannot conform to such normativities (i.e., create and maintain further invisibility for poor lesbian and gay seniors of color)—in sexual minority communities. Third, it is important to discern between media visibility and quality of such representations; for invisible populations such as aging sexual minorities, more visibility is not automatically and necessarily good. For example, the British sitcom *Vicious*, distributed by PBS in the United States, presents an older gay male couple verbally abusing each other for comedic effect, and must be examined dialectically (e.g., how does the show reinforce and maintain cultural stereotypes while simultaneously disrupt such stereotypes and offer new possibilities for living and loving). Finally, media images are not simply mirrors of society; they can offer possibilities for social transformation through queering representations of identity. Halperin elaborates:

> It is from the eccentric positionality occupied by the queer subject that it may become possible to envision a variety of possibilities for reordering the relations among sexual behaviors, erotic identities, constructions of gender, forms of knowledge, regimes of enunciation, logics of representation, modes of self-constitution, and practices of community—for restructuring, that is, the relations among power, truth, and desire.[39]

Through featuring images and representations that embody a queer position, media texts can challenge normativities. This can facilitate social transformation through offering tangible representations of alternative ways of knowing, doing, being, and loving for aging sexual minorities. While we noted throughout this chapter that media texts reproduce certain normativities while challenging others, the promise offered by queering mediated representations, which, for example, allows us to unpack cultural conceptions of age and aging as social constructions that empower certain groups and disempower others, should not be overlooked.

NOTES

1. Gust A. Yep, "Queering/Quaring/Kauering/Crippin'/Transing 'Other Bodies' in Intercultural Communication," *Journal of International and Intercultural Communication* 6 (2013): 118–26, on 119, doi: 10.1080/17513057.2013.777087.

2. Cheryl Laz, "Act Your Age," *Sociological Forum* 13 (1998): 85–113, on 108, doi:10.1023/A:1022160015408.

3. Karen I. Fredriksen-Goldsen and Anna Muraco, "Aging and Sexual Orientation: A 25-Year Review of the Literature," *Research on Aging* 32 (2010): 372–413, on 373, doi: 10.1177/0164027509360355.

4. Jim Whaler and Sarah G. Gabbay, "Gay Male Aging: A Review of the Literature," *Journal of Gay & Lesbian Social Services* 6 (1997): 1–20, on 14, doi: 10.1300/J041v06n03_01.

5. Fredriksen-Goldsen and Muraco, "Aging and Sexual Orientation," 402.

6. Sara L. Wright and Silvia S. Canetto, "Stereotypes of Older Lesbians and Gay Men," *Educational Gerontology* 35 (2009): 424–52, on 424, doi: 10.1080/03601270802505640.

7. Dana Rosenfeld, "The Homosexual Body in Lesbian and Gay Elders' Narratives," in *Aging Bodies: Images and Everyday Experience*, edited by Christopher A. Faircloth (Walnut Creek, CA: Altamira Press, 2003), 176.

8. Fredriksen-Goldsen and Muraco, "Aging and Sexual Orientation," 373.

9. Kathleen F. Slevin, "Disciplining Bodies: The Aging Experiences of Older Heterosexual and Gay Men," in *Doing Gender Diversity: Readings in Theory and Real-World Experience*,

edited by Rebecca F. Plante and Lis M. Maurer (Boulder, CO: Westview, 2010), 204–12, on 207.

10. Bill Bytheway, "Visual Representations of Late Life," in *Aging Bodies: Images and Everyday Experience*, edited by Christopher A. Faircloth (Walnut Creek, CA: Altamira Press, 2003), 29–53, on 52.

11. *Behind the Candelabra*, directed by Steven Soderbergh (USA: HBO Films, 2013). Streaming.

12. Annamarie Jagose, *Queer Theory: An Introduction* (New York: New York University Press, 1996), 1.

13. Gust A. Yep, "The Violence of Heteronormativity in Communication Studies: Notes on Injury, Healing, and Queer World-Making," in *Queer Theory and Communication: From Disciplining Queers to Queering the Discipline(s)*, edited by Gust. A. Yep et al. (Binghamton, NY: Harrington Park Press, 2003), 11–53, on 35.

14. Jagose, *Queer Theory*, 1.

15. R. Anthony Slagle, "Queer Criticism and Sexual Normativity: The Case of Pee-Wee Herman," in *Queer Theory and Communication: From Disciplining Queers to Queering the Discipline(s)*, edited by Gust. A. Yep et al. (Binghamton, NY: Harrington Park Press, 2003), 129–46, on 135.

16. David M. Halperin, *Saint Foucault: Towards a Gay Hagiography* (New York: Oxford University Press, 1995), 62.

17. Jagose, *Queer Theory*, 3.

18. Yep, "The Violence of Heteronormativity," 38.

19. Mike Featherstone and Mike Hepworth, "Images of Aging: Cultural Representations of Later Life," in *The Cambridge Handbook of Age and Aging*, edited by Malcolm L. Johnson (New York: Cambridge University Press, 2005), 354–62, on 357; Slevin, "Disciplining Bodies," 205.

20. Martha M. Lauzen and David M. Dozier, "Maintaining the Double Standard: Portrayals of Age and Gender in Popular Films," *Sex Roles* 52, no. 7/8 (2005): 437–46, on 443, doi:10.1007/s11199-005-3710-1; Tom Robinson et al., "Older Characters in Teen Movies from 1980–2006," *Educational Gerontology* 35 (2009): 687–711, on 688, doi:10.1080/03601270802708426.

21. Thomas Walz, "Crones, Dirty Old Men, Sexy Seniors: Representations of the Sexuality of Older Persons," *Journal of Aging and Identity* 7 (2002): 99–112, on 100, doi: 10.1023/A:1015487101438.

22. Ibid.

23. Ibid.

24. Michael Johnson, Jr., "Race, Aging, and Gay In/visibility on U.S. Television," in *Television and the Self: Knowledge, Identity, and Media Representation*, edited by Kathleen M. Ryan and Deborah A. Macey (Lanham, MD: Lexington Books, 2013), 227–342, on 227; Helene Shugart, "Reinventing Privilege: The New (Gay) Man in Contemporary Popular Media," *Critical Studies in Media Communication* 20 (2003): 67–91, on 87, doi: 10.1080/0739318032000067056.

25. Johnson, Jr., "Race, Aging, and Gay In/Visibility," 227.

26. Nancy J. Knauer, *Gay and Lesbian Elders: History, Law, and Identity Politics in the United States* (Surrey, UK: Ashgate Publishing Limited, 2011), 31.

27. Frank Romanelli et al., "Poppers: Epidemiology and Clinical Management of Inhaled Nitrite Abuse," *Pharmacotherapy: The Journal of Human Pharmacology and Drug Therapy* 24 (2004): 69–78, on 71, doi: 10.1592/phco.24.1.69.34801.

28. Vito Russo, *The Celluloid Closet: Homosexuality in the Movies*, revised edition (New York: Harper & Row, 1987), 48.

29. Emily Yeagley, et al., "Hypersexual Behavior and HIV Sex Risk Among Young Gay and Bisexual Men," *Journal of Sex Research* 51 (2014): 882–92, on 882, doi: 10.1080/00224499.2013.818615.

30. R. W. Connell, *Masculinities*, 2nd edition (Berkeley and Los Angeles: University of California Press, 2005), 143; Wright and Canetto, "Stereotypes of Older Lesbians and Gay Men," 426.

31. Johnson, "Race, Aging, and Gay In/Visibility," 233.

32. Richard Dyer, "Stereotyping," in *The Columbia Reader on Lesbians and Gay Men in Media, Society, and Politics*, edited by Larry Gross and James D. Woods (New York: Columbia University Press, 1999), 297–301, on 300.

33. Connell, *Masculinities*, 77.

34. Dyer, "Stereotyping," 300.

35. Aaron J. Blashill and Kimberly K. Powlishta, "Gay Stereotypes: The Use of Sexual Orientation as a Cue for Gender-Related Attributes," *Sex Roles* 61, no. 11–12 (2009): 783–93, on 789, doi: 10.1007/s11199-009-9684-7.

36. Michelle M. Johns et al., "Butch Tops and Femme Bottoms? Sexual Positioning, Sexual Decision Making, and Gender Roles among Young Gay Men," *American Journal of Men's Health* 6 (2012): 505–28, on 506, doi: 10.1177/1557988312455214; Susan Kippax and Gary Smith, "Anal Intercourse and Power in Sex between Men," *Sexualities* 4, no. 4 (2001): 413–34, on 418, doi: 10.1177/136346001004004002.

37. Cele Otnes and Mary Ann McGrath, "Perceptions and Realities of Male Shopping Behavior," *Journal of Retailing* 77 (2001): 111–34, on 112, doi: 10.1016/S0022-4359(00)00047-6.

38. Nick Trujillo, "Hegemonic Masculinity on the Mound: Media Representations of Nolan Ryan and American Sports Culture," *Critical Studies in Mass Communication* 8 (1991): 290–308, doi: 10.1080/15295039109366799.

39. Halperin, *Saint Foucault*, 62.

Chapter Six

Overcoming the Villainous Monster

The Beginnings of Heroic Gay Male Aging

Dustin Bradley Goltz

> They are afraid of what they know is somewhere in the darkness around them, of what may at any moment emerge into the undeniable light of their flash-lamps, nevermore to be ignored, explained away. The fiend that won't fit into their statistics, the Gorgon that refuses their plastic surgery, the vampire drinking blood with tactless uncultured slurps, the bad-smelling beast that doesn't use their deodorants, the unspeakable that insists, despite all their shushing, on speaking its name.
>
> —Christopher Isherwood[1]

What does a heroic depiction of an aging gay male look like? How does heroism, as a concept, inform the politics of gay representation in main-stream media? The short answer is that, according to dominant discourses, the ideas of "gay male aging" and heroism are paradoxical, for a lineage of media representation and cultural mythology have placed these ideas at odds with one another. The aging gay male body has been coded with threat, fear, and as a space of danger—a story of villainy that George, in Christopher Isherwood's *A Single Man*, finds mapped onto his body by the neighborhood children. Mainstream understandings of heroes and heroism have historically been coded as heterosexual, whereas the aging gay male has been written as villainous—the "Gorgon," the "vampire," and the "bad-smelling beast" of Isherwood's "unspeakable."

This monstrous predatory depiction marks the cultural and representation-al history of the aging gay male, which constrains—but also anticipates and potentializes—a distinct form of heroism emerging in contemporary gay rep-resentation. The aging gay male hero rejects the depressed and miserable cautionary tales of the previous decades and allows a new model, image, and

possibility for gay male aging to enter mainstream discourse. While bold and
daring in its own right, this hero's journey is less about defeating sinister
villains (with evil plots to destroy the world?) than deconstructing vilifying
legacies in order to live, love, and love living in the face of social stigma,
homophobia, and cultural ageism.

Thus, this chapter sets a historical context for how aging and gayness
have been produced in mainstream media over the last fifty years, arguing
the presence of a developing heroism in contemporary representations of old
gay men—specifically considering the character of Hal Fields in the 2010
film *Beginners*. In these pages, heroism is approached as the bold push
against, and successful destabilizing of, oppressive representational legacies.
Heroism is not merely how one is situated within their own individual storyline, or what one does (or does not do) in a specific story, but also the
rhetorical significance of one's representation within this legacy of broader
cultural discourses and meanings. Heroism sets forth an alternative possibility beyond oppressive cultural myths, confronting and overcoming social
stigmas that precede the hero and work to narrate him in limited and confin-
ing ways. Thus, the hero is challenging a cultural legacy and representational
lineage that precedes him—a story that works to present him as villain.
Directly engaging and complicating stereotypes around gay male sexuality,
gay cultural youthism, aging gay male isolation, and the neoliberal depoliti-
calization of gayness, this chapter examines how the heroic narrative of Hal
Fields embodies a bold and audacious confrontation of the legacy of the
blood-slurping twilight creatures of mainstream history.

SAD VILLAINS AND YOUTH-OBSESSED GORGONS

The song, "The Ballad of the Sad Young Men," originally part of the 1959
score for *The Nervous Set*, narrates the depressed anxiety and drunken misery
that defined mainstream stereotypes of male homosexuality in the 1950s and
early 1960s. It is the sad young man who must "kiss [his] dreams goodbye,"
as he sings by himself in the cold evening, struggling to forget the awareness
that he is growing older. In pre-1960s Hollywood, during the era of the Hays
Code, explicit reference to homosexuality in film was restricted. The winks,
whispers, hints, and coded gestures that spoke softly to queer audiences
shifted in the late 1960s, when gay characters emerged from the shadows and
onto the big screen—as villainous monsters.[2] As paranoid mythologies of the
wretched twilight creatures, these cautionary tales of dangerous homosexuals
began to take explicit form in Hollywood, offering a slew of doomed and sad
"bad guys" determined to do harm and in need of punishment.

The appearance of homosexuality was a dark and depressing affair. Rhe-
torically, for decades, the primary function and effect of aging gay male

representation in Hollywood has been a tale of failure and horror that results from the departure from the heterosexual ideal.[3] Gayness, and specifically gay aging, was a cautionary tale of the wrong path because gay characters were "pathological, predatory, and dangerous: villains and fools, but never heroes."[4] Homosexuality was the murderous psychopathic foil used to establish the inherent heroism and rightness of heterosexuality.[5] "By stepping into the limelight of explicit representation, homosexuality gave heterosexuality its coherence, its heroism, its opportunity to 'save the day' and further construct homophobia as virtuous."[6]

Older audiences and queer media scholars know this history all too well, a history that for many might seem far away in the post–*Will & Grace* land of *The New Normal* and *Modern Family*. This "wrong path" narrative of villainous monstrosity that was exemplified in the late 1960s and 1970s has changed over time, and has gone through some significant shifts, yet has not fully disappeared. The feared, punishable, sight-gag, or self-loathing queers of *Freebie and the Bean, Midnight Cowboy, Cruising,* and *The Boys in the Band*[7] shifted in the 1980s following the emergence of the AIDS pandemic. *Longtime Companion, Parting Glances, An Early Frost,* and several other AIDS-themed films presented a more sympathetic image of gayness to mainstream audiences, yet one that was constructed through the impending death of the gay character. Reflective of the horrific outbreak of HIV/AIDS, we watched a generation of young gay men die.

The politics of age play an interesting role in these narratives, as the villainous representations of the 1960s and 1970s were far more willing to use older bodies to tell these villainous tales. Yet the films in the 1980s worked to build sympathy and audience identification by often enlisting younger (and white, cis-gendered) characters and actors. When you consider the actors who defined the "face" of the '80s and early '90s AIDS narrative in Hollywood—Dermot Mulroney, Aidan Quinn, Steve Buscemi, Bruce Davison, Tom Hanks, Campbell Scott, Robert Carradine, Ian McKellen, Antonio Banderas[8] —it was a face of often younger and primarily white gay men. The rhetorical work of creating this "face" has many dimensions and implications far beyond the scope of this one chapter, such as the use of whiteness to bridge audience identification for the pandemic. Yet these narratives used age (alongside race, gender performance, and class) to produce a familiar, less threatening, and sympathetic face. Young, weak, and dying, these images of the "boy next door" demanded compassion and recognition from a homophobic society and the shamefully and inhumanely silent U.S. government.

This face also posed a powerful rhetorical argument by working to humanize and de-vilify (some) gay males on the cultural screen and by enlisting a range of normative identifications (young, masculine, white, middle-class, educated) to exploit recognition and affinity. These representations did the

difficult and necessary work of humanizing the pandemic for the mainstream, yet this was accomplished by leveraging existing systems of social
normativity and privilege. These representations carry through the 1990s and
into the new millennium, setting the landscape for the evolving—yet normatively confined—image of mainstream gay representation.

AGING VILLAINS AND THIS NEW NORMAL

The 1990s has been marked as a period of time when there was a significant
emergence of more "positive" gay representation. The closeted and self-
hating Steven Carrington of 1980s *Dynasty* is replaced with the out-and-
proud Matt Fielding on *Melrose Place*. Ellen came out, Will found Grace,
and suddenly explicitly gay characters were appearing on *Roseanne*, *Sex and
the City*, *Dawson's Creek*, daytime TV, reality TV, and Must See TV. Patrick
Swayze and Wesley Snipes dressed in drag for *To Wong Foo, Thanks For
Everything, Julie Newmar* and it seemed suddenly Hollywood was as "queer
as fuck." Amidst this wave of "positivity," which has been strongly criticized
by queer media scholars,[9] representations of gay male aging or positive
images of the future were relatively absent.[10] The twenty- to thirty-year-old
face of '80s gayness continued to be the mainstream representation, whereas
the cautionary tale of the lecherous and lonely older gay male at the corner of
the bar continued to circulate at the periphery of mainstream images and in
the dark tacit corners of gay narratives. While gay (white, thirty-something,
usually lawyers) bodies were centralized, the rare appearance of older gay
males served as a joke or a threat/warning of danger, sexual predation, or
failed development. In other words, they often appeared in order to manifest
heterosexual fears for what their gay children might become, or cautionary
tales of why younger gay men feared aging. Gay aging is equated with
perpetual loss, self-hatred, isolation from the youth-centeredness of gay culture, disciplined through myths of sexual predation, and a sad disconnected
existence for not knowing when it is time to "leave the party." Still struggling
to survive the end of the film or TV series, older gays established a legacy of
what *not* to do, be, or hope for.[11]

The implications of these representations are significant in two specific
ways. One, they perpetuate a false mythology that older gay men are depressed, lonely outcasts, barred off from the youth-driven twenty-four-hour
(strobe light beaming and house music thumping) party of gay male culture.
It tells a story of "live fast and die young" that constructs gay youths as
sexual objects of desire and victims of the ticking time clock of age, for it
will never get better than it is when you are young. This story, which has
been commonplace in mainstream depictions of gay culture for years, has
historically been unfounded in the actual research on gay male cultures,

wherein aging gay men continually report as much, if not more, satisfaction in aging as heterosexuals.[12] Research on gay communities dispels the dominating myth that equates aging with perpetual loss, misery, and isolation. Yet, the "unspeakable" old sad man at the bar staring at doom in his glass of rye is a cultural tale that Hollywood is slow to do away with. Hostetler argues that this image of the sad older gay man in the youth-centered culture "provides a cautionary tale about developmental failure"[13] to many younger gay men.

Secondly, 1990s representation worked to reify the "wrong," "harder," and "sad" path of non-heteronormative gay aging[14] that is used to justify and privilege the "normal" and "healthy" thirty-something gay males that came to dominate mainstream TV. Post-2000 representations of gayness take the white, middle class, male, thirty-something lawyer into their forties through the scripting of "straight time"[15]—a heteronormative orientation toward time and maturation that is defined through systems of marriage, procreation, and stories of happily ever after. This modern (gay) family man, as this "new normal," paves an evolving image of what a "successful" aging gay male might look like when articulated through a mainstream, heteronormative, neoliberal model of suburban life, depoliticized gay identity, consumerism, and whose primary social definition is narrated through the biological family (rather than a queer community, a political community, a community of friends or lovers, etc.). Stated another way, cultural norms have narrowly expanded to provide a space for "successful" gay male aging, so long as those images worked to faithfully declare the rightness and correctness of heteronormativity. Thus, the increase of "positive" gay representations continues to offer stories of age and future that emulate the idealized script of straight time.

BEGINNERS: HEROIC GAY MALE AGING IN FILM

Oliver: You rewrote Jesus's death?

Hal: It was far too violent. We need new stories.[16]

While there are surely arguments that can be made for how Hollywood's new normal for gay male representation is heroic in some respects, especially in thinking about heroism in bolder and more audacious terms, the film *Beginners* presents an aging gay male hero who works to disrupt decades of cultural myths, stereotypes, and apologetic representation with complexity, bravery, and a unique commitment to queer sexuality and history. At its core, *Beginners* is the story of man in his thirties, Oliver, who is processing the recent death of his father, Hal Fields. His father, played by Christopher Plummer, has already passed away at the opening of the film. Thus, we are

introduced to and only see Hal through a series of flashbacks that are re-
played in Oliver's memory. Hal's wife of forty-five years, Oliver's mother,
had passed away four years earlier, and following her passing, Hal makes the
decision to come out of the closet as a gay male. The Internet Movie Data-
base (IMDb) summarizes the film as, "A young man is rocked by two an-
nouncements from his elderly father: that he has terminal cancer, and that he
has a young male lover."[17] This framing, while effective for advertising the
film to a mainstream audience, misrepresents the tone and undercuts the
more heroic themes of the film. To equate Hal's coming out and his cancer is
a problematic parallel, yet it also implies that the film is about Oliver "dealing" with these issues that have "rocked" him. Hal's cancer and his partner,
Andy, are painted as two problems to face, assuming a straight audience who
can identify with the shock of having to "deal" with a father with "a young
male lover." Rather, while Hal's cancer claims his life, it is Hal's coming out
as gay (which is then followed by his relationship with Andy) that honors his
spirit and, inevitably, helps Oliver find the courage to live with bravery and
emotional courage.

Arguing that the representation of Hal Fields provides a unique form of
filmic heroism, this analysis moves through a series of thematic arguments to
detail this position. First, I argue that the use and recurrent presence of
history and cultural memory is significant in the constructed heroism in the
film. Next, the film's direct and fearless engagement of aging gay male
stereotypes is examined. Third, I consider the heroic significance of representing an aging gay male community, wherein the isolated aging gay male is
rescripted within a vibrant and supportive collective. Finally, a unique heroism is produced through Hal's active mobility and agency in his navigation
of his older gay life.

The heroism of the film is due, in part, to the historical framework that is
explicitly drawn to contextualize Hal's life, his desires, and his choices. At
several moments within the film, Oliver pauses and insists that the viewer
make sense and read his father and his father's life within specific historical
contexts, cultural events, and political moments. Flashes of still images are
shown as Oliver narrates that each image depicts what love or family looked
like at a specific moment in time (in the mainstream imaginary). He points
out places of events and moments that historicize the choices, relations, and
norms that defined his parents' lives. From the 1950s and 1960s into the
1970s and 1980s, Oliver reflects on what it was to be gay, a man, and an
American throughout the decades of his father's adult life. Resisting the
historical amnesia that is common to so much of the neoliberal homonorma-
tive models of contemporary representation, the film sets a context where we,
as viewers, are called on to remember. The film holds up the history of
bathroom cruising, police raids, public outings, the Stonewall Riots, and
AIDS so as to never forget the political and cultural implications of Hal's life

in the closet, as well as his decision to come out. The significance of this filmic and narrative choice is inherently political. Resisting a normative neo-liberal trend of depoliticized identity and privatization (wherein a gay character is localized in a family relation or situation that is distanced from historical or broader sociocultural systems of heteronormativity and oppression), Hal's story is produced in time and within a political moment. His story carries traces of history that cannot be erased within the perpetual now. He is not just a chipper older gay man who emerged in a narrative after the millennium. He chose, under duress, to live in the closet, to marry, to meet men in restrooms for sex, and to not come out for decades. He watched violence, hatred, and homophobic cruelty that marks and defines the present in ways "positive" 1990s representation often hides, obscures, and downplays. Resisting privatization and amnesia, Hal's story is not, nor can it ever be, just Hal's story, but a life lived in a sociopolitical context.

Secondly, as a man who comes out at age seventy-five, Hal is refreshingly unapologetic about his sexuality and his sexual desires. He's not ashamed about what turns him on and what gets him off. Historically, this is a delicate tightrope to walk, as previous representations either side with the hypersexed "creepy old man" predator tale, or a saintly asexual grandfather figure. As IMDb makes a point of labeling Andy as his "young male lover," and thus suggesting this age/gay combination is scandalous enough to "rock" Oliver's world, it is not presented with this level of alarmist drama in the film. When coming out, Hal says matter-of-factly to Oliver that he wants to "explore this side" of himself. Although the chronology of events in the flashbacks are not fully clear, it appears Hal's first trip to a gay bar, after coming out, is a hip Silverlake spot in the early 2000s called Akbar.

Reflecting on the experience, we see Hal briefly walk through the younger and hipper bar with excitement, awe, and a sense of wonder. Although this evening sends Hal home to an empty bed, the visual depiction of him inhabiting the space with pride, excitement, and a sense of feeling welcomed is discursively significant. On the phone with Oliver later that evening, he says, in a matter-of-fact tone, "Young gay men don't go for older gay men. You have it easy." He does not seem disciplined or shamed by this realization, but comfortably aware that his sexual desire for men younger than he will not usually be reciprocated. In an effort to reach out to younger men who would be interested in reciprocating his sexual attentions, he writes a personal ad. Proudly displaying a picture of his seventy-five-year-old self, he speaks of his sexual interests and attractions alongside his hobbies and biographical information. It's bold and daring in that his self-expression is simply honest. It's admirable and human, rather than something constructed to solicit an audience response of mockery or wincing. Hal speaks his desire, his hopes, and his identity without accommodation or shame.

This sex- and age-positive personal ad is a significant artifact throughout the film. It is the item Oliver discovers in the first frames of the film, and it is the text he shares with Anna, his love interest, in the closing frames of the film. It is the text that fuels Oliver to stop Anna from running away and gives him the inspiration to stop pushing her away. After hearing this personal ad, Anna states, in poignant discovery, "He didn't give up." This speaks to the bold spirit that Hal infused the last four years of his life with, but also remarks on a cultural expectation or assumption that he might have given up—that it was too late for him. Rather than adhering to the cultural script that seventy-five, for the gay man, is the end, Hal lived with audacious abandon. Seventy-five was his beginning, and he refused to lie sexually or romantically dormant and let convention define him. This model of heroism, this lesson on living one's desire, is the thing that saves Oliver in the end. He is "rocked" by his father's life and death, but not in a way that sets his perfect life off center. Rather, his father's example infuses Oliver's dulled, quiet, and drab existence with an urgency to risk and defy the things that hold him down.

Through a few brief but significant peripheral sequences, the community of gay men that surrounded and celebrated Hal works to dislodge and push against a series of negative gay aging stereotypes. It is mentioned briefly that Hal joins the Prime Timers, a national social club for older gay men, and the film is quick to establish the presence of a supportive, vibrant older gay male community that has embraced Hal. For example, near the beginning of the film, Andy and a dozen or so other men set off a sequence of fireworks in an open field in honor of their friend, Hal, who was clearly loved. The men laugh and cheer, overcome with emotion. In other scenes throughout the film, while flashing back to Hal's life, there are shots of his friends jovially drinking wine in Hal's hospital room, attending lively parties at Hal's home, and working alongside Hal to politically organize for the gay community. These scenes narrate an older gay male relational context of support, love, passion, and community.

Contrasted with Oliver's fairly isolated and sterile social life in his thirties, Hal's life is grand, bold, whooping, and communal. In another flashback, Oliver is concerned about Andy moving in to his dad's home, as Hal is very sick. But Hal and Andy resist his sobered seriousness by dancing and playing in the living room with reckless abandon. The stories of the isolated, depressed, lonely old gay man simply do not take root in this narrative, as Hal, at seventy-five, paints a uniquely different portrait about gay family, gay aging, and gay community.

While testing cultural myths, the film also works to dislodge some of Oliver's core heteronormative assumptions about relationships and community. Oliver is surprised to find that his mother, before marrying Hal, knew about Hal's same-sex desires. Oliver is also surprised and uneasy when he is casually informed about Andy and Hal's open relationship. Hal argues, "If Andy wasn't going to be monogamous, why should I be?" Attempting to shame his father for breaking norms of decorum (that cultural wince we would expect when older gay men express sexual desire), Oliver replies, "Jesus, Pop!" Hal quickly rejects this disciplinary move, replying "Jesus, yourself!"

It is Oliver who comes to ask the question, "How do you keep hold of friends? Or boyfriends?" In a significant twist, it is Oliver's social life that is isolated and lonely. As an older gay male, it is Hal who holds the secrets to success, living, loving, and happiness that Oliver struggles to make sense of. Family and community surround and hold Hal up in ways that not only substitute heteronormative models, but in many ways, criticize and trouble these logics. After Hal's passing, it takes Oliver a long time to realize that Andy is, has been, and will be family to him—even (and especially) after the passing of Hal. Oliver, somewhat ignorantly and normatively, dismissed this very real and important part of his father's (and his own) life, only coming to understand the importance of Andy later in the film, and thus the extended possibilities of family, relationships, and community.

Finally, Hal's heroism is embodied and represented through his own agency, for Hal plays an active role in the crafting and navigation of his short, but full-out gay life. The cultural stories that work to shame, discipline, contain, or restrict what an older gay man can, should, or ought to do simply do not work to define Hal. He enters Akbar and does not let his age diminish his worth, even if he is not attractive to the younger men there. He pursues relationship ads, works to find a gay community, invests his energies in gay politics, and takes active steps to "explore this side" of himself. He argues, "I don't want to just be theoretically gay. I want to do something about it." This is significant, as the myths and stories that precede and frame Hal, while given recognition, do not fully determine who he is and who he can choose to be. Neither blind to, nor immobilized by, the ways age, sexuality, history, and family have worked to write his movements, Hal heroically writes his own story against and on top of these previous tales.

Hal's agency, and thus his heroism, however, is not without some critical complication. Hal's heroism is tied to some key systems of privilege, including the financial mobility that is demonstrated by a beautiful home, shopping, and a life working in museums. He is educated, white, and has lived in the story of a heterosexual male for the majority of his life. Thus, the ability to assume and claim agency is both resistant, but also highly normative. In this respect, his heroism is still built on normative logics that help make him identifiable and relatable to the mainstream. While he can push boundaries in terms of his unapologetic sexual desires and young male attractions, which are bold and heroic steps against cultural conventions, this work is partially accomplished through his normative alignments and identifications.

As a father and a married man for forty-five years, he is coded with some safety and cultural normativity. His time in the closet might earn him, in the eyes of a heteronormative audience, a sacrifice that works to justify his sexuality. After all, we only meet Hal after we know he has died, which undercuts his threat, ushers in empathy through the image of a mourning son, and continues a long lineage of older gay men who fail to survive through the final shots of the film. In short, his agency is both heroic, yet mobilized through his relation to normativity and privilege. Still, as a single representation that humanizes the older gay man, it stories him in a community that supports and celebrates rather than demonizes his sexual desires, as well as insists that we position stories in political and historical context. This single representation is surely a worthwhile beginning.

Visible, proud, unapologetic yet identifiable, and not defined by their sexual obsession with youth and youthism, the notion of successful gay aging (which has been paradoxical for too long) is slowly being negotiated within mainstream representation. Highlighting the heroic representation of Hal Fields, this analysis works to underscore the importance and significant break from gay male representation over the last decades—a trend that will hopefully continue in newer texts such as HBO's *Looking* and the PBS series *Vicious*. These representations, in a sense, have the potential to enact "heroism" in terms of role model and inspiration, but also in presenting heroic pioneers that queer a discourse of gay aging that reshapes how gay age and gay future are storied within U.S. popular culture.

NOTES

1. Christopher Isherwood, *A Single Man* (1964; New York: Quality Paperback Book Club, 1992), 26–27.
2. Vito Russo, *The Celluloid Closet: Homosexuality in the Movies*, revised edition (New York: Harper & Row, 1987).
3. Dustin B. Goltz, *Queer Temporalities in Gay Male Representation: Tragedy, Normativity, and Futurity* (New York: Routledge, 2010), 47; John R. Yoakam, "Gods or Monsters: A Critique of Representations in Film and Literature of Relationships between Older Gay Men and Younger Men," in *Midlife and Aging in Gay America*, edited by Douglas C. Kimmel and Dawn Lundy Martin (New York: Harrington Park Press, 2001), 65–80.
4. Russo, *Celluloid Closet*, 122.
5. Ibid., 186.
6. Goltz, *Queer Temporalities*, 29.
7. In addition to Russo's *Celluloid Closet* and Goltz's *Queer Temporalities*, see Fred Fejes and Kevin Petrich, "Invisibility, Homophobia, and Heterosexism: Lesbians, Gays and the Media," *Critical Studies in Media Communication*, no. 10 (1993): 395–422; Larry Gross, *Up from Invisibility* (New York: Columbia University Press, 2001); and Suzanna Danuta Walters, *All the Rage: The Story of Gay Visibility in America* (Chicago: University of Chicago Press, 2001).
8. See the films *Philadelphia*, *Longtime Companion*, *As/Of*, *An Early Frost*, *And the Band Played On*, and *Parting Glances*.
9. See Kathleen Battles and Wendy Hilton-Morrow, "Gay Characters in Conventional Spaces: *Will & Grace* and the Conventional Comedy Genre," in *Critical Studies in Media Communication*, no. 19 (2002): 87–105; Bonnie J. Dow, "Ellen, Television, and the Politics of

Gay and Lesbian Visibility," *Critical Studies in Media Communication* 18 (2001): 123–40; Helene A. Shugart, "Reinventing Privilege: The New (Gay) Man in Contemporary Popular Media," in *Critical Studies in Media Communication* 20 (2003): 67–91; Steven Seidman, *Beyond the Closet: The Transformation of Gay and Lesbian Life* (New York: Routledge, 2002); Walters, *All the Rage*; and Gross, *Up from Invisibility*.

10. Goltz, *Queer Temporalities*.

11. For a detailed analysis of aging gay men in post-1980s representation and the rhetorical production of gay male futures, see Goltz, *Queer Temporalities*.

12. See Raymond M. Berger, "Realities of Gay and Lesbian Aging," *Social Work* 29 (1984): 57–82; Raymond M. Berger and James J. Kelly, "What Are Older Gay Men Like: An Impossible Question," in *Midlife and Aging in Gay America*, edited by Douglas C. Kimmel and Dawn Lundy Martin (New York: Harrington Park Press, 2001), 55–64, on 62; Lester B. Brown, Glen R. Alley, Steven Sarosy, Gerramy Quarto, and Terry Cook, "Gay Men: Aging Well!" in *Midlife and Aging in Gay America*, edited by Douglas C. Kimmel and Dawn Lundy Martin (New York: Harrington Park Press, 2001), 41–54; and Rachel Dorfman, Karina Walters, Patrick Burke, Lovinda Hardin, Theresa Karanik, John Raphael, and Ellen Silverstein, "Old, Sad, and Alone: The Myth of the Aging Homosexual," *Journal of Gerontological Social Work* 24 (1995): 29–45.

13. Andrew J. Hostetler "Old, Gay, and Alone? The Ecology of Well-Being among Middle-Aged and Older Single Gay Men," in *Gay and Lesbian Aging*, edited by Gilbert Herdt and Brian deVries (New York: Springer, 2004), 143–76, on 160.

14. Dustin B. Goltz, "Investigating Queer Future Meanings: Destructive Perceptions of 'the Harder Path,'" *Qualitative Inquiry* 15, no. 3 (2009): 561–86.

15. Judith Halberstam, *In a Queer Time and Place: Transgender Bodies, Subcultural Lives* (New York: New York University Press, 2005).

16. *Beginners*, DVD, directed by Mike Mills (2010; Universal Studios, 2011).

17. "*Beginners* (2010)," IMDb, http://www.imdb.com/title/tt1532503/ (accessed October 28, 2014).

Chapter Seven

The Power of Performance

Tyler Perry's Madea as Village Sage and Superwoman

Carlos D. Morrison, Jacqueline Allen Trimble, and
Ayoleke D. Okeowo

Tyler Perry has produced and/or starred in fifteen films and five plays, and
has written three books and six soundtracks. His movies alone have grossed
nearly $700 million. A large measure of his success rests on the recurring
central character of Mabel Simmons, also known as Madea, a gun-wielding,
quick-tongued force of nature, who dispenses wisdom, particularly to young
women in crisis, and serves as a paragon of female strength even as she
engages in slapstick antics. In short, she is as much village sage and superwoman as fool. Donning a gray wig and Mammy-like bosom, Perry transforms himself into a feisty, indignant matriarch to perform the feminine
across three genres: stage, screen, and television. While some scholars have
addressed a variety of critical issues related to Perry's work such as black
authenticity, class, race, spirituality, gender, and sexuality, in this chapter we
examine Madea as village sage and aging superhero. [1]

To this end, we will rely on Judith Butler's notion of "gender as performative acts"[2] to show how Madea the African American matriarch, as Perry
performs her, functions as an aged heroine who is all-knowing, village sage,
and has superpowers, as a superwoman. Therefore, our chapter begins with a
brief background discussion of Tyler Perry and his Madea character, followed by a discussion of Butler's theory of gender as performance; we then
provide a critical analysis of Madea's function as village sage and aging
superwoman.

FROM EMMITT PERRY, JR., TO TYLER PERRY:
A LIFE TRANSFORMATION

Tyler Perry was born Emmitt Perry, Jr., on September 13, 1969, in New Orleans. Perry, who has two older sisters and a younger brother, legally changed his name when he was sixteen in reaction to physical abuse he suffered at the hands of his father Emmitt Perry, Sr., a local carpenter. "I just started telling people my name is Tyler. I didn't want to carry my father's name. I didn't want to be his Jr. I have no idea where I got the name from."[3] Perry also endured sexual abuse by family members and spent much of his time fighting depression and suicidal thoughts. To deal with his anguish, Margena Christian reports that he turned to writing: "While watching Oprah Winfrey's talk show, [Perry] learned that writing could be 'cathartic' and began to journal. In his late teens, he wrote his first stage play, *I Know I've Been Changed*, about adult survivors of abuse."[4]

In 1990, Perry moved to Atlanta, Georgia, to distance himself from the pain caused by his family life in New Orleans. He was in his early twenties and took jobs as a construction worker, used-car salesman, and bill collector while he pursued his theatrical aspirations. Perry "lost his job [as a bill collector while] trying to pursue a career in visual arts because he couldn't get time off from work. [He] ended up homeless"[5] but never stopped chasing his dream of becoming a renowned playwright. His first play, the musical *I Know I've Been Changed*, deals with Christian themes such as forgiveness, love, and self-worth and initially attracted a disappointing audience of only about thirty when it premiered in 1992. Perry spent the next six years refining the play, and in 1998, it enjoyed successful runs in Atlanta at both the House of Blues nightclub and the Fox Theater. Over the next decade, Perry produced a series of financially successful productions, geared toward an African American audience, that have also become movies, including *I Can Do Bad All By Myself* (1993), *Diary of a Mad Black Woman* (2001), *Madea's Family Reunion* (2003), *Madea Goes to Jail* (2005–2006), *What's Done in the Dark* (2006–2007), and *Madea's Big Happy Family* (2010).[6]

Mabel "Madea" Simmons appeared for the first time in *I Can Do Bad All By Myself*. Twelve years later, Perry introduced the character to movie audiences in the feature film *Diary of a Mad Black Woman* (2005). Madea (whose name derives from the contraction of "mother" and "dear") became a popular recurring character and, according to Perry, is based on a combination of his mother and aunt, who live in Georgia.

GENDER AND TYLER PERRY'S MADEA PERSONA: THE THEORY

Tyler Perry's cross-gendered portrayal of Madea evokes the scholarship of Judith Butler, who sees gender identity as a flexible construct that can best be understood as performance.[7] Traditionally, sex has determined gender, and individuals have been relegated to one of two fixed categories—male or female. Butler, however, argues that "sex, sexuality, gender, and identity are all located within a matrix [as opposed to rigid categories] of power and discourse that produces and regulates how we understand the terms, among others, *man, woman, masculinity,* and *femininity.*"[8] To be recognized as masculine or feminine, an individual has to perform the appropriate gender role. For example, Martin Lawrence adopted the persona of Big Momma in order to play a credible undercover agent in the 2000 movie *Big Momma's House,* and Brooke Shields adopted a male persona so she could participate in an African safari race in the 1984 movie *Sahara.* Both cases illustrate that "gender is what we do rather than who we are; it is a verb and not a noun. . . . Gender . . . is real to the extent that it is performed."[9]

The Madea persona is rooted in Butler's notion of gender performativity. Perry reconfigures his masculine identity into female guise and offers a feminine/masculine performance or, as several scholars suggest, a "gendered performance from a male perspective."[10] Madea's facile use of language may align her with the feminine, though her aggressive behavior and her massive size may traditionally seem more masculine. Indeed, it is Perry's performance of the feminine that allows Madea to get away with behavior that would be unacceptable if she were not wearing a wig and a dress. This idea is exemplified in *Madea Goes to Jail* when, explaining why she would not go to an anger management program, she says, "I told you I ain't got no anger management problem . . . [because] before I get got, I'm goin' get my Glock." A large black man waving a Glock is perceived as dangerous; an old black woman waving a Glock is a conduit for communal wisdom and a comedic display of feminine power. Perry's masculinity, cloaked behind age and a feminine gender, allows Madea the authority and autonomy she needs to function as both village sage and superwoman.

MADEA AS VILLAGE SAGE

The village sage is generally defined as male elder who transmits the cultural knowledge of the villagers using the power of the spoken word—stories, proverbs, and oral wisdom. The oldest member of the Simmons clan, Madea, like the village sage, is an elder who occupies a position of authority and influence in the family. Because of her perceived advanced age (which she never reveals), Madea's family tolerates her unorthodox ways and her belief that years of living as a "trash-talking, gun-toting Black matriarch of an extended family of children, relatives, family and friends"[11] entitle her to do and say as she pleases. While Perry's Madea persona is the amalgamation of both feminine and masculine identities, it is Perry's performative acts of hegemonic masculinity, an idealized form that emphasizes control, authority, and toughness,[12] that infuse Madea's discourse. In other words, her elder status and authority as matriarch are grounded not in the nurturing affection of dear mother, but in a frank, violent sternness often associated with masculine behavior. Madea's reaction to the distress of younger women characters is rarely to sympathize or coddle, but rather to empower them to fight back or exact revenge, whether that be by destroying the clothes of a wayward husband as in *Diary of a Mad Black Woman* or pouring grits on an abuser as in *Madea's Family Reunion.*

As a village sage, Madea is also the embodiment of the Harriet Tubman myth or "mythoform" articulated by Molefi Assante.[13] In a modern Western context, science and technology are mechanisms by which reality is explained and understood, and myths, Asante observes, are considered to be stories viewed as false and superstitious; however, in an African or non-Western context, he notes that myths are real stories or tales "of a traditional nature that [have] functional value for society."[14] For example, the myth of Harriet Tubman was a real story, epic in nature, that told of a woman who, after gaining her own freedom from slavery, returned to the South (gun in hand) to free other enslaved Africans. Tubman repeatedly put herself in harm's way for the freedom of others. The value of the Harriet Tubman myth for present-day "villagers" is that it shows them how to take control of and overcome life's obstacles, emphasizing the importance of the collective as opposed to the individual, and teaching them how to reach back and help others. Through the discourse of wisdom and straight talk, Madea allows the villagers to see their troubles as something they have the power to overcome.

In *Tyler Perry's Madea Goes to Jail* (2009), inmates Madea, Candace (Keshia Knight Pulliam), T. T. (Sofia Vergara), and Donna (Vanessa Ferlito) attend a required lecture led by the prison counselor, Ellen (Viola Davis).[15] As Ellen engages the inmates in dialogue about forgiveness, Madea gets more and more fed up with the inmates blaming others instead of taking responsibility for their own mistakes. She forcefully admonishes the inmates to stop playing the victim, take responsibility for their actions, and forgive the individuals who led them down the path to prison (read "slavery" for purposes of the Tubman analogy). Madea says,

> You [all] in jail because of what you did. Learn to take responsibility for yourself, for your own stuff. I can't stand folks wanna be the victim. "This person did this so I'm this way." Everyone in this place got a story. Your

momma and daddy gave you life. . . . It's up to you to make something of it. Suck it up and shut the hell up.[16]

In the above example, Madea, acting as Harriet Tubman, employs a language of wisdom, albeit a kind of crude straight talk, to transform the inmates from victims to victors. Compelled by Madea's language coupled with her commanding vocal expression, the inmates choose to "suck it up and shut the hell up!"[17] Her involvement in the inmates' lives is also a testament to her concern for the collective. Madea could have easily spoken to the inmates individually; however, she was attuned to the collective irresponsibility in the village, eliciting strong public verbal and nonverbal responses from her as village sage.

Madea's use of language is rooted in the African oral tradition[18] manifested via black communication,[19] which is defined by Evelyn Dandy as "a system of speaking behaviors" that places an emphasis on, among other features, moral teachings through proverbs and wise sayings.[20] This imparting of wisdom through specific kinds of language is the final characteristic shared by Madea and the village sage. In his book, *Don't Make a Black Woman Take Off Her Earrings*, Perry, writing in Madea's spoken perspective, provides commentary on topics such as marriage, family, money, and sex, among others. While conventional wisdom tells us it is important to play the game of life well to be successful, Madea, whose advice is anything but conventional, claims, "It's not how you play the game, but if you win" the money from the late-night card game.[21] And when it comes to managing money, Madea says that "if you're going to make money, do the right thing with it. Get you some hard assets. Get you a house," as opposed to living life lavishly in the "projects."[22] Concerning credit, Madea has a few words for the young people: "Don't go out there messing up your credit. Do the right thing. That credit's going to score you and everything [you do] in life—it ain't black, it ain't white, it's the credit."[23] In case of poor credit, Madea's words of wisdom are, "A little bit of suffering is a good thing."[24] If the erstwhile villagers take Madea's wise sayings to heart, they will live as victors. If they do not abide by her wisdom, they will remain victims until they learn otherwise. Either way, Madea fulfills her role as village sage who uses the power of language to impart teachings and wisdom to the people.

As suggested earlier, Tyler Perry's feminine/masculine performance of Madea as elder, embodiment of the Harriet Tubman myth, and communicator of wisdom requires the costume of femaleness (hair, makeup, and dress) to be supported by the cultural power and authority of masculinity, which provides Madea the autonomy to speak her mind. Perry, who is physically tall and broad for a man, makes an imposing woman. His Madea costume barely hides his masculine form, but the performance of the feminine in this manner is certainly a source of her humor (numerous jokes about, and references to,

Madea's unattractiveness) and may be a source of her power. After all, the word "sage" in common usage is a synonym for "wise old man," suggesting again that Madea's role is dually gendered, as is Madea's other role, that of superwoman.

MADEA AS SUPERWOMAN

The black woman as superwoman is a topic of debate within the black scholarly community. One argument is that the dehumanizing and brutal conditions facing the black woman during antebellum slavery created a situation where she *had* to fend for herself and her children, thus taking on superwoman-like qualities. The black man could not protect her (or himself for that matter) from being beaten and raped, emasculated as he was by the strictures of his enslavement. According to Michelle Wallace in her book, *Black Macho and the Myth of the Superwoman,*[25] the black woman, as a result of the conditions she faced in a plantation system, came to be viewed in a mythical superhero-like manner:

> [She is] a woman of inordinate strength, with an ability for tolerating an unusual amount of misery and heavy, distasteful work. This woman does not have the same fears, weaknesses, and insecurities as other women, but believes herself to be and is, in fact, stronger emotionally than most men. Less of a woman in that she is less "feminine" and helpless, she is really more of a woman in that she is the embodiment of Mother Earth, the quintessential mother with infinite sexual, life-giving, and nurturing reserves. In other words, she is a superwoman.[26]

Charisse Jones and Kumea Shorter-Gooden question the idea of black woman as superwoman.[27] Wallace contends that the black woman as woman and not superwoman is aware of her human weaknesses and vulnerabilities in light of the social, political, and economic conditions she faces.[28] In focusing on her humanity, the black woman becomes less of a superwoman with uncanny abilities.

Our stance is that Tyler Perry's Madea possesses both an awareness of her human frailty and her superhero powers. One of the best examples of Madea's humanity concerns her feelings about death, particularly with regard to healthy eating. For Madea, "Death is something that a lot of people have been afraid of, but it's something that we all got to do."[29] Because she sees death as a natural consequence of living, Madea is unapologetic about her love for fried foods: "My favorite food is fried. Period. Whatever's fried, that's my favorite. The deeper you fry it . . . the better. I love fried everything: fried chicken, fried catfish, fried potatoes, [and] fried collard greens."[30] Madea's attitude about eating can be best summed up when she says, "Every day I wake up. I eat whatever the hell I want to eat. I'm happy. So if I die of anything, it's because I was eating happy. Hell, put me in a closed casket if it bothers you so much."[31]

Her weakness for unhealthy food may also be read as a sign of her superwoman invincibility. Neither death nor clogged arteries hold any sway with her. While Madea is quite human, there are, however, three traits that define her as a superwoman: (1) an alter ego; (2) a reputation for getting things done, and (3) an ability to act, unconstrained by society's laws.

Superheroes, female or male, often have alter egos that constitute part of a dual identity. In the DC Comics universe, Diana Prince's alter ego is Wonder Woman, while Dr. Barbara Gordon's alias is Batgirl. Mabel Simmons's alter ego is Madea. Simmons becomes a superhero when she defends a woman from an abusive husband: "I went over there and beat the hell out of him. He was a pretty big man, and I surprised myself with my own strength . . . I learned that I have more than the strength of a man."[32] The joke that Madea is, in fact, played by a man masquerading as a woman hovers below the surface throughout the Perry films and in her statement. Of course she has "more than the strength of a man"; she has the dual strength of both genders. As with many superheroes, Madea's superheroic act was misunderstood. Though the woman asked Madea to leave her house and leave her husband alone in the end, Madea came to the realization that "I . . . was something special and that I shouldn't waste my superpowers. I found out that when I and my big old 68 DX that's on my chest enter the room, we can make a difference. Wonder twins activate."[33]

A second characteristic that defines a superwoman is her recognition by relevant others for getting things done. A good example of this characteristic can be found in the movie *Tyler Perry's Madea's Witness Protection.*[34] In the movie, George Needleman (Eugene Levy) is the chief financial officer of a major Wall Street firm at the center of a Ponzi scheme with Mafia ties. Needleman is made the scapegoat for the Ponzi fiasco, and to clear his name and avoid prison, he decides to become a government witness. He and his family—wife Kate Needleman (Denise Richards), mother Barbara Needleman (Doris Roberts), and children Cindy (Danielle Campbell) and Howie (Devan Leos)—must go into hiding until the federal trial can take place. Madea's nephew, Brian Simmons (Tyler Perry), the federal attorney in Atlanta handling the case, is assigned the responsibility of finding a safe house for the Needleman family because the federal witness protection program has been compromised and can easily be infiltrated by the mob. Brian Simmons, the relevant other, concludes that the best place for the family is at Madea's house. He persuades Madea to take the family into her home by telling her that she will be paid four thousand dollars a month for doing so.

Brian Simmons believes Madea is capable of protecting the family because, as he tells his aunt, "You pack [have a gun] so I know you can hold it down [manage the situation]," and because she understands "the streets," required knowledge if she is going to hide a white family in a black neighborhood. Simmons's faith proves well-founded. As Madea and Kate sit on the porch one night, Madea not only gives Kate good parenting advice, directing her to "speak [her] damn mind" to rein in her daughter Cindy's bad behavior, but also she tells her, "I'm going to give you some better advice. White folks ain't supposed to be out here on this front porch in the middle of the night, let's go in the house." Keeping Kate and the rest of the family safely protected is a superwoman responsibility, which Madea does by making the white family invisible in a predominantly black neighborhood.

Madea's protection doesn't stop at simply housing the family. Indeed, like any good superhero, she uses her powers to make things right and save the Needlemans from danger. Disguised as a wealthy New York socialite, Precious Jackson (Perry doubles the identity paradigm here, as a man performing a feminine identity performing a different feminine identity), Madea goes to the New York bank housing the illegal account and, using a bravado and wit lacking in the other characters, convinces the bank manager to transfer the ill-gotten money back to the legitimate charities from which it was taken. Not only does she mitigate the Needlemans' troubles, but also she restores what had been taken from the community.

A final characteristic that defines Madea as a superwoman is that she acts without being constrained by society's laws. In *Madea Goes to Jail*, when a fellow motorist takes a parking spot that Madea had been waiting for at the shopping center, Madea "rights" the wrong by removing the motorist's car from the parking spot with a forklift and then destroying the car by dropping it on the pavement. On the surface, her actions seem brash and irresponsible, and yet what she does may mirror the desire of audience members who have been victims of rude parking lot behavior. Madea's over-the-top action was illegal, but to her way of thinking, ethical. Madea demonstrates a disregard for the law and risks arrest to accomplish what she believes is the right thing to do.

Madea's greatest power to right wrongs in her own way benefits those who are unable to fight for themselves. In *Diary of a Mad Black Woman*, Madea forces Helen, her granddaughter, unceremoniously kicked out of her home by her wealthy husband Charles, to return to "her house," get what she can, and exact revenge on him. When Charles catches Helen taking money from his office, Madea, who is upstairs about to fight his mistress, having challenged her to "call the PoPo, Ho" and telling her she is not afraid of the law, perks up as if she has heard a distress call when Charles's raised voice reaches her. Slapping the mistress on the head, Madea hurries downstairs, bursts through the doors to the study, and, waving her gun, begs Charles to hit Helen so that Madea can kill him for "putting his hand on my granddaughter." Though Madea eventually takes her gun and leaves the study, the

sound of a chain saw indicates her intention to make good on the pronounce-
ment that "half of everything in this house belong to [Helen], and I ain't
leaving here til she get it." In her estimation, Charles has crossed a line, and
though he may never face justice from the legal system, he will face Madea's
justice as she cuts furniture, pillows, and piano in half with a chain saw.
Though this stunt gets her put on house arrest, Madea's response is to throw a
party where she rolls up the bottom of her jeans and shows off her monitor-
ing device.[35]

CONCLUSION

Tyler Perry's creative works have generated hundreds of millions of dollars
in revenue, making him one of the most successful entertainers in Hollywood. The African American community has supported Perry's artistic work
and has made Madea a beloved, often quoted, heroic character. Why? What
is so appealing about this feisty African American matriarch who "speaks her
damn mind" and dares anyone to say anything about it or there will be "hell
to pay" when she pulls her gun out of her purse? The answer may lie in her
unconventional conventionality. Despite her angry exterior, her real superpower lies in her ability to shelter the vulnerable in their time of need. In
Diary of a Mad Black Woman, Madea takes in a granddaughter kicked out by
her husband; in *Madea's Family Reunion*, she houses a teenager with no
place to go; in *Madea Goes to Jail*, she counsels a young prostitute; in
Madea's Witness Protection, she saves a family. Again and again, she performs the role of communal grandmother, providing a safe space and plenty
of hard truths for the downtrodden and the troubled.

Madea's age exempts her from caring about the consequences of her
actions and frees her from the constraints of so-called polite society. Madea
often does what others wish they could, but dare not. She says what's on her
mind, threatens wayward children with physical discipline, never backs
down from a fight, and even, in *Madea's Big Happy Family*, drives her car
into a fast food restaurant when a nonchalant clerk tells her they are out of
ham. Though she does not reveal her age, she makes it clear she is far too old
to be constrained and that her authority is absolute.

As a village sage, Madea imparts knowledge and wisdom to family members, friends, and even strangers if necessary. Yet it is Madea's enactment of
the Harriet Tubman myth that is her crowning achievement as the village
thinker of the community. Just as Harriet Tubman escaped from slavery and
returned to the South to lead other slaves to freedom, Madea reaches back to
lead the villagers from a land of problems, challenges, and hardships to a
place of peace, self-respect, and tranquility, even if she has to slap them
there. Asante's assertion that "we are confronted by the Tubman example in

the daily interactions of our lives, from the extended-family philosophy to the assistance to the needy in our churches . . . a heroine, not as an individual, but as a caring, assisting person,"[36] is also true of Madea, who often provides tough-love insight and learning to others.

In addition to being a village sage, Madea is also superwoman, displaying both human and superhuman qualities. Madea acts when no one else can or will, and relevant others such as Brian Simmons or George Needleman know this to be the case. When Madea acts, she does so without feeling constrained by society's laws. Madea also establishes herself as a nexus between young and old African Americans via the concept of "identification." Identification is the idea that persuasion can come about symbolically by "speaking the same language, wearing similar clothing, exhibiting common tastes, espousing the same cause, [or by] buying into the same ideology and playing by its rules. Any mode of symbolic action can be a source of identification."[37] In so doing, Madea positions herself as an elder in her community who can relate to or identify with a new generation of young blacks. She is unashamed to share that she "worked as a stripper" rather than go on welfare.[38] Her wisdom, knowledge, and heroic actions as an aged superwoman are embraced by both the young and the old. And as a result, there is a little less division in her black community.

NOTES

1. See Jamel Santa Cruze Bell and Ronald L. Jackson II, eds., *Interpreting Tyler Perry: Perspectives on Race, Class, Gender, and Sexuality* (New York: Routledge, 2014).

2. Judith Butler, "Performative Acts and Gender Constitution: An Essay in Phenomenology and Feminist Theory," *Theatre Journal* 40 (1998): 15–31.

3. Margena A. Christian, "Becoming Tyler: Bill Collector Turned Billion-Dollar Media Mogul Was Molded from Pain, Promise and Persistence," *Ebony* (October, 2008) 74–76.

4. Ibid., 76.

5. Ibid., 78.

6. Ibid., 74.

7. Butler, "Performative Acts," 519.

8. Jonathan Wyatt, "Performativity of Gender," in *Encyclopedia of Identity*, ed. Ronald L. Jackson II et al. (Los Angeles: Sage, 2010), 539.

9. Wyatt, "Performativity of Gender," 539.

10. Tina M. Harris and Emily Porter, "Archetypes of Regression: Depictions and Reflections of Black and Familial Culture in Tyler Perry's Family Reunion," in *Interpreting Tyler Perry: Perspectives on Race, Class, Gender, and Sexuality*, edited by Jamel Santa Cruze Bell and Ronald L. Jackson II (New York: Routledge, 2014), 300–312, on 307.

11. Bryant Keith Alexander, "Bootlegging Tyler Perry/Tyler Perry as Bootlegger: A Critical Meditation on Madea's Family Reunion" in *Interpreting Tyler Perry: Perspectives on Race, Class, Gender, and Sexuality*, edited by Jamel Santa Cruze Bell and Ronald L. Jackson II (New York: Routledge, 2014), 15–31, on 17.

12. For a discussion of the military and hegemonic masculinity, see Carlos D. Morrison, "The Evolution of an Identity: *G. I. Joe* and Black Masculinity," in *Communicating Marginalized Masculinities: Identity Politics in TV, Film, and New Media*, vol. 11, edited by Ronald L. Jackson II and Jamie E. Moshin (New York: Routledge, 2013), 99–113, on 111.

13. Molefi Kente Asante, *The Afrocentric Idea* (Philadelphia: Temple University Press, 1998), 107–8. According to Asante, myths can better be understood as mythoforms. Mythoforms are "deep utterances that operate at unconscious levels . . . mythoforms are the all-encompassing deep generator of ideas and concepts in our lived relationships with our peers, friends, and ancestors" (108). So, for example, the idea of "going back in order to bring others alone" evokes the mythoform of Harriet Tubman. In the African oral tradition, myths are associated with real people like Tubman, while the idea of "returning to help others" is the form, that is, the unconscious utterance that is "made" conscious when "acted or spoken out" by those within the community.

14. Assante, *Afrocentric Idea*, 107.

15. *Tyler Perry's Madea Goes to Jail* is still Perry's most successful film to date. While the film received mixed reviews at the time of its debut in 2009, it is still number one in terms of gross box office receipts, having earned over $90 million at the time of its release.

16. *Tyler Perry's Madea Goes to Jail*, directed by Tyler Perry (2009; Santa Monica, CA: Lions Gate Home Entertainment, 2009), DVD.

17. *Madea Goes to Jail*.

18. The African oral tradition (storytelling, tonal semantics, wise sayings, etc.) speaks to the centrality of the spoken word in the life of African peoples. When enslaved Africans were brought to the Americas, this oral tradition was passed on to Africans in the Americas as Africanisms. For a context-specific discussion of Africanisms (i.e., Africanisms found in African American music, language, etc.), see Joseph E. Holloway, *Africanisms in American Culture*, 2nd edition (Bloomington: Indiana University Press), 2005.

19. Black communication or African American communication is culturally specific patterns of discourse such as rapping and storytelling that are rooted in the oral tradition of Africa. The function of African American communication is to transmit the history, culture, and identity of African American people. For a thorough discussion of African American Communication, see Michael L. Hecht, Ronald L. Jackson II, and Sidney A. Ribeau, *African American Communication: Exploring Identity and Culture*, 2nd edition (Mahwah, NJ: Lawrence Erlbaum, 2003).

20. Evelyn B. Dandy, *Black Communications: Breaking Down the Barriers* (Chicago: African American Images, 1991), 11–13.

21. Tyler Perry, *Don't Make a Black Woman Take Off Her Earrings* (New York: Riverhead Books, 2006), 231–32.

22. Ibid., 183.

23. Ibid., 183.

24. Ibid., 223–24.

25. *Black Macho and the Myth of the Superwoman* (New York: Dial, 1979) is Michelle Wallace's best-known and most-criticized work. The book is a black feminist critique of black patriarchy, the black male, and the black power movement. Wallace's central thesis was that the black woman existed both in the home and in the black power movement in a "marginalized space" that was detrimental to her well-being. Black male power was the "tool" used to keep her in her "place."

26. Wallace, *Black Macho*, 107.

27. Charisse Jones and Kumea Shorter-Gooden, *Shifting: The Double Lives of Black Women in America* (New York: HarperCollins, 2003), 18–22.

28. Wallace, *Black Macho*, 107.

29. Perry, *Don't Make a Black Woman*, 152.

30. Ibid., 122.

31. Ibid., 124.

32. Ibid., 12.

33. Ibid. Madea makes reference to her prodigious breasts (68 DX probably refers to a mythical bra size), naming them after Zan and Jayna from the Hanna Barbera cartoon, *Super Friends*. The twins, whose super powers were activated when they touched, would yell, "Wonder Twin powers activate!" whenever they called on their powers. They later appeared in DC Comics. Her use of this phrase locates her superpowers in her very large breasts.

34. *Tyler Perry's Madea's Witness Protection* is Perry's second-highest revenue-generating film, having grossed over $65 million in 2012.

35. *Tyler Perry's Diary of a Mad Black Woman*, directed by Darren Grant (2005; Santa Monica, CA: Lions Gate Home Entertainment, 2005), DVD.

36. Asante, *Afrocentric Idea*, 117.

37. Gerard D. Hauser, *Introduction to Rhetorical Theory* (Prospect Heights, IL: Waveland, 1986), 132–33.

38. Perry, *Don't Make a Black Woman*, 12.

Chapter Eight

"Not Bad for an *Abuela*, Eh?"

The Representation of the Power of Age in
Maya & Miguel

Emily S. Kinsky and Amanda Gallagher

"¡*Ay*! So much work to do! I have to make these tamales for my friend's granddaughter's *quinceañera*. Maya, do you know I haven't updated my home page in *three weeks*? Maybe we can do that together soon, eh?"[1]

Abuela Elena is a plump, graying grandmother in *Maya & Miguel*. Her words to her granddaughter, above, may not be what you would expect from an older adult; however, just as *Maya & Miguel* was groundbreaking in that it was the first animated show to feature a Latino American family, the portrayal of Abuela Elena is also similarly groundbreaking. Instead of being frail, Abuela Elena is a superhuman figure: a master problem solver, a confidant, and a quick-to-respond source of support. With this in mind, in this chapter, we examine *Maya & Miguel* to gain a deeper understanding into how aging Latino Americans might be perceived. To this end, we will review how an important aging character, Abuela Elena, might be regarded not only as a hero, but a superhero. But, first, let us briefly review the importance of children's television and then describe *Maya & Miguel* as well as the animated characters in the series.

IMPORTANCE OF MEDIA AND CHILDREN'S TELEVISION

The influence of mediated images is so pervasive that, as John Fiske argues, "we live in a world of media events and media realities."[2] Rather than simply reflecting or fictionalizing our reality, mediated portrayals on television actually influence how we perceive and interact in our worlds. For example, George Gerbner and his colleagues introduced the idea of the "mean world syndrome," in which heavy television viewers perceive and interact as if the world is far more dangerous than it really is.[3] These viewers might be so wary that they take unnecessary precautions that then limit and constrain their lives. These impacts also extend into children's television, as electronic media is "one of the most significant influences in the lives of modern children," and it can educate young viewers on a variety of topics including interpersonal relationships.[4] Additionally, "children's television does impart knowledge, it is both entertaining and instructive"[5] and aids "children in the task of growing up."[6] Thus, television also socializes and teaches children about the world.[7]

Television's representations of different social groups can influence viewers' perceptions of other races, ages, and gender roles.[8] The children's television show *Sesame Street*, for example, promotes mutual understanding between African American and white children.[9] *Maya & Miguel* may be especially influential on viewers because it is among the few television shows that portray Latino families and strong aging characters. When few representations exist, the small numbers that do exist are important to examine. With this concept in mind, we next offer a short introduction to the background and characters of *Maya & Miguel.*

ABOUT *MAYA & MIGUEL*

Maya & Miguel is an animated children's program that debuted on October 11, 2004, on Public Broadcasting Service (PBS) channels in the United States.[10] It follows the (mis)adventures of the twin title characters, along with a diverse supporting cast of family and friends. *Maya & Miguel* was groundbreaking in television because the show was the first original series produced by Scholastic Productions[11] and the first animated program to focus on a Latino family in the United States.[12] *Maya & Miguel* uses natural-sounding code-shifting—switching from English to Spanish and back again—within conversations in the family. Each character was developed by Scholastic in a way to show his or her distance from immigration; much of this is portrayed via accents. Abuela Elena has a thicker accent than her daughter, and Maya and Miguel, having been born in the United States, have no Mexican accent at all. Because of this diversity and the show's use of language for teaching non-native speakers, *Maya & Miguel* earned significant grants from the Corporation for Public Broadcasting ($9.2 million) and the U.S. Department of Education ($5 million).[13] In fact, the grant from the Corporation for Public Broadcasting was the largest awarded to date. In addition to broadcast networks airing the program worldwide, some of the series is also available on the subscription service Netflix.

Maya & Miguel was and still is an extremely important marker in American children's television because of the scarcity and negativity of Latino portrayals on television. In a study of prime-time programming in 2005, only 3.9 percent of the 1,488 characters present were Latino.[14] This same study found that Latina characters were portrayed with the worst work ethic of all of the characters, and Latinos were portrayed as less articulate than other racial/ethnic groups. Thus, "from the perspective of cultivation theory, the nature of these portrayals is consequential as heavy, long-term exposure to these persistent images should ultimately result in a belief in the authenticity of these characterizations."[15] In the realm of children's television, shows portraying Hispanic/Latino characters include *Dora the Explorer*, *Go Diego Go*, and *Handy Manny*. Unfortunately, none of them include a parent or grandparent in a major role.

Maya & Miguel differs from other Latino portrayals because of the show's underlying message: "Shared happiness is greater than personal gain."[16] This message is clearly reflected in the theme song:

> Working together is what they do best
> Helping their family and friends, that's a start
> They make a great team as they each do their part

At a broader level, Scholastic sought to promote a culturally diverse society, stating in the supporting parents-and-teachers guide that:

> respect and appreciation of differences is at the heart of the Maya & Miguel TV series. The program shows people from a variety of cultures who take pride in their traditions, families and native languages, while participating actively in a diverse U.S. neighborhood. In addition, the characters show a respect and empathy toward one another.[17]

As part of that diversity, one of the key purposes of the program is to help Spanish-speaking children learn English "through the presentation of language in a natural context with a special emphasis on vocabulary."[18] Most importantly, shows such as *Maya & Miguel* are notable because such programming efforts are important to children's television, as the show provides both educational and entertainment value with relatable story lines, important lessons about life, and—especially—likeable characters.

CHARACTERS ON *MAYA & MIGUEL*

Maya and Miguel Santos are U.S.-born, ten-year-old twins. In a nod to *I Love Lucy*, Deborah Forte, creator of the program, modeled Maya after Lucy

Ricardo and Miguel after Lucy's husband Ricky.[19] They are represented as two halves of a whole circle. Maya loves animals and, like Lucy, she is known for her zany ideas that almost always go completely haywire. Miguel, as Maya's more sensible twin brother, keeps a tab on his sister's misadventures. He loves sports (including soccer, basketball, and baseball), likes to draw, and enjoys playing his drums. As this children's program was designed to educate young viewers in a variety of areas (such as disability, race, language, and age), it revolves primarily around the titular twins, Maya and Miguel, but also includes other characters who share the twin's mis/adventures.

Their father, Santiago, comes from Puerto Rico and their mother, Rosa, is from Mexico. According to project director Mindy Figueroa, both Rosa and Santiago moved to the United States when they were children, and though they "have adapted the cultural traits of their new home country," they "take pride in maintaining their home language and culture."[20] Rosa and Santiago "speak to each other, show affection, and convey their values in a way that is representative of their cultural heritage."[21] Rosa and Santiago own a pet shop, and the family lives above it.

Although Rosa and Santiago are important and honored in the text, the most revered character—the aging heroine—is Abuela Elena Chavez. She is Maya and Miguel's maternal grandmother and a widow from Mexico. Abuela Elena "serves as the cultural bearer and teacher. She conveys the behavioral norms to be followed by the kids and, in many aspects, by the entire family."[22] In the United States, she once owned a restaurant, La Cocinita, with her late husband Ernesto and has two children: Rosa (Maya and Miguel's mother) and Ernesto. As a grandmother, she engages in traditional activities such as cooking, but she is also Internet savvy and is a member of a book club. In addition to Maya and Miguel, Abuela Elena has another grandchild, Alberto (Tito), who is the son of Teresa and the younger Ernesto. As a recent immigrant from Mexico, Tito speaks with a thick Mexican accent and struggles with homesickness.

Another key character is the family's pet parrot, Paco. He was incorporated into the story line by Scholastic to help with their educational goals because the parrot often repeats key words and phrases in both Spanish and English.[23] He also adds quite a bit of humor to the stories by misunderstanding English idioms. For example, he is afraid when Miguel tells him that "it's raining cats and dogs out there"[24] and deeply disappointed when he finds out the expression "the early bird gets the worm"[25] does not involve an actual worm.

Maya's best friends are Maggie and Chrissy. Together, they call themselves *Las Tres Amigas*. Maggie is of Chinese descent, loves to dance, and is interested in fashion. Chrissy is of Afro-Dominican descent and likes cats, the color pink, and cheerleading. Chrissy tends to be more agreeable to Maya's zany ideas, whereas Maggie is often more sensible.

Miguel's best friends are Andy and Theo. Andy is of English descent and loves sports. He has a physical disability in that he was born with one full arm and one that stops below his elbow. He is introduced in the third episode of Season 1 as having just moved from Wisconsin, and the children soon befriend him. He is Caucasian with blond hair and blue eyes. Theo is African American; he loves to read and play sports. He can sometimes be a sporting rival for Miguel. He is often portrayed as the "brain" of the group, frequently inventing tools for them to use in their adventures.

Additionally, several other older adults make appearances in various episodes throughout the series. These characters include Señor Obregon (the butcher), Mrs. Salviati (a retired dancer), and Señor Felipe (the mailman). Santiago's mother—Maya and Miguel's paternal grandmother, referred to as Tata—appears only in an episode titled, "The Perfect Thanksgiving." Thus, the primary older adult present throughout the series is Abuela Elena. In fact, she appears more often than the children's mother, and her prominence on the show signals the vital function she plays in providing guidance, stability, and knowledge for the children.

As previously noted, while *Maya & Miguel* is focused on the younger characters, older characters are also featured prominently in most episodes. Such representations of older characters are not typical in children's programming. Often children's programs do not feature adults or, if they do, they do not present them positively. For example, in the *Charlie Brown and Snoopy Show* (1986), as well as various *Peanuts* television specials, adult faces are never seen during interactions. Also, in the very rare instances when adults are heard, we only hear a muffled trombone sound effect, "wa-haaah whah," and these adults are often no help to the children.

Maya & Miguel counters these portrayals by featuring not only a grandmother as a major character, but also, as we will demonstrate, portraying her as heroic. Therefore, Abuela Elena is important to examine because she is one of the very few portrayals of an underrepresented group in the media, and those media portrayals may be extremely influential in how individuals perceive and interact in their social worlds. With this in mind, let us next demonstrate how Abuela Elena is a superhero to her family.

ABUELA AS A SUPERHERO

Abuela Elena fits as a family superhero because she is an authority on history and culture, and is full of skills, as well as an ingenious problem solver. She is the master of all trades and is able to think on her feet, so there is no problem that Abuela cannot solve. Abuela rescues adults and children no matter what the task or problem at hand. She is truly the glue that holds the family together.

Authority on History and Culture

The older characters on *Maya & Miguel*, including Abuela Elena, have gained most of their knowledge through personal experience. Of course, the children are less experienced because of their youth and, as such, they rely on the adults (especially Abuela) to lead them on the right path.

Many times the adult guidance is given by Abuela Elena and occurs through her nostalgic stories, such as in the episode "La Nueva Cocinita." When the twins come to visit her, Abuela answers the door dressed up in a lavender feather boa and a purple flamenco hat with pom-poms. She tells Maya and Miguel these clothing items "attracted a second look way back when." She invites them in and explains that she was "sorting through my trunk of treasures." When they ask Abuela to pull out her recipe book and cook some of the recipes from La Cocinita, Elena says they are just for memories now because she cooked them together as a team with Ernesto, the twins' deceased grandfather. Abuela tells them stories of the restaurant and how she and Ernesto would cook for each other and taste each other's recipes. In the episode, we see her memories come alive as they are shown in sepia tone to match the photos from the trunk.

Abuela is revered for her knowledge of the past and how she shares that knowledge through stories. When Maya talks the family into a weekend camping trip in "Family Time," she mentions what each family member's role will be. For Abuela Elena, she says, "*Abuelita* can tell her stories about Mexico." In one of the final scenes in the episode, we hear Abuela in the middle of a story that results in laughter by the whole family. Everything went wrong on the camping trip, and she told Maya and Miguel, "And now you kids will have even more stories to tell your grandchildren, eh?"

As seen in "La Nueva Cocinita," food is an important part of Abuela Elena's culture and serves as another touchstone from which she draws her knowledge. Her clear connection with food comes across in many other episodes. Abuela demonstrates that she knows what is best for the well-being of the children, and her knowledge serves as a source of guidance for Maya. Food, especially that prepared by Abuela's own hands, reinforces the notion that Abuela knows what is best for everyone.

Throughout the series, Abuela is often shown in the kitchen making traditional Mexican dishes such as tamales and flan. In "La Nueva Cocinita," Maya says they will make a restaurant "using *Abuelita's* magical, delicious, fantastic recipes from La Cocinita." When Miguel is hesitant, she asks, "Didn't *Abuelita* tell us that her recipes could cheer up the grouchiest customer? That one bite could bring people together?" Not surprisingly, the children fail to recreate Abuela's dishes, but when she discovers what they are doing, she steps in to fix everything.

Food is a focal point in a scene in "Prince Tito," too.[26] Maya thanks Abuela Elena for making them dinner, though she has been too distracted to eat.

Maya: Thank you for making us dinner, *Abuelita*.

Abuela: But you hardly touched any of it. Not even my delicious flan. [Maya was too upset to eat]

Miguel: I'll help you out with that!

However, as soon as Abuela makes a suggestion for how to solve her problem, Maya grabs her plate of flan.

While flan comes up in several episodes, tamales are mentioned in even more. In "Tito's Mexican Vacation," Maya is determined to help her cousin Tito with his homesickness for Mexico.

Maya: *Abuelita*, you know how you like making tamales?

Abuela: *Si*, I love making tamales. They remind me of Mexico.

Maya: *Exactemente*. Do you think you could make a few of them by tomorrow?

Abuela: Hmm, how many is a few?

Maya: Hmm, I don't know. Maybe a hundred?

Abuela: *¿Cien tamales?* By tomorrow?! Maya, what is this all about?

Maya: I don't want anyone to give the surprise away. Trust me. It's for someone special.

Abuela: It had better be someone *really* special.

Maya: Oh, I knew you could do it! *Gracias, Abuelita*! You are the best!

Later in the episode, Abuela delivers a tray piled high with tamales: "One hundred beautiful tamales for my beautiful granddaughter!"

Moreover, in "The Bully and the Bunny," Rosa, Santiago, and Elena meet their new neighbors, and Elena brings a plate of cookies. Also, in "Family Time," Abuela offers to "make my tortillas like my *abuela* did when we went camping." When Maya throws a surprise birthday party for her friend

Chrissy in "Surprise, Surprise," we see Abuela Elena pulling a cake out of the oven and then making Chrissy's favorite dish, *arroz con leche.* Just as Elena serves as a cultural guide for the family history, she also draws in Maya to help with these two desserts.

Maya: Look, *Abuelita*! I finished decorating the cake.

Paco: Mm, *el pastel.*

Abuela: Not for you.

Paco: Oh.

Abuela: It's beautiful, *mija.* Why don't you help me with the *arroz con leche?*

Paco: Mmm, *arroz con leche!*

Abuela [to Paco]: That's not for you, either. [To Maya] Here, help me fill these cups.

Maya: This is going to be a great party!

In addition to her knowledge of traditional Mexican cooking and her stories of her childhood home, Abuela Elena is also shown sharing family photos with Maya when she wants to help Tito with his homesickness. This is yet another way that Abuela can teach the children based upon her vast array of life experiences. Maya says if she cannot take Tito back to Mexico, "We're going to bring Mexico to Tito!" and she goes to Abuela for help.

Abuela: *Mi linda,* I'm glad you want to learn about Mexico. Let's look at some pictures of the family.

Maya: Is this Tito as a baby?

Abuela: *Si, que chulo, no?* That is the house where your aunt and uncle, Tia Teresa and Tio Ernesto, lived. It's where Tito was born. And these are Tito's cousins.

The cultural training the children receive from Abuela is demonstrated again in the episode, "La Calavera," as Maya announces to the whole family at dinner that she has chosen to do her oral report on Mexico:

Abuela: *¿De verdad?* The land of my birth? *Ay, mija,* that makes me so happy to see you're so proud of your culture.

Maya: I was hoping it would. That's why I picked it.

Miguel [picking up a taco]: I'm proud of my culture, too, and I LOVE the food.

Abuela: *Mi vida*, if you need any help with your report, don't hesitate to ask.[27]

Later Maya goes to Abuela's apartment for items to use in her oral report. Abuela allows her to dig through a trunk:

Maya: Wow, *Abuelita*! You have so many beautiful treasures from Mexico in here.

Abuela: *Si, mi reina.* Since I can't visit my country as often as I'd like, these things help me feel close.

Maya: They must be very special. Are you sure it's OK to borrow something to share with my class?

Abuela: Ha ha! *Absolutamente!* Nothing would make me happier than you getting a good grade on your oral report. I'm proud that you're helping your friends learn more about Mexico. You can take anything.

Maya: *Padrísimo !* This is cool! [picks up the sugar skull]

Abuela: Except that.

Maya: Well, why not?

Abuela: You know, I made this *calavera* for your Abuelo Ernesto when we were young. I put it on his altar every year for the *Dia de los Muertos.*

Maya: That's why I think it's perfect. Instead of just talking about Mexican culture, I can actually show my class something we do to celebrate the Day of the Dead.

Abuela: I understand, *mi amor.* But I'm worried that something might happen to it.

Maya: It's exactly what I need to get a good grade.

Abuela: I don't know.

Maya: O, *por favor*, *Abuelita*. Please, please, pretty please. You said nothing would make you happier than if I got a good grade.

Abuela: No, *no me hagas esos ojitos.* [Maya blinks her eyes at Abuela] Oh, all right.

Maya: Yes!

Abuela: But only if you make sure to take very good care of it and return it in perfect condition. *¿ Me prometes?*

Maya promises to take good care of the *calavera,* but she ends up losing it and then breaking it. She dreads letting Abuela know because it was such a prized possession that cannot be replaced:

Maya: I'm so sorry, *Abuelita.* I know how much the *calavera* meant to you. I'll do anything to make it up to you.

Abuela: I can't believe you waited all afternoon to tell me . . .

Maya: I know. *Me siento tan mal.*

Miguel: She felt so bad that she couldn't tell you.

Abuela: . . . about how well you did on your oral report.

Maya: Huh?

Abuela: I'm so proud of you. You made me very happy.

Maya: Happy? But aren't you sad I broke the *calavera*?

Abuela: Yes, it meant a lot to me. But I'm sure you didn't break it on purpose. Besides, you mean more to me than a sugar skull.

Maya: *Gracias, Abuelita.*

The episode ends with further training as Abuela teaches Miguel and Maya how to make *calaveras* together.

Not only does the series show Abuela Elena as a cultural leader for her grandchildren, but she is also shown training her grown daughter. For example, in "The Perfect Thanksgiving," the adult women (Rosa, Elena, and Tata) are grocery shopping for Thanksgiving. Abuela and Tata, Santiago's mother, both have their recipes memorized. Rosa, however, looks to Abuela and Tata for approval for some of the produce she picks in the store. Rosa's search for approval is an example of a difference in the representations of middle-aged adults compared to older adults in the series.

Skillful

Beyond being the family's expert on culture and history, however, Abuela Elena is also extremely skillful. In addition to knowledge about Mexico's culture and food, Abuela Elena also has surprising mechanical skills and a great deal of knowledge regarding technology. According to Figueroa, the use of the Internet was included by Scholastic as a "literacy element," so that the show would be "reflective of the current environment."[28] This broad expertise is referenced, for example, at the beginning of "Abuela Upmanship":

> Maya [showing off her new skirt to her friends at school]: Ta da! *Abuelita* made it for me!"
>
> Maggie: Your grandmother is the coolest ever!
>
> Chrissy: It's like she can do ANYthing!
>
> Maggie: She makes the best food, she makes the best clothes, AND she even has her own website with the best graphics!
>
> Chrissy: *Tu abuela es la mejor del mundo.*
>
> Maya: *Gracias, amigas*! Yes, my grandmother IS the best grandmother in the world.[29]

This scene points to several of Abuela's abilities, as well as the admiration she has earned from the other characters.

Her handy skills are also clear in "La Nueva Cocinita." Abuela Elena opens her apartment door, surprised to see one of her grandchildren, Tito, standing there. He asks his grandmother to come closer: "I need help with my airplane, *Abuelita.*" As she comes closer, six other children sneak behind her back. Though she first tries to invite him into her apartment and offer him hot cocoa instead, he insists she come across the hall because it's important. His intent is to stall her—to cover for his cousins and friends. He brings her to a table strewn with model airplane parts. She says she's not good at things like this, but she will try. All of a sudden, she whips the plane together in no time. "Not bad for an *abuela*, eh?" she asks.[30] In addition to putting together a model plane in seconds, in "Soccer Mom," she quickly assembles a foot massager—something that her daughter could not figure out how to do after working on it all day.

Throughout the series, Abuela Elena mentions using the computer and updating her website. In "Surprise, Surprise," Maya plans a surprise party for Chrissy's birthday and wants to invite her favorite singer who has come to town for a sold-out concert. Miguel points out, "We don't even know where Enrique is staying, and even if we did, *Mama* and *Papi* would *never* let us go there by ourselves!" Enter Abuela Elena, who promptly sits down at the computer, cracks her knuckles and starts typing at superhuman speed:

Maya: *Abuelita,* what are you doing?

Abuela: Checking Enrique's fan sites for the hotel where he's staying. Aha! Here we go. Enrique's home site. Blah, blah, blah, blah, blah. Bingo. Enrique's staying at Hotel Dominico.

Maya: You really found it?

Abuela: And look at this! In his biography, it says Enrique and I were born in the same town in Mexico. *¡Que interesante!*

She is then able to use this information she found online to help the children meet Enrique. When things start falling apart for the surprise party, it is Abuela's technological skills that save the day. This story of tracking down the teen idol also points to Abuela's ingenuity in solving problems for her family.

Ingenious Problem Solver

In addition to tracking down Chrissy's favorite pop star, Abuela Elena also demonstrates an ingenious idea: bringing a goat to meet Enrique when she learns information about his background.

Miguel: *Abuelita* just got the same look on her face you get when you have a big idea! Scary!

Abuela: And look at this! When he was a boy, he used to have a pet goat. Maya, Miguel, *tengo una idea*!

Miguel: Not you, too.

Abuela asks Santiago to find a goat, and she and the kids head to Enrique's hotel. Two doormen block the door, but the goat manages to run past them. Maya, Miguel and Abuela Elena chase the goat into the building.

Doorman: Señor Enrique, I am very sorry. These crazy fans of yours brought a goat into the hotel, and it got loose. They'll be leaving right away this minute.

Enrique: A goat? Do you know I used to have a pet goat when I was a boy?

Maya: *Si, en Aguascalientes.* That's where my *abuela* grew up!

Enrique: Really? You come from *Aguascalientes*?

Abuela: Born and raised.

Miguel: We thought the goat might remind you of your childhood.

Maya: And help you relax before your big concert tonight.

Enrique: Well, it sure does. *Gracias*! You are very kind. Please give your names to my people and we will send you my latest CD.

Maya explained that what she really wanted was for him to sing "Happy Birthday" to Chrissy at her birthday party. Enrique shows up at her party and invites all the children to his concert. The episode ends with Miguel's voice-over: "Who would have thought a goat would get us into an Enrique concert?" Clearly Abuela Elena saw the possibility and acted on it.

In "Team Santos," Abuela Elena, her three grandchildren, and Paco compete in a carnival competition against another family (the Flanigan brothers and their dog, Crusher).[31] After a few events, the teams are tied. The competition is going to be determined by a tie-breaker and it involves finding a flag in a maze. Abuela Elena proclaims, "Out of my way, there is nothing in the world I love more than a good puzzle. *Vamos!*" In contrast, Team Flanigan, with the four brothers, becomes hopelessly lost in the maze. They ask for Maya's help, to which she responds, "Just follow my *abuelita*!" After the Santos family is announced as the winners, one of the boys from Team Flanigan offers his congratulations. He says, "Congrats. You guys, you were tough, but I gotta say, your grandma is awesome!" Abuela Elena responds, "And don't you forget it."

Some scenes demonstrate both Abuela's surprising energy and her wisdom for solving a problem for the children. In the top row of the baseball stadium—row Triple Z, Abuela Elena leaps in the air and catches Orlando Flores's home run ball in "The Autograph." She is later able to use that ball to negotiate for Flores's autograph for Miguel. Maya had gone to great, crazy lengths to try to restore the baseball card that had been accidentally destroyed, but it is Abuela Elena who saves the day.

Thus, Abuela Elena's status is that of a familial superhero, especially to the children because she is culturally wise, technologically skillful, and a brilliant problem solver. Now that we have described some of Abuela Elena's characteristics, let us next discuss how she is similar to, as well as different from, some existing portrayals of aging.

DISCUSSION

Abuela Elena is a familial superhuman character, especially to her grandchildren, because she is always available to help them, no matter how big or impossible the problem. While she displays some characteristics associated with that of an older grandmother character, she also leverages them to help other characters as they experience problems. For example, Abuela Elena is often pictured in the kitchen. While she is a good cook, especially of Mexican food, she also shows that she cares for her family through that food. She cooks for the children when their parents are absent, uses food to comfort a child in distress, or offers hot cocoa to make a Sunday afternoon movie even more special. She also spends the time to make labor-intensive dishes such as tamales. Therefore, we suggest that her focus on food fits expectations of not only her role as a grandmother, but also her portrayal as a Mexican American woman.

In addition, Abuela Elena is known for her stories of the past. She has used these stories as parables to educate her children and grandchildren about family traditions and cultural mores. Because of these stories, her grandchildren know about her home country of Mexico, their grandfather, and important traditions and events such as the Day of the Dead. Another aspect that is consistent with other portrayals of aging characters is her knowledge from her life experiences. She knows how to sew (which is a skill much more common in grandmothers than their daughters or granddaughters) and makes numerous dresses to be raffled in a fundraiser for the children's school in "Abuela Upmanship." In addition to knowing how to sew and cook, she knows how to make *calaveras* (a cultural skill that she imparts to the children).

However, Abeula Elena also breaks with existing mediated portrayals. Unlike most depictions of elderly people, Abuela Elena is presented as an inventive problem solver. With her ingenuity, she helps her grandchildren out of precarious situations (e.g., the restaurant in the apartment, the kids' arrest at the baseball field). She also turns a home run baseball into a new, signed baseball card for Miguel. She comes up with the idea of a goat to get access to the pop star Maya wanted to meet on Chrissy's behalf. Instead of conforming to some aging portrayals of helplessness, she resists them because she is a resourceful, ingenious problem solver.

Finally, Abuela Elena's characterization is different from many other elderly characters because of the portrayal of her seeming superpowers. From energetically walking home with the children from the grocery store to leaping in the air to catch a home run ball, Abuela Elena shatters expectations. She has the power to fix things like model planes and foot massagers, the power to run a website, the power to help her grandchildren when Maya's plans go awry, and the power to lead her community because of the respect she has earned. This power she has been granted in the story lines is why we call her the superhero of the family.

CONCLUSION

Abuela Elena solves problems, demonstrates surprising skills, and leads the way for her family's cultural identity. Abuela Elena is a superhero, not only because she confirms, as well as resists, some representations, but also because she is a heroine to her grandchildren and the greater community. Abuela Elena's powerful presence on *Maya & Miguel* is especially noteworthy because of the lack of older Latinas on television. With few representations of grandparents on children's animated programs, each one has a greater likelihood of influencing viewers' perceptions of older adults, especially if they do not have contact with many older adults in their daily life. Signorielli explains that "for those who do not regularly interact with minorities, television tells its audience about these groups and how they may be similar and/or different from other people."[32] With few representations of Latina women in leading roles, Abuela Elena's presence in the story line also holds great power and the potential to influence people's conceptions of Latinas, especially if they have not had personal experiences with Mexican American women.

Latino/Hispanic cultures have notable differences compared to mainstream U.S. culture. For example, "Mexican Americans place high value on the family as a central point in their lives."[33] In addition to differences in the role or level of importance of family, older family members are often treated differently than in the mainstream: "Age connotes status in [Mexican American] culture, and younger people are expected to behave respectfully towards elders."[34] Even for Mexican Americans who have lived in the United States for a long time, like Abuela Elena's character, cultural differences remain; "Despite the fact that Mexican Americans are increasingly acculturated into the U.S. mainstream culture, the command honor thy parents, remains a strong moral duty in their communities, perhaps due to culturally based, religious beliefs."[35] These differences help explain why Abuela Elena lives in the same building with Maya, Miguel, and their parents and why she is so present in their lives.

Maya & Miguel made a huge step in the portrayal of a diverse group of people working and playing together in harmony. This diverse group includes older adults who are often absent from television scripts, especially those in children's television. The program shares a positive depiction of the role grandparents can have, as well as the life of Hispanic/Latino families and women in particular. We hope this is the first step of many.

NOTES

1. *Maya & Miguel*, "Family Time," episode 114, directed by Tony Kluck, written by Luisa Leshin, PBS, 2004.
2. John Fiske, *Media Matters* (Minneapolis: University of Minnesota Press, 1996), xv.
3. George Gerbner, "Cultural Indicators: The Case of Violence in Television Drama," *Annals of the American Academy of Political and Social Science* 388, no. 1 (1970): 69–81.
4. Maire M. Davies, *"Dear BBC": Children, Television Storytelling and the Public Sphere* (Cambridge: Cambridge University Press, 2001), 79.
5. Ruth Inglis, *The Window in the Corner: A Half-Century of Children's Television* (London: Peter Owen Publishers, 2003), 188.
6. Davies, *"Dear BBC,"* 58.
7. George Gerbner, "What Do We Know?" [foreword], in *Television and Its Viewers: Cultivation Theory and Research*, edited by James Shanahan and Michael Morgan (Cambridge: Cambridge University Press, 1999), ix–xiii.
8. Nancy Signorielli, "Aging on Television: Messages Relating to Gender, Race, and Occupation in Prime Time," *Journal of Broadcasting and Electronic Media* 48 (2004): 279–301, on 297.
9. Shalom M. Fisch, Rosemarie T. Truglio, and Charlotte Cole, "The Impact of Sesame Street on Preschool Children: A Review and Synthesis of 30 Years' Research," *Media Psychology 1* (1999): 165–90.
10. Deborah Forte, *Maya & Miguel* (New York: Scholastic Media, 2004).
11. Joyceann Cooney, *"Maya & Miguel*'s Mosaic," *License!* 7 (2004): 26–38.
12. Debra Smith, "Cartoon Culture: How Maya and Miguel Excel Beyond the 1990 Children's Television Act," in *Americana: Readings in Popular Culture*, edited by Leslie Wilson (Hollywood: Press Americana, 2006), 105–12.
13. Lily Dei, "PBS Heads *Maya* Way with Scholastic," *Daily Variety*, June 3, 2003, 5.
14. Dana E. Mastro and Elizabeth Behm-Morowitz, "Latino Representation on Primetime Television," *Journalism and Mass Communication Quarterly* 82, no. 1 (2005): 110–30.
15. Ibid., 125–26.
16. "*Maya & Miguel*: Parents & Teachers: About the Program," PBS Parents, http://www.pbs.org/parents/mayaandmiguel/English/program /index.html (accessed September 21, 2014).
17. "Maya & Miguel: Parents & Teachers: About the Program: Frequently Asked Questions," PBS Parents, http://www.pbs.org/parents /mayaandmiguel/english/program/faq.html (accessed September 21, 2014).
18. Mindy Figueroa, email to the authors, September 14, 2006.
19. Cooney, 2004; Eunice Sigler, *"Maya & Miguel*: The Latest Bilingual Kids' Show Features Twins," *Hispanic* 17 (2004): 68.
20. Figueroa, email.
21. Ibid.
22. Ibid.
23. Mindy Figueroa, telephone discussion with authors, December 7, 2007.
24. *Maya & Miguel*, "La Nueva Cocinita," episode 106, directed by Tony Kluck, written by Andy Yerkes, PBS, 2004.
25. *Maya & Miguel*, "Maya and Miguel, Come on Down," episode 122, directed by Tony Kluck, written by Rachelle Romberg, PBS, 2005.

26. *Maya & Miguel,* "Prince Tito," episode 112, directed by Tony Kluck, written by Chris Nee, PBS, 2004.

27. *Maya & Miguel* , "La Calavera," episode 109, directed by Tony Kluck, written by Chris Nee, PBS, 2004.

28. Figueroa, telephone conversation.

29. *"Maya & Miguel* , "Abuela Upmanship," episode 133, directed by Tony Kluck, written by Evelina Fernandez, PBS, 2005.

30. "La Nueva Cocinita."

31. *Maya & Miguel,* "Team Santos," episode 127, directed by Tony Kluck, written by Chris Nee, PBS, 2005.

32. Signorielli, "Aging on Television," 297.

33. Hsueh-Fen S. Kao, Mary Lynn, and Kyungeh An, "Development of the Mexican American Family Loyalty toward Elderly Relatives Scale," *Journal of Theory Construction & Testing* 16, no. 2 (2012): 38–44, on 39.

34. Ibid.

35. Ibid.

Chapter Nine

Babes and Crones

Women Growing Old in Comics

Caryn E. Neumann

Comics entertain by focusing on certain aspects of our daily lives and then surrounding them with adventure, romance, and comedy. They also help us examine those aspects as a form of parable. For example, in the *X-Men* series, the tensions between Professor Xavier and Magneto, both fighting for the cause of mutant rights, paralleled the real struggle for civil rights in the 1960s and the tensions between Martin Luther King, Jr., and Malcolm X.[1] Additionally, these comics also allowed spaces to resist and change some of these oppressive aspects. For instance, and with regard to issues of gender, William Marston created Wonder Woman as a strong female character and role model to fight against prejudice against women, both on and off the page. As such, these comics are useful for examining discourse surrounding aging in popular culture.

   In the pages of graphic novels, readers might find adventures with aliens, vampires, mutants, superheroes, androids, as well as anthropomorphic animals and plant life. However, despite this great diversity of characters and characterizations, the aged woman remains extremely rare. Thus, similar to other texts in popular culture, comics have long denied the existence of highly capable, attractive, mature women, which also reflects negative Western societal attitudes about aging women. For example, Superman's female counterpart is Supergirl, a nubile subordinate. Batwoman was created to challenge gay rumors surrounding Batman and Robin. She had a brief existence before being replaced by Batgirl, a sexy subordinate. The male creators of Wonder Woman designed Wonder Tot and Wonder Girl, but never any Amazons with lines on their faces. This includes Wonder Woman's mother, Queen Hippolyta. Meanwhile, mature and accomplished older men can be found in graphic short stories and novels, including characters such as Superman; Lex Luthor; Flash; Clark Kent's editor, Perry White; Batman's butler, Alfred; Brit; Green Lantern; Spiderman's boss, J. Jonah Jameson; and of course, everyone's favorite senior citizen, Professor Xavier. With this in mind, I examine discourse about aging women in comics by focusing on the superhero genre, with a comparison of attitudes toward male characters who have gray hair and wrinkles. I review women and aging in comics, aging superheroines across two comic series, and conclude with the commercial viability of aging heroines. But first, let me start by broadly discussing some discourse surrounding aging.

EXISTING DISCOURSE OF AGING IN WESTERN SOCIETY

It does not exactly come as a shock to learn that many countries in Western society are obsessed with youth. For example, many American women use potions, dyes, injections, and elective invasive medical procedures to ward off the appearance of aging. In fact, anti-aging is a product category in the marketing and sales of "beauty" products for women. Furthermore, the word "youth" is actually part of the product names in this category, including youth recovery, youth code, youth-infusing, youth surge, youth-activating, youth-renewing, and pro-youth.[2] However, while the search for the Fountain of Youth predates Christ, social historians have marked the cultural forces set in motion after World War II as influencing both men and women to seek everlasting youth. Lynne Luciano, in her work on male body image, links the belief that immaturity is superior to maturity to the 1960s "youth quake."[3] Baby Boomers, very visible by their vast numbers, became contemptuous of the older generation and prompted youth to become more desirable.

No clear link has been established between the appearance of wrinkles and a loss of physical or intellectual power. However, characters in the comics, especially superheroes, typically do not show any appearance of aging. Thus, comic book creators seem to have made an assumption that age is synonymous with weakness and that characters should not appear weak. For example, Captain America has to be placed in suspended animation so that he will be perpetually youthful and able to battle evil with his shield and fists. Superman gains a few gray hairs, but retains his testosterone and the muscles that it builds. With the notable exception of various X-Men characters, many of the men and women in the inked pages show few signs of frailty. It is part of the appeal of these characters that they are supermen and superwomen. But the link between aging and ill health weakened throughout the twentieth century.

Aging in the twenty-first century is not the same as aging in the 1930s, when Superman first donned his tights. In fact, life expectancy in the 1930s was a little under sixty years old. However, from 1930 to 1960, the number of people over sixty in the United States more than doubled, with women significantly outliving men.[4] With generous old-age pensions, medical advancements, and fewer child care obligations than previous generations, wealthier Americans increasingly saw middle age and beyond as a time of health, leisure, and enjoyment.[5] Women pursued diets that would keep them healthy, viewed menopause as liberating, and cultivated a positive attitude toward the calendar. But older women in the pages of comics do not reflect health and happiness. On the rare occasions when older women do appear, they are marked as decrepit.

WOMEN AND AGING IN COMICS

Women have had to battle poor images of older women in all forms of media as negative views of aging pervaded popular culture in the twentieth century.[6] While women saw the possibility that they could be still be beautiful, vigorous, and useful into their middle years and beyond, the images and texts in popular culture communicated a contrary message. This message has continued into the twenty-first century, particularly in the pages of comic books.

A youthful appearance is so desirable partly because it is perceived to be linked with inner beauty. In other words, heroes and heroines cannot be old and ugly, because they are good people. As social and cultural historian Sander Gilman elaborates, "This is a very Western or Calvinist notion—that God selects people in very special ways for either punishment or rewards . . . beauty and goodness are equal—that if you're beautiful you're healthy, and if you're healthy you're good."[7] An extreme version of this thinking can be seen in the comics. Dick Tracy is handsome while his nemeses have names that reflect their inner and outer ugliness: Flattop, Pruneface, and Mole.

It is, perhaps, too shocking for sensibilities to give older women such descriptive names, but an older woman is still an ugly woman in much of modern American culture. In the United States, the "ideal age of beauty" for women is twenty-nine, according to a mid-2000s study by the Dove cosmetics company.[8] Not coincidentally, our heroines are also young women, or women who look young. Promethea, Alan Moore's Arab heroine, is born in Alexandria about A.D. 400. She comes back to life, aged about twenty-nine, in the bodies of a series of twentieth- and twenty-first-century women. One of these women, Barbara Shelley, ages into middle age, though not in the pages of the comic. Nicknamed "Fat Babs," we only see her when she "huffs" at physical exertion and laments that she "must be nuts, getting into this at my age," all while she is in the form of the forever-young Promethea.[9]

Heroines, for the most part, do not age past youth in the pages of comics, as evident in the large number of characters named "Girl": Power Girl, Wonder Girl, Star Girl, Batgirl, Supergirl. The "girls" are typically adults when they don their heroic suits. In contrast, the only major male hero given a juvenile name is Superboy, who is generally an earlier, and much younger, incarnation of Superman. (In the unique universe of comics, Superboy is sometimes a clone of Superman and Lex Luthor.) In the rare instances they appear, the older women are marginal and weak characters, such as Spiderman's Aunt May, who needs constant rescuing. In other words, aging women are often bystanders or victims, but occasionally criminals. Barbara Shelley spends much of her time in the first issues of Promethea in a hospital bed as a victim of a supernatural villain. Mostly, women past the bloom of youth, like Shelley, are simply nonexistent, not even worth the ink.

Such dismissals have ramifications beyond the comic book pages because popular culture images influence attitudes toward women in society. Mike Madrid, in his book on comic book heroines, notes that many female superheroes are never allowed to reach their potential. They are given powers that are weaker than their male compatriots, and positions of lesser importance. Also, any power that they may have is often overshadowed by their overly sexualized images.[10] Thus, by making female superheroes less fun than male superheroes, comic book creators encourage all readers to identify with the stronger male characters.

AGING SUPERHEROINES IN THE JUSTICE SOCIETY OF AMERICA

The Justice Society of America (JSA) is a DC Comics superhero group that first appeared in 1940, and the typical treatment of aging women can be seen in its history. The JSA reappeared in the 1950s after a brief absence, to cooperate with the Justice League of America (JLA). The series featured middle-aged JSA superheroes interacting with their younger JLA counterparts. However, only the men are middle-aged. In contrast, Wonder Woman, the immortal Amazon, and Black Canary, a martial artist, were not allowed to age. *Comic Buyer's Guide,* long the most influential publication reporting on the comics industry, ranked both Black Canary and Wonder Woman as among the sexiest women in comics.[11] They are both highly attractive young women, members of JSA, but unlike their male counterparts they are not allowed to age, because an old woman is not an attractive one. In other words, neither character shows any signs of advancing past her twenties, whereas the men could age gracefully.

In addition to their appearances, this unequal treatment of aging women is also apparent within the JSA plotlines. For example, the "Gentlemen Ghost" series in 2006 prompts some of the characters to discuss aging as they fail to subdue the ghostly thief. Flash, the original 1940s superhero who is Jay

Garrick, has sideburns turned to white and a few wrinkles on his forehead. He is close friends with Alan Scott, the 1940s-era Green Lantern, who has a slightly wrinkled face but no other signs of aging. Another character notes that Green Lantern is "not as young as he used to be" and that "even with the miracles you two have experienced, you still pay a price for age." But the men do not pay a price. They have the same skills as they did when younger as well as the same bodies, despite real-life men losing testosterone and muscles as they grow old.

In sharp contrast, women do not pay that same price. Joan Garrick, Flash's wife, is a frail old woman with white hair and a face appropriate for an elderly woman. In the same series, Lois Lane is bedridden while Superman has his usual strapping build, but with a face of wrinkles as his only sign of aging into his ninth decade. The faces of male characters age but, unlike the fate of women, little changes as a result. They remain vital and virile.

The sexual turnoff of an aging woman is touched upon in *Superman Red Son*. The comic features a hero who lives for millennia but picks up nary a gray hair or wrinkle over the many centuries. This version of Lois Lane turns into an old woman, as does Wonder Woman, who sacrifices her youth to save Superman's life. As soon as a flash reveals a stunned Diana with white hair but the same body, the old Amazon stops being Superman's potential love interest despite their shared immortality. She is still able to fight; only her hair has aged. Yet she effectively drops from the center of Superman's world and is later easily defeated by the Man of Steel. In other words, old men are potent, but old women have little value.

AGING SUPERHEROINES

Another potent old man is Brit, a character who appeared in 2007 in an Image Comics series. His existence is a wonderful example of the different treatment of aging male and female comic book characters. Brit has no superpowers except for indestructibility. His father, determined not to lose another loved one to the grave, gave Brit a serum in 1917 that allows him to survive gunshots, bombs, and assorted alien attacks. Brit ages, but he does so very slowly. However, by the time that he appears in a comic, he is an elderly man with the physique of Superman. Only Brit's white hair and wrinkles, along with the reactions of other characters, indicate that he is old. The creators of the character make much of his vigorous sexuality, as his girlfriend acknowledging at one point that, "I know you're not a one-woman man." As the owner of a strip club and special operations soldier, Brit marries a much-younger woman and fathers a son with her in a rather ludicrous story line in which the hero rebukes his new father-in-law for being upset that his daughter dropped out of law school to become a stripper. Thus, Brit is virile and portrayed as being vital to the survival of the United States.[12]

In contrast, his sister, Britney, is not. She was born about 1920, is twenty years younger than her brother, and received the same indestructibility serum from their father. She also gained super strength, and her aging halted almost completely. One character, Slitter, describes her as "You sound just like [Brit]. . . . A marginalized troublemaker—too powerful to release but too volatile for mainstream deployment. You're almost perfect, a Brit with a vagina."[13] While Brit saves the world, his sister has been shunted off to complete obscure assignments for the Drug Enforcement Agency (DEA). Unlike her brother, she has no partner, no offspring, and no sexual life. Like *Superman Red Son*'s Wonder Woman, an old woman is not a vital woman. Britney, too, has marginal value.

A young woman is sexy, and that is the only sort of woman who counts with the men who create and sell comics. Robert Kirkman, the creator and editor of *Brit*, discussed his thoughts on Britney's characterization in addendums to the volumes in the series, explaining, "Originally she was going to be old, like Brit—but I figured it wouldn't be a bad idea for her to be a pretty girl—I mean, that sells comics right? I'm always trying to be commercial."[14] Kirkman envisioned an audience that finds an elderly man appealing but rejects the thought of a sexy older woman. He and Nate Bellegarde, a penciler and inker, discussed their thoughts about Britney in the third volume of the series. Bellegarde lamented giving Britney a costume as "the bra-revealing dress shirt really worked for her . . . or just designed one so you see more of her, how to put it tactfully—huge boobs."[15] Brit winds up without his clothes so often that one character actually comments on it, but the creators of the comic do not consider Brit's body to be worthy of extended discussion. It clearly goes without saying that an old man is attractive while an old-appearing woman is not worth much ink.

Brit is a product of Image Comics, but larger representatives of the comic book industry reflect the same negative attitudes toward women. DC Comics' Catwoman, a thief who is generally portrayed as having some maturity, though the body of a twenty-year-old, has had enough of a fan club to make the move into 1960s television before entering the Batman series of movies as a major character. A sketchbook of character designs by one of her artists, Guillem March, includes these lines: "Is she a stripper? No, she's going to kick some ass."[16] Catwoman is fundamentally sexy. Therefore, her body is her most important attribute, although she is also smart, witty, and Batman's equal. Catwoman cannot age without losing a basic element of her identity, according to her male designer.

Kirkman and March may be in error with their assumptions that older women are not good for sales. Mainstream comic creators, largely male, have never explored the marketability of a mature, crime-fighting woman. Wonder

Woman, celebrated by feminist Gloria Steinem as an icon, is probably the superheroine who is most popular among women, with much of her popularity deriving from the 1970s television show that featured actress Lynda Carter in the starring role. Steinem celebrated Wonder Woman's strength, not her appearance.[17] Men tend to focus on her appearance.[18] Yet older female characters, who are not in the superhero branch of the comics industry, do sell books to a growing segment of the comic-buying audience.

COMMERCIAL VIABILITY OF AGING HEROINES

Comics were initially aimed at boys. Even Marston, the creator of Wonder Woman, aimed at a male audience though girls like Steinem clearly did pick up the books. As American society roiled with all of the changes of the late 1960s, women's liberation activists began to celebrate the smart, self-sufficient crone. Some of these women drew comics, and they drew them for other women. These artists often reflected the society in which they lived, a multigenerational one with vivid women at every step. The term "crone" referenced older women in ancient matriarchal societies and sought to restore respect and power to mature women.[19] Comics aimed at female audiences have given power and intelligence to mature women.

For example, Alison Bechdel's "Dykes to Watch Out For" is a syndicated comic strip that appeared from 1983 to 2008. It is one of the products of the women's movement, appearing in women's newspapers and reflecting many of the aspects of the women's movement such as a feminist bookstore, Madwimmin Books. Set in a small city in the United States, "Dykes to Watch Out For" chronicled generations of lesbians. In Bechdel's world, life for women did not stop at age twenty-nine. In fact, older women were featured, not marginalized, and they had sex lives. Jasmine, old enough to be the mother of a teenager, dated Lois. Jezanna Ramsey, a bookstore manager, struggled with financial issues and gave advice to younger women, as did college professor Dr. Sydney Krukowski. As one of the most successful comic strips, "Dykes to Watch Out For" lasted longer than many mainstream strips. The range of characters in the strip helped its marketability as it appealed to generations of women.

The Hernandez brothers, possessing a feminist sensibility, continued this trend of recognizing mature women by creating strong older characters like the matriarch, Luba, in the *Love and Rockets* series. The brothers, Gilbert and Jaime, are best known for *Love and Rockets* though each has worked on his own. With a minimalist, Latin American style, both brothers have become widely respected creators of American fiction. The women in their graphic novels are full human beings, albeit with the exaggerated breasts typical of the art form. They are based on women whom the brothers knew while growing up and, as such, are very much real women.[20]

The work of the Hernandez brothers challenges the notion that older women have little value. The characters are vital and appealing, perhaps because they are not based on an archaic image of mature women. Luba, a creation of Gilbert Hernandez, managed to rank sixtieth in *Comic Buyer's Guide* of the sexiest women in comics despite advancing in age from an infant in a Central American village to a middle-aged migrant to the United States. Her large breasts might have helped with the ranking as the voters were presumably male, but she is also one of the most popular characters in graphic novels. Luba is a strong woman, and age does not weaken her spirit.[21]

Thus, we can see that fiction, especially in comics, plays a valuable role in society by allowing people to put themselves in the shoes of characters who are unlike themselves. Such shifting permits people to empathize with others and understand the challenges that they face. By eliminating older women from comic books, creators have made life more difficult for actual older women. Thus, in many comics, aging women are to be ignored, rather than recognized or celebrated in the style accorded to older men.

NOTES

1. John M. Trushell, "American Dreams of Mutants: The X-Men—'Pulp' Fiction, Science Fiction, and Superheroes," *Journal of Popular Culture* 38 (2004): 149–68, on 154.

2. Products include serums and creams from lines such as Christian Dior, Clinique, Clarins, Lancôme, L'Oreal, and Origins.

3. Lynne Luciano, *Looking Good: Male Body Image in Modern America* (New York: Hill and Wang, 2002), 75–100.

4. W. Andrew Achenbaum, *Old Age in the New Land: The American Experience since 1790* (Baltimore: Johns Hopkins University Press, 1978), 59–60, 91.

5. Catherine Carstairs, "Look Younger, Live Longer: Ageing Beautifully with Gayelord Hauser in America, 1920–1975," *Gender & History* 26, no. 2 (2014): 332–50, on 333.

6. Lois Banner, *In Full Flower: Aging Women, Power, and Sexuality* (New York: Alfred Knopf, 1992).

7. Quoted in Beth Teitell, *Drinking Problems at the Fountain of Youth* (New York: Harper Luxe, 2008), 184–85.

8. Quoted in Teitell, 189.

9. Alan Moore, J. H. Williams III, and Mick Gray, *Promethea* (New York: DC Comics, 2000).

10. Mike Madrid, *Supergirls: Fashion, Feminism, Fantasy, and the History of Comic Book Heroines* (San Francisco: Exterminating Angel Press, 2009), vi.

11. Bret Frankenhoff, *Comics Buyer's Guide: 100 Sexiest Women in Comics* (Iola, WI: 2011).

12. Robert Kirkman et al., *Brit: Volume One: Old Soldier* (Berkeley, CA: Image Comics, 2007), n.p; Robert Kirkman et al., *Brit: Volume Three: Fubar* (Berkeley, CA: Image Comics, 2009), n.p.

13. Robert Kirkman et al., *Brit: Volume Two: AWOL* (Berkeley, CA: Image Comics, 2008), n.p.

14. Robert Kirkman, "Sketchbook," in *Brit: Volume Two: AWOL*, n.p.

15. Robert Kirkman, "Sketchbook," in *Brit: Volume Three: Fubar*, n.p.

16. Judd Winick and Guillem March, *Catwoman: Volume 1: The Game* (New York: DC Comics, 2012), n.p.

17. Gloria Steinem, ed. *Wonder Woman* (New York: Holt, Rinehart and Winston and Warner Books, 1972).

18. Bradford W. Wright sees Wonder Woman as entertainment for men in *Comic Book Nation: The Transformation of Youth Culture in America* (Baltimore: Johns Hopkins University Press, 2001).

19. Barbara G. Walker, *The Crone: Woman of Age, Wisdom, and Power* (New York: Harper & Row, 1988).

20. Frederick Luis Aldama, *Your Brain on Latino Comics: From Gus Arriola to Los Bros Hernandez* (Austin: University of Texas Press, 2009).

21. Gilbert Hernandez, *Luba* (Seattle: Fantagraphics, 2009).

III

Being a Man?
Masculinity and Aging Heroes

Chapter Ten

Aging Masculinity in Popular Culture

The Case of Mad Men*'s Roger Sterling*

Patrice M. Buzzanell and Suzy D'Enbeau

How gender is portrayed in popular media has intrigued media and communication scholars and popular audiences alike, because media has the power to both reinforce and challenge gender norms and expectations.[1] Yet until very recently, the vast majority of this commentary has focused on women and femininity despite the fact that the preferred or normative privileging of men and masculinity performances dominates lived and mediated contexts.[2] Even so, these preferred performances of men and masculinities coincide with stereotypic representations that not only become evident when juxtaposed with those of women and femininities, but also still offer only narrow images of men and masculinities. These gendered stereotypes indicate that men are supposed to be stoic, anti-feminine, competitive, individualistic, successful, and heroic.[3] Notably, these stereotypes are premised on a sexy, successful, attractive *young* man. What is missing is a consideration of how age factors into such portrayals so that men and masculinities across the lifespan can be better understood.[4] Depicting the nuances and complexities of ordinary men and masculinities in mediated contexts provides a window for observing and potentially changing contemporary gender stereotypes and gender relations throughout individuals' lifetimes.

More than ever, popular media are grappling with the unrealistic nature and instability of masculinity stereotypes, especially with regard to age. For instance, viewers can watch a high school chemistry teacher with a life-threatening disease enter the dangerous world of drug trafficking in an attempt to secure his family's future (*Breaking Bad*); an Italian American mobster challenged by the competing demands of his home life and leading a criminal organization (*The Sopranos*); and a father negotiate political differences and work-life issues among his family (*Last Man Standing*). These characters "are in a constant process of change, but most of the men exist in a state of being endlessly bewildered by how to handle situations in their lives in a way never fully or clearly resolved at the conclusion of each episode."[5] This is the crux of contemporary popular cultural portrayals of aging and masculinity: popular culture represents how older men attend to the various dilemmas and contradictions that surface in their attempts to adhere to ideal masculinity standards. Thus popular cultural representations of men and masculinity can reinforce limiting interpretations of masculinity, but also offer opportunities to push back and redefine what it means to be a man. The aim of our chapter is to explore one such portrayal, that of *Mad Men*'s Roger Sterling.

Currently in the middle of its seventh and final season, *Mad Men* depicts the men and women working in Madison Avenue advertising agencies in 1960s New York. The series follows Don Draper, the most successful creative director in advertising, and his fellow employees at Sterling Cooper Draper and Pryce (SCDP). Roger is a partner at SCDP (an offshoot of Sterling Cooper, an agency cofounded by his father in 1923), a U.S. Navy veteran of World War II, a notorious womanizer, and a heavy drinker. He is known for his lighthearted demeanor, which makes him liked by most of his SCDP colleagues, especially his mentor, Bertram Cooper. Over the course of seven seasons, Roger divorces his long-term wife, remarries an SCDP secretary, has a child from an ongoing affair with another SCDP secretary (now business partner), consumes copious amounts of alcohol and the occasional illicit drug, openly struggles with his relationship with his daughter, and suffers two heart attacks, all the while working to attain and maintain lucrative clients for SCDP over business lunches, dinners, and cocktails. In this analysis, we take Roger as the focus and rely on theory and research about masculinity as socially constructed to situate this particular characterization and to explore the tensions that emerge as discourses of masculinity and aging intersect.

Mad Men offers a compelling case to explore the intersections of aging and masculinity for several reasons. First, *Mad Men* has received numerous awards and critical acclaim for its historical portrayal of gender and workplace processes. *Mad Men* represents the 1960s as a "televisual memory weighted by an era and American identity in tumult, where the thing remembered is increasingly mediated by television itself."[6] Second, popular cultural commentary lauds *Mad Men* for insightful depictions, commentary, and critique of shifting norms and ideals around masculinity.[7] That is, fascination with *Mad Men* has less to do with "its gleeful portrayal of socially repudiated attitudes and behaviours, or even its much-vaunted visual elements, than with its diversification of the way in which popular culture talks about men."[8] The few popular culture and academic articles that do explore *Mad Men* and masculinity focus exclusively on the lead character, Don Draper, and are thus missing a critical opportunity to consider how aging influences masculinity.

Third, *Mad Men* offers viewers a glimpse into a time when lives were presumably simpler, especially with regard to masculinity norms and expectations. Indeed, leading experts in men and masculinities contend that although the world has changed in terms of gender, many young men still cling to what they perceive as the more clearly defined gender roles and ideals of *Mad Men* masculinity.[9] More specifically, "the changes in how men are valued are brought into stark relief" when comparing *Mad Men* male characters to twenty-first-century contemporaries.[10] Finally, *Mad Men* provides a savvy representation of how gendered processes and workplace practices can both constrain and transform gendered constructions and performances.[11] In this way, *Mad Men* offers a popular cultural space for viewers to reflect on how things have presumably changed and to reflect on their own practices.[12]

Thus, our reading of Roger Sterling proposes that he is an unlikely popular culture hero who transcends the false dichotomy between aging and masculinity. To develop our analysis, we explore Roger as a paragon of aging masculinity in terms of professionalism, intimacy, and (grand)fatherhood. We contend that Roger presents possibilities for viewers to contemplate successful aging, reflective masculinities, and a rearticulation of what it means to be an older American man. In the following pages, we explore the tensions that surface when dominant discourses of masculinity bump up against discourses of aging in popular culture.

THE PARADOXES OF MASCULINITY AND AGING IN POPULAR CULTURE

Most iterations of preferred masculinity privilege competition, independence, aggression, and logic, while also promoting anti-feminine behaviors.[13] Additionally, proving one's manhood is thought to be "one of the defining experiences in American men's lives."[14] In popular culture, there is no greater example of preferred masculinity and proving one's manhood than the hero. The hero is a man who transcends the mundane, excels in what he sets out to accomplish, mystifies others, symbolizes success and conquest, and does it all without noticeable assistance from others. That ordinary masculinity is held up to this standard makes the achievement of it a tall order. Indeed, scholars contend that "the hero figure, as the ideal against which masculinity is judged, simultaneously denotes manhood and demotes male identity. It largely defines the masculinity to which many Western men aspire and just as thoroughly defines their inevitable failure."[15] Specifically, the hero identity is undergirded by a set of masculine ideologies that dictate "how a man earns respect, what makes a man successful, what it means to be a good father, what qualities make a man heroic, and so on" and that are circulated throughout popular culture.[16] In short, the hero persona translates to a set of unattainable criteria to which ordinary men often aspire.

Furthermore, youthfulness is embedded as a taken-for-granted criterion of both successful manhood and heroism. Indeed, the paradox of the hero—that he both defines preferred masculinity for ordinary men and is unattainable by ordinary men—is nowhere more pronounced than for aging men. Aging men are arguably rendered invisible by these dominant narratives of masculinity and heroes for two reasons. First, older people are typically constructed as ungendered, and, second, gender is consistently constructed as a static, unchanging entity.[17] According to Spector-Mersel, "the absence of cultural guidelines for being both a 'true' man and an aging person constitutes the context within which contemporary older men struggle to build acceptable identities."[18] Moreover, when we do consider the intersections of age and gender, dominant aging discourses contradict dominant masculinity and hero discourses. In specific, aging is associated with feminine-typed attributes such as dependence, reflection, support, and a lack of autonomy.

To address the conspicuousness of an aging masculinity framework, a lifespan perspective contends that "masculinities are bound to social clocks that ascribe different models of manhood to different periods of men's lives."[19] That is, how men perform masculinity and what ideal masculinity scripts actually look like change over time. From a life-span perspective, older men have an opportunity to (re)define successful, aging masculinity norms and expectations. Consider the Disney Pixar movie, *The Incredibles*, which follows middle-aged Mr. Incredible's return to the superhero life following a fifteen-year hiatus in the suburbs where he and his wife, Elastigirl, raised their superhero family. The movie pokes fun at the challenges Mr. Incredible faces as he attempts to access his superhero powers and defeat bad guys with his bulging, out-of-shape, middle-aged body. Moreover, he is only able to defeat the villain with the help of his family. In this example, the masculine hero as a young, autonomous man is problematized, exposing a transgressive portrayal of an aging hero who effectively works with others, an image that has the potential to inform how we think of aging masculinity.

To summarize, age is a key definer of masculinity, although it is often overlooked. Both theoretical underpinnings of masculinity and popular culture offer entrée into an exploration of masculinity-aging intersections. First, "masculinities are configurations of practice that are constructed, unfold, and change through time," and what it means to be masculine is defined through social interaction and can change with context.[20] In other words, definitions of preferred manhood and masculinity are not static but change over time, indicating that older men have the power to (re)define a newer version of masculinity that accounts for successful aging. We see this gap as an opportunity to consider alternative constructions of masculinity in the context of aging heroes—those men who transcend the limiting tensions between age and gender and reinstate age as a key determinant in how we think about ideal manhood. Second, popular cultural representations have the capacity to both reinforce *and* transform how we think about gender, inviting a reconsideration of stereotypical versions of gender. We turn to *Mad Men*'s Roger to elucidate (a version of) aging masculinity.

AGING MASCULINITY: FRIENDSHIP, PROFESSIONALISM, INTIMACY, AND FATHERHOOD

Our reading of Roger depicts how he successfully navigates the tensions between masculinity and aging to (re)define how older men perform manhood. This is what makes Roger so interesting, attractive, and likable despite his numerous transgressions as a womanizer and heavy drinker. Our reading of Roger also explores his transformation from early seasons to the final seasons of *Mad Men*, and focuses on major incidents and milestones in Roger's life that encourage reflection and showcase the tensions of aging masculinity. We propose that Roger is a complex and paradoxical character who reimagines masculinity and transcends the dichotomy between aging and gender through professional trickery, recursive intimacy, and reflective (grand)fatherhood.

Professional Trickery

The first way in which we consider aging masculinity and Roger is through the masculine and archetypal role of the trickster. The trickster emerges as an engaging but very troublesome character because of his cleverness, desire to disrupt human lives for the sheer joy of causing chaos, and ability to ensnare unwitting humans into playing parts in not well-thought-out schemes. In the end, something good sometimes comes of the trickster's deeds, but the course is precarious, at best. [21]

Roger maintained his childishness, petulance, lack of foresight, arrogance, and self-centeredness despite heart attacks, negative feedback from others, and unfulfilled opportunities to assist the new SCDP agency. In this way, Roger exemplifies the rebellious nature of masculinity in which the class clown is privileged over the serious worker. [22] For example, when Roger was alerted that one of the agency's biggest clients, Lucky Strike, was going to drop SCDP, he informed no one until it was too late, and he had a month to appeal their decision. In fact, when the other partners were devastated by the news, Roger acted as if he hadn't known, faked a call to Lucky Strike in front of the other partners, and even faked a trip to North Carolina to purportedly attempt to save the account.

Roger eventually admitted to his mistress, agency secretary-now-partner Joan Harris, that he knew about Lucky Strike's decision before anyone else did but was unable to do anything about it. He was a trickster with a conscience, and this facet of his personality may have assisted his eventual transformation. That is, Roger played the role of a trickster who disobeyed normal rules, refused to take blame for his misdeeds, and who could be heroic and foolish simultaneously. He also took no responsibility for SCDP's financial woes. His cleverness was most evident in his constant verbal quips. Eventually, however, he turns his intellect toward agency transformation.

By the end of the first half of the final season, the agency is in financial trouble. Roger works out a deal that can potentially solve the agency's problems by inviting a larger agency to buy a 51-percent stake in Sterling Cooper as an independent subsidiary. Roger explains that he would be the president of Sterling Cooper, and that Don Draper would be back as creative director. The deal passes with a partners' vote as the remaining partners are left bewildered but pleased by Roger-the-trickster's ability to successfully attend to the dilemmas of the agency. In sum, discourses of aging masculinity allow Roger to retain the class-clown qualities of the masculine rebel, but when viewed through the lens of the trickster, he has the ability to also transform the status quo.

Recursive Intimacy

Traditional masculinity suggests that men should engage in sexual conquests and that men should be emotionally detached from their multiple sexual partners. Yet these stereotypical expectations do not fully capture the complex human desire for intimacy and connection that transcends age and gender. That is, intimacy and sexual desire are thought to be the purview of the young, despite a growing body of research that suggests otherwise.[23] Admittedly, Roger is a womanizer who has a foolish and unmet desire to feel young. He engages in countless affairs with younger women and even throws away his twenty-two-year marriage to wife Mona for a young SCDP secretary, Jane. Roger seems fascinated by young women and their presumed naiveté, sense of fun, and humor. He is careless and carefree, forever the sexist clown who makes comments denigrating marriage or objectifying a woman's body, as when he tells Joan that he was grateful to "roam those hillsides." His commentary suggests that Roger is no different than a lothario who privileges multiple sexual partners over sustained romantic intimacy.

However, beneath his carefree facade, he seems to want more than just a sexual conquest. He desires intimacy and answers for bigger questions about life. Roger's longtime affair with Joan best illustrates this desire. Certainly, their affair is not without problems. In one scene, Roger claims he is tired of sneaking around and wants to get Joan an apartment in the city. Joan quickly replies that she knows men very well and that the "sneaking around" is what they desire most. She says, "Roger, if you had your way, I would be stranded in some paperweight with my legs stuck in the air. We both know I'll find a more permanent situation and you'll find a new model." Joan claims she doesn't want to leave her roommate and live alone so, during their next hotel rendezvous, he surprises her with a pet bird in a cage to counteract her loneliness. This gift also ironically represents his desire to keep Joan all to himself. As the pair leave the hotel separately, Joan is carrying the bird, and she does not get an apartment in the city.

Their relationship, however, grows in intensity over the next few seasons. When Roger returns to the office after suffering a heart attack, Joan assists him in applying some makeup foundation to improve his pale coloring. She begins to cry as he admits that he regrets a lot of the things he has done but not his relationship with her. Later, when Roger is married to Jane, he attempts to rekindle his romance with Joan when her husband is called to Vietnam. Roger tries to comfort Joan, and tells her that he wishes she would talk to him about things. He recalls that when he thinks back on all of the good things in his life, Joan is always there. He longs for an intimate connection with her, but she remains guarded until they are surprised by the sudden death of an older SCDP secretary. Joan and Roger share cheesecake and drinks to console each other, and on their way home, they are mugged. The robbery leaves them both out of sorts, and they end up briefly rekindling their affair, resulting in Joan's pregnancy. When the two discuss what to do about the pregnancy, Roger suggests that maybe he is in love with Joan. But he fails to ever take full responsibility, and Joan, forever guarded, does not force the issue with him. When the couple consults a doctor about a possible abortion, the doctor accuses Roger of using Joan and of being selfish and irresponsible. But Roger fails to reflect truly on this accusation. It merely lingers beneath the surface of their relationship.

In terms of aging masculinity, Roger's desire for intimacy contradicts the assumption that men do not want more than a physical connection. The fact that Roger keeps returning to Joan, and keeps replaying the same mistakes and failing to assume responsibility, demonstrates a form of recursive intimacy in which men are only capable of emotionally impoverished relationships.

Reflective (Grand)Fatherhood

The final way in which we consider aging masculinity is through (grand)fatherhood. Fatherhood is yet another realm that is linked to dominant discourses of masculinity, although research suggests that grandfatherhood provides men with the opportunity to reconstitute their own version of masculinity.[24] Specifically, whereas men may feel limited in their roles as fathers by restrictive stereotypes and expectations that constitute fathers as breadwinners instead of caregivers, grandfatherhood offers greater flexibility for men "to reengage with family life."[25] In the case of Roger, our reading proposes that he engages in reflective fatherhood and grandfatherhood, as shown best through his relationship with his daughter, Margaret.

Over the course of nearly the entire series, Roger is attempting to better understand Margaret. When viewers are first introduced to Margaret, she is a preteen in need of a haircut. When Mona brings the ever-disgruntled Margaret to the office to find out where to get a haircut, Roger remarks that her ponytail makes her look young and he likes that. Margaret quips back that she likes his haircut because it makes him look old, revealing an underlying tension in their relationship. In another scene at a dinner with Roger, Mona, and Don and his wife, Mona explains that Margaret is going to see a psychiatrist. She does not see this as a big deal since Margaret is the last child in their apartment building to seek psychiatric help. But Roger mumbles that he "can't wait for that girl to be another man's problem."

Instead of speaking to his daughter, in scene after scene, he asks other women about Margaret and her issues. For example, after sleeping with a woman who is not much older than his daughter, he asks her why his daughter is always so angry and why she always rolls her eyes at him. When Roger is in the hospital following his first heart attack, he does not want Margaret to see him that way. She disregards his request and walks into his hospital room, and then they share an emotionally charged embrace, one of the few times in the early seasons of *Mad Men* that viewers see both in familial intimacy. He is both intrigued and annoyed by his daughter, yet fails to account for his role or responsibility in her upbringing. His fatherhood performance is shaped by rigid stereotypes: he is emotionally distant and physically unavailable, subsumed by his breadwinner role. Margaret seems to want more from their relationship, yet she remains frustrated and is frequently disappointed.

When Roger becomes a grandfather, he tries to maintain a close relationship with Margaret's son. But when Roger inappropriately takes him to see *Planet of the Apes*, she angrily tells him that he can never see her son again. Then, at the opening of Season 7, Roger is awakened by the phone ringing. His daughter is on the phone, inviting him to brunch. He immediately perks up and agrees to meet her. She seems ethereal, bright-eyed, and open. He is suspicious because she doesn't ask him for anything. She just wants to let him know that she has come to terms with their relationship and with her life. Later, Mona contacts Roger in a state of panic because Margaret is missing. Mona insists that she and Roger travel to find their daughter, who is living on a commune. They find Margaret, now calling herself Marigold, in a ragged skirt, messy hair, no makeup, and living in an abandoned farmhouse with no electricity. She is pleased to see them, as long as they do not try to take her away. She asserts that she is happy there.

Mona cannot handle the situation and leaves Roger to sort things out. In this case, Roger's carefree attitude and amicable personality come in handy as he is welcomed by the commune members and is able to adapt, briefly, to their lifestyle. He rolls up his shirt sleeves, smokes marijuana, and sleeps in a sleeping bag. He does not try to force anything onto Margaret, but instead attempts to truly understand where she is coming from. His attitude changes, however, when he watches her sneak away in the middle of the night to have sex with a man in the commune. The following morning, when he breaks down and insists that she cannot just abandon her son, she retorts that Roger did just that to her. He physically tries to remove her, and the two fall into the mud as Margaret runs away. Roger leaves the commune without Margaret, and it is one of the first times viewers see him somewhat despondent, perplexed about what to do next, and unable to make light of a difficult situation. At the close of 2014 and the first half of Season 7, the tensions between Roger and Margaret remain unresolved, and Margaret remains in the commune.

In sum, Roger is constantly reflecting upon his own fatherhood, drawing on his own childhood, his relationship with his first wife, and his confusion about his daughter. No matter the situation, he is constantly befuddled by his daughter's behavior and her detachment from him but fails to account for his own behavior. However, once he becomes a grandfather, he attempts to reengage his daughter and her family. It is in these moments that viewers bear witness to his attempts to redefine his own manhood through his (grand)father performance.

THEORIZING AGING MASCULINITY

In this chapter, we considered *Mad Men*'s Roger as an unlikely aging hero who reconstitutes aging masculinity. We've explored three different sites of aging masculinity in terms of professionalism, intimacy, and grandfatherhood. In pulling together the different threads of our reading, we suggest that aging masculinity reinserts age as a crucial and integral factor in considerations of manhood. Our reading takes a life-span perspective in documenting how Roger reinvents himself over the course of the seasons. Roger is both magnetic and threatening. He transforms from merely a class-clown rebel who is unreliable, selfish, and forever making light of difficult situations, to a redeemer who earns professional respect from his colleagues. His performance of masculinity is not static, but ever-changing over time and across contexts. Specifically, how Roger performs professionalism, intimacy, and grandfatherhood is based on particular interactions and sociocultural contexts. These different themes work in concert with each other to reveal the nuances, complexities, and contradictions of a reimagined masculinity that both conforms to and pushes the boundaries of hegemonic, youthful masculinity.

Related to this, reflection and transformation are key facets of each theme. Roger is not perfect—he refuses to take accountability and responsibility, and often glosses over the truth. But these transgressions reveal the contradictions of aging masculinity. Roger clowns around as a way to enact the rebel don't-take-me-too-seriously persona, but this also functions as a security blanket that protects him from his own insecurities and failures. This is not surprising given that, in the 1950s, although men were "responsible breadwinners and devoted fathers, they were still anxious about overconformity but unable and unwilling to break free of domestic responsibilities to become rebels on the run."[26] Future explorations of *Mad Men* and masculinity should compare the multiple ways in which manhood is performed on the show.

In closing, Roger's character is portrayed as a complex human being who, in some ways, epitomizes traditional hegemonic masculinity and yet also redefines aging masculinity. He takes organizational risks, engages in competitive interactions in the workplace, drinks heavily, romances the agency's office manager, and leaves his long-term wife for a much-younger second wife. He does not portray himself as thinking or feeling deeply, but as being a man situated primarily in the present and focused on the here and now. Yet our reading depicts the moments of disruption in his performance of masculinity, moments that are informed by discourses of aging masculinity.

NOTES

1. Bonnie J. Dow, "Gender and Communication in Mediated Contexts: Introduction," in *The Sage Handbook of Gender and Communication*, edited by Bonnie J. Dow et al. (Thousand Oaks, CA: Sage, 2006), 264.

2. Amanda D. Lotz, *Cable Guys: Television and Masculinities in the 21st Century* (New York: New York University Press, 2014), 21.

3. Douglas B. Holt and Craig J. Thompson, "Man-of-Action Heroes: The Pursuit of Heroic Masculinity in Everyday Consumption," *Journal of Consumer Research* 31 (2004): 425–40, on 426.

4. Gabriela Spector-Mersel, "Never-Aging Stories: Western Hegemonic Masculinity Scripts," *Journal of Gender Studies* 15 (2006): 67–82, on 67.

5. Lotz, *Cable Guys*, 58.

6. Rodney Taveira, "Inside the Mad Men: Don Draper and American Masculinity," *The Conversation*, April 10, 2014, http://theconversation.com/inside-the-mad-men-don-draper-and-american-masculinity-24800 (accessed November 3, 2014).

7. Taveira, "Inside the Mad Men."

8. Nicky Falkof, "The Father, the Failure and the Self-Made Man: Masculinity in *Mad Men*," *Critical Quarterly* 54, no. 3 (2012): 31–45, on 33.

9. NPR Staff, "The New American Man Doesn't Look Like His Father," *All Things Considered*, June 23, 2014, http://www.npr.org/2014/06/23/323966448/the-new-american-man-doesnt-look-like-his-father (accessed October 20, 2014).

10. Amanda D. Lotz, "Don Draper's Sad Manhood: What Makes *Mad Men* different from *Breaking Bad, Sopranos*," *Salon*, April 11, 2014, http://www.salon.com/2014/04/11/don_

drapers_sad_manhood_what_makes_mad_men_different_from_breaking_bad_sopranos/ (accessed November 3, 2014).

11. Patrice M. Buzzanell and Suzy D'Enbeau, "Intimate, Ambivalent, and Erotic Mentoring: Popular Culture and Mentor-Mentee Relational Processes in *Mad Men*," *Human Relations* 67, no. 6 (2014): 695–714, on 695; Suzy D'Enbeau and Patrice M. Buzzanell, "The Erotic Heroine and the Politics of Gender at Work: A Feminist Reading of *Mad Men's* Joan Harris," in *Heroines of Film and Television: Portrayals in Popular Culture,* edited by Norma Jones et al. (Lanham, MD: Rowan & Littlefield, 2014), 3.

12. Katie Milestone and Anneke Meyer, *Gender and Popular Culture* (Cambridge: Polity Press, 2011).

13. Patrice M. Buzzanell, "Gaining a Voice: Feminist Organizational Communication Theorizing," *Management Communication Quarterly* 7, no. 4 (1994): 339–83, on 344.

14. Michael Kimmel, *Manhood in America: A Cultural History* (New York: Oxford University Press, 2011), 1.

15. Kevin Alexander Boon, "Heroes, Metanarratives, and the Paradox of Masculinity in Contemporary Western Culture," *The Journal of Men's Studies* 13 (2005): 301–12, on 304.

16. Boon, "Heroes, Metanarratives," 326.

17. Spector-Mersel, "Never-Aging Stories," 67.

18. Ibid., 68.

19. Ibid., 70.

20. R. W. Connell and James W. Messerschmidt, "Hegemonic Masculinity: Rethinking the Concept," *Gender & Society* 19, no. 6 (2005): 829–59, on 852.

21. Helena Bassil-Morozow, *The Trickster in Contemporary Film* (New York: Routledge, 2013), 3.

22. Holt and Thompson, "Man-of-Action Heroes," 428.

23. Brian de Vries, "Sexuality and Aging: A Late-Blooming Relationship," *Sexuality Research & Social Policy: Journal of NSRC* 6, no. 4 (2009): 1–4, on 1.

24. Penny Sorensen and Neil J. Cooper, "Reshaping the Family Man: A Grounded Theory Study of the Meaning of Grandfatherhood," *The Journal of Men's Studies,* 18 no. 2 (2010): 117.

25. Sorensen and Cooper, "Reshaping the Family Man," 123.

26. Kimmel, *Manhood in America,* 185.

Chapter Eleven

Aging Superheroes

Retirement and Return in Kingdom Come *and*
Old Man Logan

Nathan Miczo

With the continued "graying of America," scholars and researchers should keep step by examining facets of aging, including media portrayals of the elderly.[1] Also, as superheroes are still extremely popular on both the big and small screens, it follows that we should take this opportunity to focus on how they are portrayed in media as a way of examining aging. Immediately, one confronts a conundrum: where are they? Although many of our most popular superheroes have been around for decades (Batman turned seventy-five in 2014), we see few, if any, aging superheroes across television, film, and graphic novels. Rather, superheroes simply don't age. In many cases they conveniently possess powers that include aging very slowly, or get a periodic reboot, restarting storylines all over again, with their youth intact.[2] Therefore, stories that portray an aging superhero stand out. They tend to be stand-alone narrative arcs that reside outside of other continuities. Two stories of aging superheroes with several parallels are DC Comics's *Kingdom Come*[3] and Marvel's *Old Man Logan*.[4] Both of these stories depict aging superheroes precisely because the passage of time is portrayed in a meaningful way.

The passage of time in both narratives is indicated by the retirement of the aging heroes from their superhero roles. Retirement is often a status marker, indicating the transition into the category of "older person" or "elderly."[5] As noted by many scholars, Western societies tend to be ageist, showing a marked preference for youth over older age.[6] However, the expression of that preference is more complicated because both negative and positive stereotypes of aging persist in society and popular culture. This ambivalence is also evident when examining the media: the elderly have been described as noticeably absent from media,[7] and when they are present they are variously portrayed as evil and malignant forces, or as good-natured but bumbling and incompetent.[8] However, neither of these depictions suitably characterizes Superman (a.k.a. Kal-El, or Clark Kent) or Wolverine (a.k.a. Logan). They are superheroes who fight on the side of the "good and the right."[9] Therefore, examining their narratives as aging heroes may expand the range of characterizations for reflecting on media portrayals of aging.

Given that age is relevant in both stories, what challenges does it pose for the retired superhero? One interesting similarity between the narratives is that the plots do not center on a conflict between the hero and a villain. To be sure, there are villains, and they are dealt with in the course of events. However, the crux of the dilemma for both heroes is an internal struggle over who they are and what their role is in a changed world. This is the same struggle faced by many aging individuals who confront doubts about the value of their contributions to society. The chapter begins by describing the basic plots of the stories. Following that, criteria of successful aging are developed by examining three theories of aging. Themes of retirement and return are then explored in the stories of Superman and Wolverine. Finally, implications for successful aging are discussed.

BACKGROUND OF THE STORIES

Both stories open with heroes who have withdrawn from the world. In *Kingdom Come*, we are first introduced to Norman McCay, a preacher grown "utterly despondent" over the state of the world. He is visited by the Spectre, the spirit of vengeance whose charge is to punish wrongdoers. Drawn to McCay's desire for justice, the Spectre tells him that they must both be witnesses to a coming Armageddon, brought on largely by the superheroes. They then travel to a "Midwestern farmland," where our first image of the retired Kal-El (Superman) shows him wearing overalls, without a shirt, his hair long and pulled back in a ponytail. It becomes clear that this is an older Kal-El by the whitish-gray beard, mustache, and sideburns, as well as the streaks of gray in his black hair. When they first spot him, Norman McCay says to the Spectre, "The farmer looks familiar." The Spectre responds, "You know him by a name he has not used in ten years." The passage of time is confirmed with our first close-up of Kal-El's face, which shows deep lines across his forehead and brows.[10]

In *Old Man Logan*, the opening panels depict a bloody and battered Wolverine staggering off over a forested ridge. The narration tells us that he "hasn't raised his voice or popped his claws in close to fifty years." The next page reveals a back view of a heavy-set man with close-cropped white hair, riding a tired horse toward a battered homestead. The first frontal view confirms that the man on the horse is indeed Logan (Wolverine), and, as with Kal-El, his sideburns, like the rest of his hair, are whitish-gray, and his face is deeply lined and scarred. Given the potency of Wolverine's well-known healing factor, the presence of scars becomes significant in revealing a certain loss of efficiency in its functioning. Like Kal-El, Logan's withdrawal from the world involves the taking up of farming. The first spoken word is "Pa?" and we learn that Logan has a wife and two young children.

Importantly, in the wake of their retirement, the world has become a worse place. As we learn from McCay, the world in *Kingdom Come* is filled with the children and grandchildren of the heroes of yesterday. Having rid the world of supervillains, this new breed of heroes "no longer fight for the right. They fight simply to fight, their only foes each other." The problem is not just the surplus of undisciplined, unprincipled powerhouses, however. In the wake of Superman's withdrawal from the world, the rest of the Justice League members have retreated to their own individual spheres of influence. Batman jealously guards Gotham City, Green Lantern sits high above the Earth waiting for extraterrestrial threats, the Flash endlessly patrols Keystone City, and Hawkman has turned the Northwest into his own private nature sanctuary.

Old Man Logan takes place fifty years after the villains defeated the heroes and divided the country up into zones of influence. Logan's farm, located near Sacramento, falls under the sway of the Hulk and his "Banner family" gang of thugs, who regularly extort rent payments from the locals. However, things are no better elsewhere. Having deposed Magneto, the Kingpin rules the zone from Arizona north to Idaho through fear and intimidation; the Midwest is overrun with dinosaurs imported from the Savage Land, and the president is none other than the Red Skull. Further, moloids, a race of subterranean creatures, have begun sinking cities and towns into the earth. According to Hawkeye, "some folks reckon they're the planet's immune system" released by the earth "to thin us all out." Thus, although the two stories present opposite visions of a dystopian future (i.e., a world overrun by superheroes and a world overrun by supervillains), both present a world without hope.

In both stories, the retired heroes are visited by an old friend and cajoled out of retirement. Following a superhero battle led by the "hero" Magog that decimates Kansas and a great portion of the Midwest, Wonder Woman visits Kal-El and tries to persuade him to return to the world. Although he initially seems uninterested, he does ultimately return to his role as Superman and attempts to curb the damage wrought by the new breed of hero. Logan is visited by Hawkeye, who asks his help in transporting a package across the country to New Babylon (formerly, Washington, DC). Logan assumes the package is drugs, but he is strapped for cash and needs the money promised by Hawkeye in order to pay the gang his rent money. As it turns out, there is more to Hawkeye's delivery than meets the eye, as he is trying to resurrect a team of superheroes. This chain of events culminates in Logan's decision to once again "pop his claws" and don the mantle of the Wolverine. To understand the reasons for their retirement and the challenges they face when they return, we can turn to theories of aging for insight.

THEORIES OF AGING

Whereas earlier views of aging depicted society as abandoning the elderly, disengagement theory proposed that the withdrawal, the disengagement, of the elder and society is mutual.[11] According to the theory, when people are young(er), the number and variety of interactions they have with others (e.g., teachers, employers) places heavy normative constraints upon their behavior. As they age, networks shrink, the quantity of interactions decreases, and those constraints are relaxed. Consequently, aging persons experience the "freedom" of old age, the ability to display their idiosyncratic and unique ways of acting. Central to the theory is beginning to perceive oneself as "an old person," and to prepare for withdrawal, even before the transition actually occurs. In this approach, therefore, aging successfully means willingly withdrawing from the world in order to make way for younger generations.[12]

The notion that getting older means disengaging from the world has been criticized, and various alternatives have been advanced. One of those is socioemotional selectivity theory (SST).[13] According to SST, across the life span, the amount and kinds of social contacts that individuals desire are motivated by a variety of social goals. The importance of specific goals, however, depends on one's position in the life cycle. Young(er) people often desire and seek out new information, expanded social networks, and an enlarged view of the future. With aging comes a view of a contracting future, resulting in decreased importance placed on new information and new social contacts. This altered goal configuration results in a preference for emotionally positive and pleasant interactions with close, intimate partners. In contrast to disengagement theory, SST predicts a more careful selection of social contacts rather than a general withdrawal from social contacts.

The third approach, the social-environmental perspective, shares with SST a focus on the aging person as an active agent.[14] The social-environmental perspective states that aging persons continue to face normative demands and expectations from their social environments, but they differ in their resources for meeting those demands. Resources include personal qualities (e.g., mobility, mental acuity), relational ties (e.g., friends, neighbors), and tangible and intangible "things" (e.g., goods, money, information) that can be drawn upon and exchanged under concrete circumstances. With aging, as physical abilities diminish, networks shrink, and goods such as status decline, aging persons are at risk for negative outcomes as they perceive a poorer fit between what they possess and what is required and/or desired of them by society. However, it is also possible to occupy valued social roles, to maintain ties, and even possess wisdom and knowledge that are desired by others. Successful aging in this approach depends upon the fit between self-perceived resources and the normative demands of one's situations.

Looking across the theories, three qualities that seem especially prominent in those who age well are: 1) the capacity to experience positive hedonic states (i.e., positive moods and emotions), 2) the ability to derive meaning and purpose in life, and 3) deliberately engaging in continued goal pursuit. [15] In terms of affect, research has found that friends are even better at meeting emotional needs than family, who tend to provide more instrumental forms of support. [16] Deriving meaning and purpose involves feeling that one is a part of something that transcends the self. Nussbaum found that life satisfaction was higher for those who engaged in frequent conversations about world and local events, compared to those who dwelt on personal problems, including health issues. [17] Thus, aging well involves the ability to maintain satisfactory relations with family, friends, and the larger world.

RETIREMENT

In some ways, the depictions of Kal-El and Logan in retirement conform to aspects of disengagement theory. Both have clearly experienced a reduction in the quality and quantity of social ties. When Wonder Woman speaks with Kal-El, she references the fact that he has lost his parents and wife. In comparison, it is clear that Logan's social world revolves almost exclusively around his family. Also, it quickly becomes apparent that both men experienced a changed self-perception that preceded their withdrawal from the world. Wonder Woman tells Kal-El, "Our generation takes its lead from you. We always have." The problem, as the Spectre tells McCay, is "his inability to perceive himself as the inspiration he is." Superman wasn't forced out by the changes of the world, but rather, his perception that the world had changed caused a re-evaluation of his role in it. Similarly, Logan repeatedly tells Hawkeye that he's not "Wolverine" anymore and, on two early occasions, refuses to defend himself. As he tells a member of a gang of "Ghost Riders," "I will never hurt another living soul . . . you can do what you like to me, boy . . . but I refuse to strike you back." His decision to become a "beautiful pacifist," as Hawkeye sarcastically calls him, preceded his retirement and withdrawal from the world.

However, by the criteria put forth earlier, neither man is aging successfully. There is no evidence that either experiences frequent positive hedonic states in his retirement. In fact, both are presented as grim and emotionally disconnected. When Wonder Woman references Kal-El's losses, he replies, "Earthlings die. You know that." She responds, "They were your parents, Cla[rk]—Kal. And she was your wife. Don't call them earthlings." When Logan's daughter is provoked to ask him about his superhero past, he tells her, "You tell Becky's mom there's no such thing as superheroes. Now be a good girl and pass me those bread rolls." Later, when his wife confronts him about the interaction, he says, "It's not the baby I'm angry with. It's myself. How could I let things get this bad." Clearly, both men do not seem to be reveling in the "freedom" that is supposed to come from the release of normative constraints.

With respect to finding meaning in life and goal pursuit, both men again are failing to age successfully. When Kal-El tells Wonder Woman, "I have work to do. Here, things grow," she responds, "Really?" She touches the side of the wall, revealing that the blue sky overhead is a hologram; Superman has been living in a bubble. Logan, too, has insulated himself from the broader world. As he and Hawkeye travel through Hammer Falls, Nevada (formerly Las Vegas), Logan seems completely unaware that the location has become a tourist spot and shrine for those longing for the return of the superheroes. Retirement is clearly not functional for Kal-El and Logan.

Therefore, consistent with SST, as they perceived that the future no longer held anything of value or meaning for them, Kal-El and Logan retreated from the public world, reducing the size of their social networks to a small circle of close companions. At first glance, however, their behavior seems inconsistent with the theory's claim that maintaining positive emotional interactions becomes a central goal when one's personal time frame is reduced. That first glance might be misleading, once we realize that both men are suffering from a heavy burden of guilt and anger. Thus, consistent with the theory, emotional regulation is a central concern for them. In their case, however, the emotions they are trying to regulate and keep from overwhelming them are negative emotions.

Of course, the withdrawal and retirement of the heroes is really just the beginning in both stories. Shortly after Wonder Woman's visit, Kal-El returns to the world scene as Superman. Logan reluctantly agrees to accompany Hawkeye across the country to make his delivery. Notably, at an early stage in their return, both *Kingdom Come* and *Old Man Logan* involve interactions between the superhero and a younger hero who has turned out badly, and this can be traced, in part, to the absence of the influence of genuine heroes as role models. When Superman finally confronts Magog at the site of the Kansas devastation, the assembled crowd braces for an altercation. After taunting Superman for his decision to leave, however, Magog breaks down, falling on his knees, saying, "They chose the man who would kill over the man who wouldn't . . . and now they're dead. A million ghosts. Punish me.

Lock me away. Just make the ghosts go away." When Logan and Hawkeye arrive in Hammer Falls, they learn that Hawkeye's daughter, Ashley, has formed a "super team" and has been caught in Salt Lake City trying to take down the Kingpin. Once they rescue her, she immediately kills the Kingpin and then turns on Hawkeye. When he asks her what she's doing, she replies, "What I came here to do . . . seize control of the Kingpin's Quarter." He replies, "I thought you came here to free everybody," to which she responds, "That's because you're stupid, dad. I killed the Kingpin like he killed Magneto." Clearly, in the absence of heroic role models, Ashley has accepted the villain's creed of the survival of the fittest, where, incidentally, getting old inevitably results in being supplanted by someone younger, stronger, and more brutal.

These confrontations reveal that simply reappearing in the world may not be enough. When aging individuals withdraw from society, they take with them the inspirational potential of their wisdom and experience. In line with SST, we might predict that before Superman and Wolverine can once again become effective as superheroes, they must realign their perceptions of themselves and the world. They must rebuild their resources and re-establish effective relationships. That will be difficult if they cannot overcome their personal obstacles.

RETURN

When Superman first reappears on the world scene to stop a battle between superhuman groups at the Statue of Liberty, he is accompanied by several of his former Justice League members (e.g., Wonder Woman, Green Lantern, Hawkman). From there, they fly to the United Nations, where Superman tells the assembled crowd, "In our absence, a new breed of metahuman has arisen . . . a vast phalanx of self-styled 'heroes' unwilling to preserve life or defend the defenseless . . . a legion of vigilantes who have perverted their great power . . . who have forsworn the responsibilities due them." Superheroes, according to Superman, place their powers in service to the community by doing things such as fighting villains, rescuing civilians, and generally ensuring the workings of the rule of law. These activities are consistent with a fiduciary role. According to Morreim, a fiduciary relationship "exists when one party is far weaker than, and dependent upon, a stronger party who in turn has an obligation to promote the weaker's best interest."[18] Fiduciaries are bound by a strong set of obligations, chief among which is a loyalty to those they protect. They cannot put their own interests or a third party's interests ahead of those whom they serve. The requirements of the superhero role fit well with this description of a fiduciary relationship between superhero and public.

If we use these criteria to evaluate the behaviors of Superman and Wolverine, it is clear that, in their return, they are not fulfilling their role. Superman's role is to uphold the law, not to make the law. As McKay narrates, "Social government was never Superman's arena." Although virtually invulnerable physically, his chief power has always been inspirational, precisely because he does the right thing. His greatest temptation will always be circumventing the rule of law to impose his will in a unilateral fashion. Such a move undercuts his power by diminishing his inspirational potential and the support he derives from it. Yet, that is precisely how he proceeds upon his return. He himself says as much during that first UN press appearance: "Together we [i.e., Superman and his new justice league] will guide this new breed with wisdom . . . and, if necessary, with force. Above all, we will restore order. We will make things right." Inevitably, as the ranks of those who refuse to accept Superman's definition of "order" and "right" grow, he becomes frustrated and, at the urging of Wonder Woman, constructs a vast prison in the decimated wastelands of Kansas to contain, without due process, the metahumans who resist his rule. In the tradition of modern despotic regimes, he tells the captives that they are not there for punishment, but for "education."

In contrast to Superman, Wolverine is more of an anti-hero. Anti-heroes attempt to "balance their evil methods with their good intentions."[19] Wolverine is a killer, albeit one who constantly strives to do good in the world. By those criteria alone, Wolverine's refusal to kill, though admirable, is misplaced. The villains, after all, have taken over the country. In fact, our first image of New Babylon (Washington, DC) shows the White House redecorated with Nazi paraphernalia. More critically, Wolverine's motivation for accompanying Hawkeye is purely self-interest. He agrees to drive him across the country solely for the money. For example, when Hawkeye learns that his daughter Ashley is being held captive by the Kingpin, Logan is reluctant to help because he "will not be a party to violence." He only agrees once Hawkeye promises to double his price. Clearly, Logan is putting his self-interest and the interest of his family ahead of the common good.

In part because of their failure to live up to the normative expectations of the superhero role, both men find their relational resources difficult to draw upon. With the return of Superman and Wolverine to the world scene, one would expect old allies to rejoice. However, this is not the case. Shortly after his return, and long before the resistance grows and the metahuman prison is constructed, Superman goes to Gotham City to enlist the assistance of Batman (i.e., Bruce Wayne). Perceiving that Superman's return is not guided by the proper motivation, Bruce refuses to join his new league. Similarly, Hawkeye refuses to believe that Logan has become a "beautiful pacifist." When Logan repeats his insistence that he won't fight anymore, Hawkeye replies, "Yeah, but I didn't think you meant it." Hawkeye cannot believe that

Logan will simply sit by and let evil hold sway. The failure of former allies to support the hero upon his return stems largely from their own expectations. Both Batman and Hawkeye expect their comrades to be the people they knew before their retirement. However, as alluded to earlier, the focus of both men on their personal concerns is limiting their view of the future; yet, they are stepping back into a fiduciary role that, of all the roles that make up a society, presumes the existence of a common good and a future for the world.

Both heroes are having difficulty aligning their own goals with the expectations of others because they are bringing with them a burden of guilt and responsibility for the situations they encounter. Superman feels guilt because of his withdrawal ten years earlier. We learn that he left after Magog killed the Joker in cold blood and was then acquitted for the crime. Superman feels he has to make up for his absence by attempting to force a unilateral solution on the new breed of heroes. As a climactic battle unfolds between Superman's league and his opponents at the site of the Kansas prison, the humans unleash a trio of nuclear bombs to deal with the metahuman threat once and for all. When one gets past Batman and Wonder Woman, Superman gives Shazam the choice of deciding whether to destroy the metahumans or the humans. When Shazam detonates the bomb over the Kansas battlefield, an enraged Superman flies to the United Nations and begins wreaking havoc. At this point, McCay steps into the story, telling Superman, "You blame yourself for Captain Marvel . . . for Magog and Kansas . . . for ten years that ended today." He tells Superman to forgive himself and that "if you want redemption, Clark . . . it lies in the very next decision you make. Make it as a man . . . and make it right." When Superman sees that a number of heroes survived the blast, he chooses to partner with the humans, rather than rule them. This is the point at which he occupies his role in the distinctive Superman way.

Prior to Hawkeye's death at the hands of the Red Skull's agents, Logan eventually reveals to him what happened that "broke him." When the supervillains launched their coordinated attacks, a group of them invaded the Westchester, New York, home of the X-Men. Wolverine took them on and killed all of them, only to discover that Mysterio had created an illusion, and in reality, he had killed every last one of his X-Men teammates. He concludes, "You just try tellin' me I been a fool to hide these claws for fifty years." Hawkeye replies, "I wouldn't dare." After killing the Red Skull, Logan races across the country in the Iron Man suit with a suitcase full of money for the Hulks. He arrives back in Sacramento, only to discover the Hulks have killed his wife and children anyway, and that is the moment he finally pops his claws, telling a fellow farmer, "the name isn't Logan, bub . . . it's Wolverine." He then proceeds to eliminate the Hulk gang, including Banner himself. After burying his wife and children, he heads out and takes on the villains. When a farmer tells him, "You realize it's impossible, right?" he replies, "A friend told me there was no such word." When a woman asks, "And who might that be?" he tells her, "The same man who taught me to forgive myself." Once again, we can say that this is the point at which he returns to his superhero role in the distinctive Wolverine way.

Why is forgiveness such a prominent theme in both characters' return to their own way of taking up the mantle of the superhero? Solomon and Szwabo, drawing upon the work of Peck, describe one of the psychological tasks of growing older as managing ego preoccupation versus ego transcendence.[20] Ego preoccupation occurs when "the older man thinks solely of what he has done, what he could have done, or what he should have done."[21] Both Superman and Wolverine are suppressing their feelings about their perceived shortcomings and regrets. Forgiveness, the extension of undeserved mercy to a transgressor,[22] breaks those chains of preoccupation. When Superman and Wolverine forgive themselves, they transcend the narrow limits of the ego and make possible a new construal of the future. The possibility of acting within the world, of beginning the world anew, opens up before them.

With self-forgiveness comes the return to effective action. Both stories end on a hopeful note, and that hopefulness is embodied in the hero undertaking the training of a future generation. In *Kingdom Come*, after Bruce Wayne correctly surmises that Wonder Woman is pregnant with Superman's child, Wonder Woman asks Bruce to be the godfather to the child, specifically so that he can assist them in raising the child in the heroic mold. As the trio walk out of a superhero-themed restaurant, Superman's final words are, "let's go home . . . and dream about the future." In *Old Man Logan*, as Wolverine sets out to take on the villains, he has with him the last remaining member of the Hulk family, a small Hulk child, the "first guy on [his] new team." As the other farmers try to dissuade him, telling him "this ain't a world for super-teams and big, grand plans," he replies, "Well, they killed me fifty years ago, bub. . . . and I got better. I figure I've kept my head down long enough." There is even the faintest trace of a smile on his face as he utters these last words. The final panel depicts him riding his horse into the sunset.

IMPLICATIONS

Three implications follow from this examination of the stories of Superman and Wolverine. When our elders withdraw from society, they take with them valuable social resources. In many fields, experience can be more important than chronological age.[23] More importantly, we need our elders as guides, role models, and mentors to younger generations.[24] This is certainly true of the professions, but it is also true of more informal settings, from the family circle to the local community. Admittedly, not all elders are, or desire to be, role models. Rather than assuming that aging persons invariably desire positive interactions with a small circle of close contacts, however, scholars should focus more on what factors contribute to a desire to accumulate and share wisdom over the life span. Promoting and cultivating those qualities might result in more elders who strive to remain engaged with the world.

Second, as aging persons engage with the world, they need the support of companions, especially friends. Sometimes, it may be a literal return to the workplace in the form of a career change or a post-retirement job. In other cases, it may be the occupation of a more social role, perhaps "parenting" a grandchild or volunteering in the local community. Regardless, all aging persons will likely face the societal devaluation of their contributions, and will have to confront the internal struggle of fitting in to the changing world. In order to do that successfully, aging persons must learn to transcend their ego preoccupations and to forgive themselves for any lingering failures, disappointments, poor decisions, and mistakes they have made. As Wolverine points out, we have to be "taught" how to forgive ourselves; aging persons, too, need their role models and mentors. Friends and close companions can provide the support and encouragement to actively move out into the world, rather than allowing ourselves to be shunted aside.

Finally, we must continue to combat ageist stereotypes, and media depictions have the potential to lead that charge.[25] The stories examined in this chapter present complex characters grappling with their role in a changed world. They demonstrate that aging persons don't have to be stock characters of ill will or bumbling incompetence.[26] The lesson of Wolverine and Superman is clear: the world would be a worse place without them in it. We should be able to say the same thing about our own aging and elderly.

NOTES

1. According to a U.S. Census Bureau report released December 12, 2012, the population aged sixty-five or older will more than double between 2012 and 2060, increasing from 43.1 million to 92.0 million; proportionately, that age group will increase from one American in seven to one in five.

2. This list does not exhaust the possibilities, of course. A superhero may "die," and be temporarily replaced by someone else, usually a sidekick or mentee. Even to have a sidekick strike out on his or her own frees up the hero from the implications of time's passing.

3. *Kingdom Come* was originally published as four single issues in 1996. For this chapter, I will be referring to the graphic novel collection of those issues, published in 2008. Mark Waid and Alex Ross, *Kingdom Come* (New York: DC Comics, 2008).

4. The *Old Man Logan* storyline ran from *Wolverine* 66 to *Wolverine* 72 and was concluded in the one-shot *Giant-Size Wolverine: Old Man Logan*. Mark Millar, Steve McNiven, Dexter Vines, and Morry Hollowell, *Wolverine: Old Man Logan* (New York: Marvel Publishing, 2008–2009); Mark Millar, Steve McNiven, Dexter Vines, and Morry Hollowell, *Giant-Size Wolverine: Old Man Logan* (New York: Marvel Publishing, 2009).

5. Leslie F. Zebrowitz and Joann M. Montepare, "'Too Young, Too Old': Stigmatizing Adolescents and Elders," in *The Social Psychology of Stigma*, edited by Todd F. Heatherton et al. (New York: The Guilford Press, 2000), 334–73, on 335.

6. Erdman B. Palmore, *Ageism: Negative and Positive*, 2nd edition (New York: Springer Publishing Company, 1999). However, Montepare and Zebrowitz review evidence that negative attitudes toward aged adults are universal. Joann M. Montepare and Leslie F. Zebrowitz, "A Social-Developmental View of Ageism," in *Ageism: Stereotyping and Prejudice against Older Persons*, edited by Todd D. Nelson (Cambridge: MIT Press, 2002), 77–125, on 91–92.

7. Jake Harwood and Karen Anderson, "The Presence and Portrayal of Social Groups on Prime-Time Television," *Communication Reports* 15 (2002): 81–97, on 88, doi: 10.1080 / 08934210209367756.

8. Monisha Pasupathi and Corinna E. Löckenhoff, "Ageist Behavior," in *Ageism: Stereotyping and Prejudice against Older Persons*, edited by Todd D. Nelson (Cambridge: MIT Press, 2002), 201–46, on 219–21.

9. Jeph Loeb and Tom Morris, "Heroes and Superheroes," in *Superheroes and Philosophy: Truth, Justice, and the Socratic Way*, edited by Tom Morris and Matt Morris (Chicago: Open Court, 2005), 11–20, on 14.

10. Morgan and Kunkel distinguish between usual changes associated with aging, and inevitable changes. Usual changes are ones that are typical, but highly variable because they are associated with lifestyle choices (e.g., scars). Inevitable changes are universal, "genetically or biologically programmed or the unavoidable result of living through time." Among the inevitable changes they mention are graying of the hair and wrinkles. Thus, despite the fact that Kal-El is an alien and Logan is a mutant with a healing factor, aging is depicted in both men through the use of inevitable signs of aging. Leslie Morgan and Suzanne Kunkel, *Aging: The Social Context*, 2nd ed. (California: Pine Forge Press, 2001), 108.

11. Elaine Cumming, Lois R. Dean, David S. Newell, and Isabel McCaffrey, "Disengagement—A Tentative Theory of Aging," *Sociometry* 23 (1960): 23–35, doi:10.2307/2786135.

12. Carroll L. Estes and Karen W. Linkins, "Critical Perspectives on Health and Aging," in *The Handbook of Social Studies in Health & Medicine*, edited by Gary L. Albrecht et al. (London: Sage, 2000), 154–72, on 156.

13. Laura L. Carstensen, "Evidence for a Life-span Theory of Socioemotional Selectivity," *Current Directions in Psychological Science* 4 (1995): 151–56. doi:10.1111/ 1467–8721.ep11512261.

14. Jon Hendricks and C. Davis Hendricks, *Aging in Mass Society: Myths and Realities*, 2nd edition (Cambridge: Winthrop Publishers, 1981), 136–42.

15. Jon F. Nussbaum, Loretta L. Pecchioni, James D. Robinson, and Teresa L. Thompson, *Communication and Aging*, 2nd edition (Mahwah, NJ: Lawrence Erlbaum, 2000), 328–45.

16. Jon F. Nussbaum, "Successful Aging: A Communication Model," *Communication Quarterly* 33 (1985): 262–69, on 268, doi:10.1080/01463378509369606.

17. Jon F. Nussbaum, "Perceptions of Communication Content and Life Satisfaction among the Elderly," *Communication Quarterly* 31 (1983): 313–19, on 317, doi:10.1080/ 01463378309369520.

18. E. Haavi Morreim, "The Clinical Investigator as Fiduciary: Discarding a Misguided Idea," *The Journal of Law, Medicine & Ethics* (2005): 586–98, on 586, doi:10.1111/ j.1748–720X.2005.tb00521.x.

19. Michael Spivey and Steven Knowlton, "Anti-Heroism in the Continuum of Good and Evil," in *The Psychology of Superheroes: An Unauthorized Exploration*, edited by Robin S. Rosenberg (Dallas: Benbella, 2008), 51–63, on 62.

20. Kenneth Solomon and Peggy A. Szwabo, "The Work-Oriented Culture: Success and Power in Elderly Men," in *Older Men's Lives*, edited by Edward H. Thompson, Jr. (Thousand Oaks, CA: Sage, 1994), 42–64, on 53.

21. Solomon and Szwabo, "Work-Oriented Culture," 53.

22. Vincent R. Waldron and Douglas L. Kelley, *Communication Forgiveness* (Los Angeles: Sage, 2008), 22.

23. Robert McCann and Howard Giles, "Ageism in the Workplace: A Communication Perspective," in *Ageism: Stereotyping and Prejudice against Older Persons*, edited by Todd D. Nelson (Cambridge: MIT Press, 2002), 163–99, on 172–74.

24. Solomon and Szwabo describe a seventy-eight-year-old physician who spent four hours a week teaching medical students precisely so that "the young generation of physicians can make use of the knowledge and expertise that he has accumulated through more than 50 years of professional activities." Solomon and Szwabo, "Work-Oriented Culture," 48.

25. Valerie Braithwaite, "Reducing Ageism," in *Ageism: Stereotyping and Prejudice against Older Persons*, edited by Todd D. Nelson (Cambridge: MIT Press, 2002), 311–37, on 314.

26. Harwood and Anderson, "The Presence and Portrayal of Social Groups on Prime-Time Television," 83.

Chapter Twelve

Mr. Incredible, Man of Action, Man of Power

What If He Loses It All?

Itır Erhart and Hande Eslen-Ziya

The Incredibles (2004) is an animated film about a family of superheroes forced into retirement and anonymity. The aging superhero, Bob Parr (Mr. Incredible), now has a potbelly and a bald patch. He was discharged from his superhero duties and is now working as an insurance clerk in a claustrophobic cubicle. After work, he comes home to his non-super, normal family, and they live in the suburbs. The only outlets that the once-powerful and handsome man of action has to let him recall his past masculine and heroic identities are through occasional covert rescue missions, which he secretly performs with his aging superhero male buddy, Frozone. With this in mind, our goal is to analyze how the masculinities of an aging man are re-established. When we discuss masculinity, we will focus on the ways Mr. Incredible shapes desirable and undesirable masculinities, and identifies or disassociates with different ways of being a man. Thus, by reviewing Mr. Incredible, we wish to address how aging and demasculinization are portrayed in popular culture.

MASCULINITIES: DESIRABLE OR UNDESIRABLE?

Much of what has been written in this area concerns the construction of the masculine identity across the life span and in spheres such as education, sports, gender relations, and pornography.[1] Challenges to masculinity with advancing age have become an emerging research area in the fields of gender and aging.[2] For example, the research on late-life masculinities includes the difficulties that older men face with changes in their lives, such as widowhood and health problems. The research also addresses their strategies for coping with aging and this so-called loss of masculinities. Thus, in this chapter and through our examination of the superhero, Mr. Incredible, we aim to tackle this question: How does aging shape masculinity? With this in mind, we will discuss how perceptions of aging shape masculinities. Also, as we discuss masculinity, we will also focus on the ways Mr. Incredible shapes desirable and undesirable masculinities, as well as identifies or disassociates with different ways of being a man.

Masculinity is normally defined within the context of gender relations and composed of symbols, practices, and ideologies that are usually associated with men.[3] As the meanings and attributes that define men and the notion that masculinity changes with age, situations, and settings, that masculinity is never something static. It is not a fixed gender identity, but rather a culturally diverse and discursively constructed set of prescriptions and practices. This view also implies that within one society, different forms of hegemonic masculinities persist and are constantly negotiated and reframed.

According to Connell, masculinity is conceptualized in four major ways: hegemonic, subordinated, marginalized, and complicit.[4] These conceptualizations are based on the characteristics and performances of men. First, Connell defines hegemonic masculinity as a dominant form of masculinity in which traditional gender practices as well as the currently accepted "answers to the problem of the legitimacy of patriarchy" are re-created.[5] It is via hegemonic masculinity that aggressiveness, physical power and toughness, competitiveness, rationality, power, and heterosexuality as well as anti-femininity and the rejection of homosexuality become associated with being a real man.[6]

Subordinated, complicit, and marginalized masculinities exist outside of those heterosexual, patriarchal norms. First, subordinated masculinities include men who have characteristics and perform in opposition to heteronormative and dominant ideals. Albert in the film *The Birdcage* (1996) portrays this type of masculinity because he is a gay man who dresses in ways and exhibits behaviors that are associated with being a woman. Next, complicit masculinities include men who do not fit into those patriarchal norms, but whose behaviors are in line with those norms. Drawing further from *The Birdcage*, Albert's partner Armand is also gay, but he is the main financial provider for the family, has a son from a previous heterosexual relationship, and is the taciturn head of this household. Lastly, marginalized masculinities are men who subscribe to hegemonic norms but have characteristics that place them outside of that masculinity. In this instance, African American professional athletes may be included in this marginalized masculinity, because they are not white.

In the United States, in addition to Connell's definition of hegemonic masculinity, recent studies show that there is a growing cultural trend toward a self-oriented masculinity.[7] Branchik and Chowdhury write that this self-oriented masculinity represents itself in narcissistic and self-centered tendencies.[8] In these instances men tend to focus on their physical appearances, their well-being, and their own happiness. Similarly, Rotundo observes that in the United States, "the balance of bourgeois values has tipped from self-discipline to self-expression, from self-denial to self-enjoyment."[9] Thus, a man's focus is increasingly on himself rather than on others; that is to say, other-focused values (to join, unite, or bond in friendship, companionship, and cooperation) has declined while the proportion of self-focused values (vitality, strength, boasting, dominance, exhibitionism, being active, athletic, robust, as well as young, childlike, and resistant to aging) has increased.[10]

Given that masculinities are constructed, they are also not static, because they change and affect men during their life spans. So, a representation of an ideal around which masculinity is constructed may affect men who no longer meet the criterion of hegemonic masculinities, simply because they are getting older. For example, as a man ages, he may lose some traits, such as physical power and toughness, that are associated with being a real man. In fact, issues of masculinity and masculine competence in both public and private life arise as men age and lose access to traditional places in the family and their hegemonic masculine identity.

Since the definition of hegemonic masculinity involves being the main provider for the family, having physical power and the final say in important decisions, loss of these powers leads to masculinity crisis.[11] As men age they start losing their strong male roles as providers, active parents, and competent negotiators with public-sector entities, including the state.[12] When this happens, they start falling away from the ideals of hegemonic masculinities and into old-age masculinities. In this chapter, by looking at Mr. Incredible and his adaptation or mal-adaptation to his aging life, we wish to untangle the experience of aging and its gendered meaning.

AGING AND FEELINGS OF DEMASCULINIZATION

Masculinity is shaped through age relations. Old men position and understand themselves not only vis-à-vis young and middle-aged men, but also who they were in their past. So, they seem to reflect on their memories of youth, success, and virility and verbalize a longing for the masculinities that they once possessed. Thus, the natural act of aging itself becomes a marginalizing factor for men, as it implies loss of power and stigmatization. As Calasanti writes: "Old age does in fact confer a loss of power, even for those who are advantaged—and thus able to make different 'claims' in later life to power and resources—by gender and class."[13]

In other words, aging alters power relations in which manhood becomes associated with discourses not only about age, but also with discourses about gender, sexuality, and even class. For instance, while male sexualities are actualized via comparison with young and middle-aged men, female partners, heterosexuality, and gender roles are actualized when old men's everyday practices are taken into account. Both instances lead to feelings of demasculinization. As outlined by Kabachnik and colleagues, at the loss of the role of breadwinner, men experience a disruption and imbalance, which in return leads to feelings of demasculinization.[14] Kabachnik et al. add that such loss of power not only puts pressure on the existing labor market relationships, but also creates a tension within the household economy.[15] This, according to Erol and Özbay, causes men to feel a sense of "crisis":

> Men would normally be expected to adapt their masculine identities to these changing conditions and when they fail to do so they are tagged as "in crisis." Men also face a crisis as they get older: andropause frames the current discourse of this moment of crisis that men at a certain age may experience.[16]

In other words, when a man no longer meets the standards of hegemonic masculinity, "he is gradually deemed marginalized, dissident, excluded or subaltern."[17] He is seen as a man lacking manhood, a dichotomy in itself. As a man ages, andropause, often defined as "male climacteric" or "male menopause" or "low testosterone," becomes a significant threat to masculinity.[18] The men that come to the brink of losing their dominant form of masculinities may search for other ways of reasserting those hegemonic masculinities, both from the outside (via the relations they form) and the inside (via the very source of their own manhood). While such reassertion of hegemonic masculinities from outside may be expressed in particular instances of increased control of women by men, the overemphasis on youth admiration and body-image building might signify the reassertion of hegemonic masculinities from the very source of their own manhood.[19]

Because the male body is both seen and used as an object of heterosexual desire as well as a signifier of physical power in demonstrating hegemonic masculinity for the aging men, preserving the body becomes an important goal.[20] They do it by focusing on their body images and developing a hyperheterosexual persona to "re-sex" their aging bodies.[21] Such "re-sexing" is made attractive via steroid and testosterone advertisements that define manhood as "biological opposition to womanhood and old age" and andropause as "the loss of manhood."[22] They suggest that masculinity can be regained through the use of their products. They use slogans like "We found the fountain of youth" and "Women love a man with muscle" and "To learn how to live well longer."

Men seem also to reassert their masculinity through their "demeanor, showing little emotion, outlining their career accomplishments, and contrasting themselves with femininity and women."[23] Thus, we argue that a deeper analysis of the superhero Mr. Incredible and his coping strategies with aging and aging masculinities will provide an understanding of masculinities, as well as how these relate to ageism and even to broader spheres of gender inequality. For this purpose we analyze the character of Mr. Incredible, and the narrative of midlife crisis in the movie *The Incredibles*, and explore him through the lens of desirable and undesirable masculinities.[24] In the first half of our analysis, we focus on how desirable (self-oriented, hegemonic) ideal masculinity is constructed. In the second half, we investigate the construction of undesirable (marginalized, dissident, excluded, subaltern old-age) masculinity for a superhero through the key issues in the movie: aging, midlife crisis, and loss of power.[25]

SPACES OF TRAUMATIC MASCULINITIES

Our narrative analysis suggests that traumatic masculinities emerge as a direct consequence of both restrictions on performing superpowers and being a man of action, as well as aging. For us, this superpower is reflected through the "supers," such as super strength and super speed which "ordinary" humans lack. Being men of action means that these men do not have to play by the rules, but instead operate outside the official rules and constraints, and also have sufficient potency to vanquish whatever villain is threatening the social order. As Holt and Thompson observe, "The heroic superman vanquishes the diabolical foe, proves his manhood with panache, restores the moral order, saves society . . . gets the girl and then takes his well-deserved seat at the pinnacle of a patriarchal status hierarchy."[26] Aging is presented to the audience through the passage of time (fifteen years) as well as Mr. Incredible's aging physique (flabby muscles, loss of hair, loss of sexual desire and interest). In this section, we will first show how Mr. Incredible used to fit the hegemonic ideal (self-oriented, proud, strong man of action) and how later on, as just Robert Parr, he is demasculinized through both aging and the restrictions put on his super performances.

"I Work Alone:" Introducing the Narcissistic, Self-Oriented Man of Action

In the opening sequence of the film we see Mr. Incredible, the masked superhero, at the height of his career, answering the questions of an unseen reporter. As the "ideal" man, Mr. Incredible is constructed in the interview as being a powerful, lean, young, confident, and proud superhero. When he has trouble putting the microphone on, he says, "I can break through walls, I just can't . . . get this on," in a self-absorbed, narcissistic manner. At this stage of his life, the proud superhero sees his secret identity as a means of protection: "Every superhero has a secret identity. I don't know a single one who doesn't. Who wants the pressure of being super all the time?"

He implies that the burden of being a full-time superhero would be overwhelming for him. Yet, from the tone of his voice and body language it can be inferred that he is indeed very satisfied in this life, performing superhero duties. He compares the world to naughty children and implies that it would go out of control if he neglected his duties as its protector: "No matter how many times you save the world, it always manages to get back in jeopardy again. Sometimes I just want it to stay saved, you know? For a little bit. I feel like the maid. 'I just cleaned up this mess. Can we keep it clean for ten minutes?'" We find this statement interesting because while he identifies himself with a maid, tired of performing household duties over and over again, his gestures imply the opposite: he is happy to be repeatedly performing his masculine, superhero duties in the public realm.

He is so oblivious to his surroundings, and uninterested in what the reporter has to say, that he decides to end the interview on the previous high note where he suggests that the world would be a mess if he were not there to clean it up every ten minutes.

Interviewer: Wait, no, don't get up. We're not finished.

Mr. Incredible [with a sigh]: Sometimes I think I'd just like the simple life, you know? Relax a little and raise a family.

This comment is a foreshadowing of the events to follow. It is obvious to the interviewer (as well as the viewing audience) that a simple life would mean nothing but misery for this man whose identity is defined by his muscles and superhero work. The point is made clear through his late arrival at his own wedding with Elastigirl[27]—another super—while trying to save the world. He stops to help an old lady whose cat is stuck in a tree and keeps repeating: "I still have time." When he finally arrives at his wedding with his mask on, he finds his wife-to-be waiting at the altar. Up to this point the superhero proves himself to be a narcissistic, self-oriented man of action.

As expected of a self-oriented man, he also rejects any companionship and offers of help in his superhero work. When a ten-year-old fan, Buddy, appoints himself as his sidekick as IncrediBoy, Mr. Incredible ejects him from his car and speeds away. That very evening, Buddy comes back with his rocket boots and offers to help him fight Bomb Voyage, a supervillain. Mr. Incredible, again, rejects the boy in a dismissive manner: "Fly home,

Buddy. I work alone." He repeats his catchphrase on another occasion when his soon-to-be-wife Elastigirl comes to help him fight a pickpocket, this time in a more charming manner: "I work alone." She twists herself around him and responds "and I think you need to be more . . . flexible." The exchange between two supers, when they were both at the height of their careers, is an indication of how differently they will react to the changes in their circumstances. She is more flexible and adaptable, both metaphorically and physically.

A Relocated Superhero: Aging Man with a Midlife Crisis

Shortly after Mr. Incredible gives his interview, several lawsuits are filed against the supers. This includes one from a man who sued Mr. Incredible for stopping his suicide attempt. The government responds by prohibiting further acts of superheroism, and initiates the Super Hero Relocation Program. Similar to existing witness protection programs, the supers are anonymously relocated and forced to live using only their "secret" and ordinary identities. Thus, they are required to lead non-super lives among the ordinary citizenry, instead of fighting crime in their skintight suits, capes, and masks.

We flash-forward fifteen years, and meet Mr. Incredible again. Instead of saving the world, he has only the mundane Bob Parr identity and works in a claustrophobic cubicle for an immoral insurance company, and under a cruel boss. His daily commute involves being stuck in traffic while trying to cram his body, once muscular but now flabby, into a very small car. He is married with three children who all have superpowers. As Tregonning observes, he "is disconnected from the family unit."[28] While Elastigirl, now Helen Parr, is busy trying to hold the family together and keeping them safe by stopping their children from using their superpowers, he reads at the dinner table, does not respond to her, and is not interested in his children's problems with fitting in with ordinary people.[29] Feeling depressed and worthless, he often locks himself in his home office. In that space, he has created a virtual shrine to Mr. Incredible with pictures, news clippings, and memorabilia, including his old Mr. Incredible outfit displayed in a glass case. In short, he shows signs of the traumatic masculinities of an aging man in midlife crisis, one who longs for his past while the "precious" objects displayed in his office represent his youth and masculinities.

Dealing with the Trauma: "Reliving the Glory Days"

Mr. Incredible, as an aging superhero with flabby muscles, tries to reassert his masculinity by "reliving the glory days." He sneaks out of the house with another ex-super friend, Frozone,[30] for what he claims to be a regular bowling night. Instead of bowling, the two hide in a car and listen to a police scanner in an attempt to find opportunities to perform superheroic acts, or their traumatic masculinities. These performances have, and continue to, put his family in danger of yet another relocation, but he keeps going back for more because they help him fight the demasculinization.

For these reasons, he does not hesitate to accept a risky job requiring his superpowers, when contacted by a mysterious and beautiful woman named Mirage. This job gives him the opportunity to reclaim his masculinity by working alone and making money, as well as a chance to find personal gratification outside his dull and mundane suburban life. In this way he reasserts his masculinity and once again becomes the ideal man of his youth. So, it follows that after he completes this risky job, or performance of hero work, he comes home fully satisfied and engages with his wife and children in an unusually joyful manner.

However, this resurgence has a cost, and as Tregonning points out, "the energy and passion he finds for his family is only an expression of that gratification. . . . Dishonesty makes Bob feel more satisfied."[31] Additionally, we discover that Mirage actually works for Syndrome, the supervillain that Buddy/Incrediboy has become. When Syndrome finally confronts Mr. Incredible, the supervillain tells his former superhero idol that all he wanted was to help. However, when Mr. Incredible rejected the young Buddy, the boy declared that he would be the superhero's nemesis. At this point, it is important to note that Mr. Incredible's previous embodiment of desirable masculinities actually creates a supervillain. Furthermore, his uncontrollable urge to escape undesirable masculinities carries him right into Syndrome's trap, which puts not only him but his entire family in grave danger. In the end, ironically, Mr. Incredible—who always works alone—has to collaborate with his whole family, including his baby boy, to overcome the enemy.

In contrast, Elastigirl has been much more flexible, both literally and metaphorically, and adaptive to the changes in their circumstances and life styles throughout the narrative. In fact, she saves Mr. Incredible from Syndrome, the supervillain he created with his own masculine anxieties. It is here, we argue, *The Incredibles* demonstrates how men and women approach aging: women are more adaptive to changing circumstances, while men feel demasculinized and show a tendency to perform risky behavior.[32] This could be due to how feminine and masculine identities are constructed differently, in that masculine identity is associated with aggressiveness, physical power, toughness, competitiveness, rationality, power, and heterosexuality that co-exist with youth.

CONCLUSION

Our analysis of this movie reveals that Mr. Incredible's identity was constructed by youth and hegemonic/self-oriented masculinity. He is self-oriented because he believes that he can achieve/be successful without the help of anyone else. In fact, this characteristic leads to the creation of his nemesis, Syndrome. The presence of this nemesis in return offers him his masculinity back, at an extremely high price—the endangerment of himself and his family.

From this, we draw several interesting conclusions from our analysis, one of which is the difference between femininity and masculinity when it comes to the adaptation of changing life span circumstances such as aging and loss of power. As Kabachnik and colleagues find from research on the internally displaced persons from Abkhazia to Georgia, there is a common assumption that women are more adaptable to new situations.[33] In contrast, men seem to not adapt and instead perform their traumatic masculinities. Similarly, this movie also seems to reproduce this commonly held perception of gender roles: Elastigirl, for example, adapting to the housewife role from that of a superheroine, while Mr. Incredible goes through trauma. While Elastigirl deals with children's problems at school, he sneaks out to perform hero-work and puts their hidden identities in danger.

Another conclusion we offer concerns how masculinities are incredibly influential in men's lives. This is to say that the construction and reconstruction of masculinities shape their very identities, and challenges to those identities may lead to literal and figurative acts of self-destruction. In other words, as in the case of Mr. Incredible, the shift from desirable (self-oriented, hegemonic) masculinities to the undesirable (marginalized, dissident, excluded, subaltern, aging) masculinities creates trauma and traumatic masculinities, which in turn causes great distress and disruption.

In the end, the "man of action" who has sufficient potency to vanquish the supervillain and re-establish the social order, actually turns out to be a woman who was accompanied by her children. Thus we can argue that the ideal man is in fact a flexible, collaborative, interpersonally oriented woman.

NOTES

1. Raewyn W. Connell, *Gender and Power: Society, the Person, and Sexual Politics* (Palo Alto, CA: Stanford University Press, 1987); Raewyn W. Connell, *Masculinities* (Cambridge: Polity Press, 2005); David H. J. Morgan, *Discovering Men: Critical Studies on Men and Masculinities* (New York: Routledge, 1992); Lynne Segal, *Slow Motion: Changing Masculinities, Changing Men* (London: Virago Press, 1990); Victor J. Seidler, *Unreasonable Men: Masculinity and Social Theory* (London: Routledge, 1994).

2. Sara Arber, Kate Davidson, and Jay Ginn, "Changing Approaches to Gender and Later Life," in *Gender and Ageing: Changing Roles and Relationships*, edited by Sara Arber, Kate Davidson, and Jay Ginn (Buckingham, UK: Open University Press, 2003), 1–14.

3. Connell, *Gender and Power*; Connell, *Masculinities*; Michael S. Kimmel and Michael A. Messner, "Introduction," in *Men's Lives*, edited by Michael S. Kimmel and Michael A. Messner (Boston: Pearson, 2007).

4. Connell, *Masculinities*.

5. Ibid., 77.

6. Stephen Frosh, "Father's Ambivalence (too)," in *After Words: The Personal in Gender, Culture and Psychotherapy*, edited by Stephen Frosh (London: Palgrave, 2002), 21–34; Michael S. Kimmel, "Masculinity as Homophobia: Fear, Shame, and Silence in the Construction of Gender Identity," in *Theorizing Masculinities*, edited by Harry Brod and Michael Kaufman (Thousand Oaks, CA: Sage Publications, 1994), 119–42.

7. Blaine J. Branchik and Tilottama G. Chowdhury, "Self-Oriented Masculinity: Advertisements and the Changing Culture of the Male Market," *Journal of Macromarketing* 33, no. 2 (2012): 160–76, on 160.

8. Ibid.

9. Anthony E. Rotundo, *American Manhood: Transformations in Masculinity from the Revolution to the Modern Era* (New York: Basic Books, 1993), 285.

10. Branchik and Chowdhury, "Self-Oriented Masculinity," 164.

11. Hale Bolak-Boratav, Güler Fişek, and Hande Eslen-Ziya, "Unpacking Masculinities in the Context of Social Change: Internal Complexities of the Identities of Married Men in Turkey," *Men and Masculinities* (2014), doi:10.1177/1097184X14539511; Linda McDowell, *Redundant Masculinities: Employment Change and White Working Class Youth* (Oxford: Blackwell, 2003).

12. Jessie Bernard, "The Good Provider Role: Its Rise and Fall," in *Diversity and Change in Families: Patterns, Prospects, and Policies*, edited by Mark Robert Rank and Edward L. Kain (Englewood Cliffs, NJ: Prentice Hall, 1981), 235–54; Laura Curran and Laura S. Abrams, "Making Men into Dads: Fatherhood, the State, and Welfare Reform," *Gender & Society* 14 (2000): 662–78; Kathleen Gerson, "Dilemmas of Involved Fatherhood," in *Reconstructing Gender*, edited by Estelle Disch (Mountain View, CA: Mayfield, 1997), 272–81.

13. Toni Calasanti, "Theorizing Age Relations," in *The Need for Theory: Critical Approaches to Social Gerontology*, edited by Simon Biggs, Jon Hendricks, and Ariela Lowenstein (Amityville, NY: Baywood Press, 2003), 199–218, on 205.

14. Peter Kabachnik, Magdalena Grabowska, Joanna Regulska, Beth Mitchneck, and Olga V. Mayorova, "Traumatic Masculinities: The Gendered Geographies of Georgian IDPs from Abkhazia." *Gender, Place & Culture: A Journal of Feminist Geography* 20, no. 6 (2013): 773–93.

15. Ibid.

16. Maral Erol and Cenk Özbay, "'I Haven't Died Yet': Navigating Masculinity, Aging and Andropause in Turkey," in *Aging Men, Masculinities and Modern Medicine*, edited by Antje Kampf, Barbara L. Marshall, and Alan Petersen (New York: Routledge, 2013), 156–71, on 156.

17. Ibid., 156.

18. Rodger Charlton, "Ageing Male Syndrome, Andropause, Androgen Decline or Mid-Life Crisis?" *Journal of Men's Health and Gender* 1, no. 1 (2004): 55–59, on 56; Erol and Özbay, "I Haven't Died Yet," 156.

19. Kabachnik et al., *Traumatic Masculinities*, 3.

20. Patricia Neville, "Side-Splitting Masculinity: Comedy, Mr. Bean and the Representation of Masculinities in Contemporary Society," *Journal of Gender Studies* 18, no. 3 (2009), 231–43.

21. Blaine J. Branchik and Ellexis Boyle, "Marketing Muscular Masculinity in Arnold: The Education of a Bodybuilder," *Journal of Gender Studies* 19, no. 2, (2010); Calasanti, *Theorizing Age Relations*; Branchik and Chowdhury, "Self-Oriented Masculinity"; Susan M. Alexander, "Stylish Hard Bodies: Branded Masculinity in *Men's Health* Magazine," *Sociological Perspectives* 46, no. 4 (2003): 535–54; Harrison Pope, Katherine Phillips, and Robert Olivardia, *The Adonis Complex* (New York: Free Press, 2000).

22. Calasanti, *Theorizing Age Relations*, 361.

23. Deborah K. Van den Hoonaard, "Aging and Masculinity: A Topic Whose Time Has Come," *Journal of Aging Studies* 21, no. 4 (2007): 277–80, on 277.

24. *The Incredibles*, directed by Brad Bird (2004; Los Angeles: Walt Disney Home Entertainment, 2005), DVD.

25. Erol and Özbay, "I Haven't Died Yet," 156.

26. Douglas B. Holt and Craig J. Thompson, "Man of Action Heroes: The Pursuit of Heroic Masculinity in Everyday Consumption," *Journal of Consumer Research* 31, no. 2 (September 2004): 425–40, on 429.

27. Elastigirl has the ability to stretch her body parts up to 111 feet, and reshape her body in a variety of ways, such as a parachute and a boat.

28. James Tregonning, "My Incredible Dad: Father Figures in Pixar's *The Incredibles*," *The Scribbler Zine*, July 10, 2013, http://thescribblerzine.blogspot.com.tr/2013/07/my-incredible-dad-father-figures-in.html (accessed June 26, 2014).

29. "The Incredibles," *Heroine Content*, September 21, 2012, http://www.heroinecontent.net/archives/2010/09/the_incredibles.html (accessed June 26, 2014).

30. Frozone has the power to freeze water and moisture in the air.

31. Tregonning, "My Incredible Dad."

32. Kabachnik et al., *Traumatic Masculinities*.

33. Ibid.

Chapter Thirteen

"He Has to Be Good. The Airline Won't Settle for Less."

Gender, Age, and the Trope of the Male Pilot in Advertising

Guilliaume de Syon

In January 2009, Americans witnessed live the rescue of airline passengers emerging from an airplane floating precariously on the Hudson River in New York City. Shortly after takeoff from LaGuardia Airport, US Airways Flight 1549 encountered a large flock of birds, which disabled both of the Airbus A320's engines. Without power, the pilot decided to land on water instead of trying for a local airport. The successful water landing was a rare feat and was credited mostly to the captain of the doomed plane, Chesley Sullenberger, whose looks reflected his advanced middle age. He remarked, "One way of looking at this might be that for forty-two years, I've been making small, regular deposits in this bank of experience, education and training. And on January 15 the balance was sufficient so that I could make a very large withdrawal."[1]

Less than a year later, "Sully" retired from flying, as required by federal regulations. His fame extended across generational barriers partly because, beyond his amazing flying skills, the image of the commercial pilot in Western culture continues to emphasize the icon of the experienced flyer with silver hair in a pressed uniform. This chapter proposes to analyze the nature of this trope. In so doing, it suggests that popular culture has frozen the image of the commercial pilot into both gender and age categories that no longer reflect current conditions.

MIDDLE-AGED WHITE MALES IN AIRLINE BRANDING

The image of a middle-aged white male becoming a leitmotif of airline branding represents a peculiar exception, for two reasons. Not only does it go against the nature of what airlines sell, namely the youthful characteristic of speed, but it contradicts the overwhelming trend in male image representations in ads, as these also emphasize youthful figures.[2] Airlines, on the other hand, show serious, middle-aged, and experienced men in uniform.

The trope of an admired middle-aged master and commander is not novel, however. As literature specialists point out, there appeared in the nineteenth century a peculiar rhetoric that emphasized the hard work and spiritual diligence of the hero in the face of nihilism. This pattern, argued in reinterpretations of such Greek myths as that of Prometheus, and later echoed by Thomas Henry Huxley, emphasizes that physical and mental endeavor alone can rescue the individual in the face of heartless industrialization.[3] Put another way, the human mastery of the machine through experience builds trust in it. Pilots fit the bill of mastering the machine, but the evolution of the image is quite telling.

Common to fliers in all eras, the fashion associated with flying became an important trope of masculinity. As Jennifer Craik notes, uniforms help perform identities.[4] Not only do airline uniforms sanction the power of the pilot, they reinforce the notion of experience that airlines so strongly promote. This experience, however, is paradoxically muted through the use of uniforms. It is not creativity or flying skills that are praised, but the ability to carry a series of choreographed gestures to handle the machine. The attributes that popular culture often assigns pilots, from individuality to informality and even sex appeal, were thus in contradiction with notions of teamwork in the cockpit, rigor, and fatherly control.[5] The origins and resolution of this contradiction of a heroic image originate in the early image of the pilot as a swashbuckler and its accelerated evolution in peacetime.

So long as they were flying combat aircraft or achieving new records, a youthful image of pilots was the norm: youth after all was associated with challenge, and thus control of new realms.[6] Dashing, fresh faces much in the manner of Charles Lindbergh or World War I aces served to inspire confidence in warfare. Yet much as the association of pilot with chivalry balanced out the nihilism of industrial warfare on the ground, it did not fit the bill of commercial flight.

Starting in the 1930s, in an effort to brand themselves as a safe means of travel, airlines sought to emphasize the image of their pilots. Masculinity as shown in advertisements moved away from the daredevil image of the 1920s toward one that associated pilots with clean-cut uniforms. A primary mover in this direction was Juan Trippe, the founder of Pan American Airways.

Trippe felt that as aviation—particularly Pan Am's use of flying boats on over-water routes—derived from seafaring, it should borrow some of its traditions. While he was not the only one to argue this point, his flying boat personnel uniforms changed the norm associated with aviation by emphasizing practices borrowed from the navy, from white uniforms to marching in rank to the aircraft.[7] In so doing, Pan Am and others came to acknowledge the image of the crusty sea captain who had seen it all. The shift was not complete, however. As the records associated with the interwar years reflect, the pilots of the era were young, eager, and foolish, especially the ones who died on the job. Jean Mermoz of France, for example, epitomized the eager, unmarried man seeking to fend off danger in the name of the nation. But his disappearance during a South Atlantic mail-carrying flight, while reflecting patriotic sacrifice, emphasized youthful heroics rather than long-term safe endeavor. However, the acceleration of aviation's development in World War II would affect such visions.

THE INFLUENCE OF WAR II ON AVIATION

The Second World War's impact on aviation extended beyond the air war. New technical feats achieved in terms of airplane autonomy, transport capacity, and navigation all impacted the commercial realm, but so did new levels of standardization. The public did not see such progress, exposed instead to a mass culture that adored the air ace. Ads that American aircraft manufacturers took out showed pilots discussing their experiences with youth, and capitalized on the brashness of the pilots; one such ad featured a painting of actor Spencer Tracy as Pete Sandidge, the brash pilot-hero of the film *A Guy Named Joe* (1943), telling children "what it's like up there."[8] The excitement of flying, however, did not suggest anything safe about the undertaking.

The behind-the-scenes standardization meant that any creative practices that pilots applied to difficult situations now relied on procedures determined at the engineering level. While pilots would continue to contribute to the design and improvement of aviation, it was through experience, and not wild maneuvers, that they were expected to do so. Thus, a new image came to be emphasized: that of the wise middle-aged flier, who not only had seen it all, but made the notion of flying appear to be routine.

As airlines expanded their routes following World War II, the expansion drew in demobilized military pilots, and created a buyer's market for employers.[9] The shrinking of aviation contracts combined with the beginnings of the Cold War created a dichotomy that welcomed pilots into civilian jobs in limited numbers, but emphasized their experience to deal with the challengers of flying piston-engined, propeller-driven aircraft. Advertising dramatically followed suit, as the image of the pilot would still include a youthful smile, but the emphasis on experience that advertising agencies stressed pushed up his age, adding graying hair and a pipe to any figure in uniform.

Though such ads were not meant to portray pilots as senior citizens, they implicitly acknowledged the experience of middle age. This reflected the maturation of the World War II generation, but also the patriarchal culture of the 1950s throughout the Western world. National ads were quick to feature the airline captain as a war veteran who knew the skies and its dangers, but could also help passengers in need: "Experienced travelers fly British" clamored a British ad from 1950, featuring a pilot whose uniform looked very much like that of a wartime Royal Air Force pilot.[10] This notion of control, however, had particular resonance in the American realm.

The apogee of the middle-aged hero began in the 1950s, as airlines expanded their reach to encourage passengers to come aboard. Aside from slashing fares by introducing economy class in 1952, the branding process involved making flying seem benign. In an era when plane crashes remained frequent, projecting a safe image became central to the branding of an airline. Safety could be suggested through a variety of tropes, from a new fleet of aircraft to the motherly qualities of stewardesses caring for children. Pilots joined the set of advertising tools airlines used, and their very attributes of middle age proved central to the element of safety.

BALANCING MIDDLE AGE AND YOUTH

The balance between middle age and youth was also part of the rhetoric applied in American ads. Readers of popular magazines, where the main U.S. carriers ran their ads, could expect to see the serious pilot, but these men, whether they were hired models or actual pilots, were also expected to display characteristics associated with non-flyers. A favored trope, for example, involved the pilot who might smile at a child and was part of the seduction process that involved selling flight, convincing people of the quality of the airline, and of course inviting them to fly to distant destinations. As A. Bowdoin Van Riper notes, many such ads were "shamelessly manipulative . . . yet brilliantly effective."[11]

Whether saluting children as they climbed aboard (in posed photographs and paintings) or explaining to them how an airplane worked, middle-aged males projected the image of toughness with a tender heart. The intent was obviously to convince parents that an aircraft was safe enough to fly their offspring, but also to show how the human element mattered more than the machine. When the Douglas Corporation promoted its new DC-8 jet in 1958, for example, it encouraged potential passengers to "love" the aircraft the way pilots did, but the illustration, rather than showing the new jet in all its majesty, placed it in the background. At the forefront, seated at a departure lounge bar, a relaxed pilot explains the aircraft's maneuvers to a young boy.[12] The pilot figure himself, though pictured as excited about flying, wears the blue generic uniform and drinks coffee, a reflection of maturity, while the mother of the child looks on, smiling and trusting the experienced stranger (see Figure 13.1).

This fatherly style was intended to reflect authority without being authoritarian, the epitome of friendly grace, in marked contrast to the stern rigor that might be associated with pilots. This "friendliness" graced many ads and would continue to grace ads of various airlines well into the 1970s. In parallel, the airline pilot became a frozen image, thanks in part to safety regulations.

Airline rules came to require that senior pilots retire by age fifty-five, a restriction that would continue to apply for decades. There thus appeared a distinct dichotomy where older men in commercial ads for airlines, though clearly middle-aged, also reflected the intermediate step to senior citizenry. By contrast, the flight attendants remained an odd combination of youthful beauty and motherly concern. Such a distinction thus ennobled the senior male in control of technology: the captain was by nature an aging male hero, charged with protecting the passengers and even their youthful flight attendants.

MASTERY OF TECHNOLOGY

This image of middle-aged *homo faber* came to extend beyond aviation into the automobile industry. Several car models in the 1950s had used styling that echoed aeronautical engineering.[13] However, by the 1960s the emphasis shifted to the technological breakthroughs at one's fingertips *inside* the car, and targeted a male clientele for that purpose. Ford, for example, advertised its 1964, 1965, and 1966 Thunderbird models as having special emergency light releases that were activated from a panel in the roof, much like aircraft buttons.[14] One such illustration shows an airline captain in full uniform reaching for one of the buttons. His short hair is slightly gray, but the emphasis is on power. Aging is thus affirmed as an ally rather than a handicap in the mastery of technology, even for the commuter. In parallel to the print version, the filmed advertisement goes so far as to show a pilot driving his car to the airport to board a jet, suggesting that the car "very closely approximates the feeling of flight."[15]

What advertisers hoped would register was the transposition of the male in control of technological complexity into the popular psyche: The car would be everyman's cockpit. Yet the sway of the fascination that made middle age into a heroic life stage relied not only on the machine, but on clothing, too: the uniform was central to the image of aging heroes. To

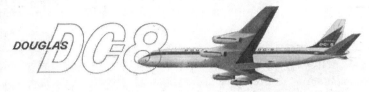

Pilots call it...*(and so will you!)* "The world's most <u>advanced</u> jetliner!"

Already, more than 500 pilots have flown the Douglas DC-8 Jetliner. Here's how they feel about the world's most modern jetliner: "It's in the DC tradition, and that's good enough for me" . . . "Remarkable approach and stability characteristics" . . . "I've flown them all and this is *it!*"

As a DC-8 passenger, you'll share their enthusiasm. You'll appreciate the many Douglas innovations. And you'll rely on the DC experience that has made Douglas the most popular aircraft in aviation.

Make a date with the DC-8, *world's most advanced* jetliner!

These world-famous airlines will soon fly you almost any-where on earth by DC-8: ALITALIA-LINEE AEREE ITALIANE · DELTA AIR LINES · EASTERN AIR LINES · JAPAN AIR LINES · KLM ROYAL DUTCH AIR LINES · NATIONAL AIRLINES · NORTHWEST ORIENT AIRLINES · OLYMPIC AIRWAYS · PANAGRA · PANAIR DO BRASIL · PAN AMERICAN WORLD AIRWAYS · SAS – SCANDINAVIAN AIRLINES SYSTEM · SWISSAIR · TRANS-CANADA AIR LINES · TRANSPORTS AERIENS INTERCONTINENTAUX · UNION AEROMARITIME DE TRANSPORT · UNITED AIR LINES

More airlines have chosen the DC-8 than any other jetliner!

Figure 13.1. **The experienced yet youthful stranger becomes the random hero of a youth. From the Douglas Aircraft Corporation, 1959.** *Copyright Boeing Co., reproduced by permission*

suggest that any family man climbing into a new sedan would automatically acquire the heroic attributes of technical knowledge stretched credibility, since the point of the ad was to show a safe ride, not one that included risk. This dichotomy would also affect the real pilot.

As airlines entered the jet age in the late 1950s, the notion of the middle-aged hero, capable of manipulating tons of flying metal, began its transformation into that of ennobled bus driving. The shift to the jet age proved trying for airline pilots, as many washed out in the process of adjusting to jet transition. Simply put, seniority aboard propeller aircraft did not translate into similar privilege aboard jets. Higher speeds, navigational complexities, and the increase in air traffic all added to the stress some experienced pilots encountered, and led in some cases to notorious crashes. To remedy this, airlines stressed pilot knowledge in the ads they published. A Trans World Airlines (TWA) advertisement, for example, summarized its pilots as the epitome of confidence because they might be a "twenty-year [company] man, but nobody at Trans World Airlines is too experienced to learn a little more."[16] Middle age would take care of the new technical challenge, and turn flying into a new routine. All that the passenger needed for flying was a ticket, not a will.

Indeed, routine as a measure of safety called for pilots *not* to act in the image that had been cast of them up until World War II. The smiling pilot offering the child a relaxed attitude does so on the ground; in the air, he shows focus, but not pensiveness. His good looks are not expected to warrant promiscuity the way characters in movies like *Airport* (1970) do,[17] but to project comfort. While Peter Lythe noticed such contradictions in the image of female flight attendants, this peculiarity is also to be emphasized in the case of male airline pilots as they acquire a separate identity from that of the fighter pilot, always a younger type.

The image of empowered middle age became routine in the 1970s, as airlines pictured members of their staff to emphasize that each company offered a special caring identity. Delta pilots pictured in a series of ads in 1977–1978 all had spent thousands of hours in flight and had put in countless more studying in order to master newer, wide-body jets. By placing actual pilots in the commercials, the feeling of genuine care and concern could be argued convincingly, thus rejuvenating the truly aging trope of the middle-aged hero (see Figure 13.2).

Figure 13.2. Finnair pilots who carried out the airline's first transatlantic flight pose in front of their DC-8 jetliner in the late 1960s. The emphasis on fearless middle-aged experience (two captains and a senior flight engineer flew that flight) is accentuated by the striped uniforms and the size of the jet behind them. *Copyright Finnair, reproduced by permission*

The practice of identifying each pilot soon disappeared, however, due to tragedy. Priding itself on its punctuality and the quality of its service, the Dutch airline KLM took out an ad in 1976 and 1977 featuring its Boeing 747 chief pilot, Jacob Veldhuyzen van Zanten. Bashful yet graying, the smiling face of the experienced pilot invited magazine readers to enjoy the charms of the Netherlands. On March 27, 1977, Veldhuyzen van Zanten commanded a delayed flight rerouted to Tenerife, in the Canary Islands. His actions on takeoff were one of the factors leading to the death of 583 passengers and crew when his plane collided with a Pan Am 747 positioned on the same runway.[18] While the image of the pilot would continue to appear occasionally in airline ads, it would no longer be as a central element of flying.

ERASING THE HEROIC PILOT

As airlines began deregulating in 1978, the trope of using male authority figures in airline commercials had given way to other approaches to wooing passengers. The advent of female airline pilots and the increase in the number of low-cost carriers brought an end to the tradition of representing the middle-aged pilot as a heroic figure. Though it sometimes reappears in airline ads, the original purpose, to suggest flight safety and mastery, is no longer present.

Consigned to memory, the vision of the middle-aged pilot as hero survives in movies and satirical skits, but is now a fantasy rather than an actual element of the flying experience. The only exception includes publicity for the actions of pilots saving planes from crashing. Captain Sullenberger's actions, as well as recent ones by other pilots flying for Qantas, British Airways, and LOT Polish airlines, all cast these pilots as middle-aged heroes through actions that challenged routine. However welcome they may have been in the public eye, these events challenged routine, and thus the very image airlines seek to project. Thus, the passing of the airline pilot as a trope of advertising represents an evolution of airlines and how they sold their product. It proved to be a necessary tool as consumers adjusted to the notion—and cost—of travel in the air. While other tropes, notably that of the flight attendant, are recurring features of airline advertising, the persons in the cockpit are no longer deemed as important in imagining an airline service: Routine has erased the pilot hero.

NOTES

1. "Capt. Sully Worried About Airline Industry," CBSNews.com, February 10, 2009, http://www.cbsnews.com/news/capt-sully-worried-about-airline-industry/ (accessed July 2014).

2. William M. O'Barr, "Representations of Masculinity and Femininity in Advertisements," *Advertising and Society Review* 7, no. 2 (2006), http://muse.jhu.edu/journals/advertising_and_society_review/v007/7.2unit07.html (accessed July 2014). The resulting parallel, however, is that flight attendants were cast as young, attractive, but also motherly; see Peter Lythe, "Think of Her As Your Mother: Airline Advertising and the Stewardess in America, 1930–1980," *Journal of Transport History* 30, no. 1 (June 2009): 1–21, on 15.

3. Anne-Julia Zwierlein, "Exhausting the Powers of Life: Aging, Energy and Productivity in Nineteenth-Century Literary and Scientific Discourses," in *Interdisciplinary Perspectives on Aging in Nineteenth-Century Culture*, edited by Anne-Julia Zwierlein, Katharina Boehm, and Anna Farkas (London: Routledge, 2013), 38–56, on 48–49.

4. Jennifer Craik, *Uniforms Exposed* (New York: Berg, 2005).

5. Ibid.

6. Joseph Corn, *The Winged Gospel: America's Romance with Aviation* (Baltimore, MD: Johns Hopkins University Press, 1983), 8.

7. Marylin Bender and Selig Altschul, *The Chosen Instrument* (New York: Simon and Shuster, 1982), 188–89.

8. "The Airlines of the United States" [advertisement], *Saturday Evening Post*, October 13, 1943.

9. Jennifer Van Vleck, *No Distant Places: Aviation and the Global American Century*, PhD dissertation (Yale University, 2009), 305–10.

10. "Experienced Travelers Fly British," [advertisement for BOAC/BEA], *Flight*, July 13, 1950.

11. A. Bowdoin Van Riper, *Imagining Flight: Aviation and Popular Culture* (College Station: Texas A&M University Press, 2003), 95.

12. "The World's Most Advanced Airliner" [advertisement for Douglas Commercial Aircraft], *Saturday Evening Post*, August 15, 1959.

13. David Gartman, *Auto-Opium: A Social History of American Automobile Design* (London: Routledge, 1994), 163–65.

14. "The Thunderbird Touch" [advertisement for Ford Motor Company], Curbsideclassic.com, http://www.curbsideclassic.com/wp-content/comment-image/211876 (accessed July 2014).

15. "1965 Ford Thunderbird Commercial," https://www.youtube.com/watch?v=EzJu9P7013c (accessed July 2014).

16. "Confidence" [advertisement for Trans World Airlines], 1962.

17. Van Riper, *Imagining Flight*, 113–15.

18. Jan Bartelski, *Disasters in the Air: Mysterious Air Disasters Explained* (Shrewsbury, MA: Airlife, 2001), 248–69.

IV

Real to Reel: Individuals Aging on and off the Screen

Chapter Fourteen

Helen Mirren and the Media Portrayals of Aging

Women's Sexuality Concealed and Revealed

Barbara Cook Overton, Athena du Pré,
and Loretta L. Pecchioni

A Linkin Park metal beat screams under an action-packed car chase and shoot-out through the narrow streets of London. We follow the driver, expertly piloting a laser-blue Lotus Exige S. From the passenger seat, the shooter dares the driver to "show me something" and then fires two guns simultaneously, arms spread, from both front windows (see Figure 14.1). The shooter targets the pursuing black Range Rover, hitting it several times. The Range Rover flips over as it crashes into a parked car. Who are these action stars? Men? Women? A man *and* a woman? How old are they? Who is driving? Who destroys the Range Rover with deadly aim and from a moving vehicle? The scene is from *RED 2* (2013), and Byung-hun Lee, age thirty-three, is driving while Helen Mirren, sixty-seven, challenges aging stereotypes by portraying a sexy, dangerous, and deadly action hero. She is an important heroine to examine because, until recently, young and middle-aged men have dominated this action genre, while much younger women are their damsels in distress and love interests.

For example, when Roger Moore played James Bond in *A View to a Kill* (1985), he was a dashing fifty-seven-year-old sex symbol. His love interest was played by thirty-year-old Tanya Roberts. Decades later, the eleven-year age gap between secret agent 007 (Daniel Craig) and his sexy companion (Bérénice Marlohe) in *Skyfall* (2012) was smaller but still notable. Outside of Bond films, twenty years separated Bruce Willis and Milla Jovovich in *The Fifth Element* (1997). Even in the *RED* franchise, Willis is nine years older than his on-screen love interest, Mary-Louise Parker. Thus, for generations, the message in the media has been consistent: Men age (to a point) in ways that are consistent with a sexy and heroic image, whereas for women, the point between "sexy" and "invisible" (in terms of their Hollywood presence) has arrived much sooner.

With regard to women, the younger-is-sexier theme has not disappeared. But, some striking texts have emerged to challenge that theme. For example, *RED* and *RED 2* have made Mirren a bona fide action star, and age has done little to diminish her sex-symbol status. At sixty-five, she filmed a topless sex scene for the movie *Love Ranch* (2010). In late 2014, Mirren was signed as the new face for one of the world's largest cosmetics company, L'Oreal. Amid the ensuing news coverage, Mirren was described as "living proof that age need be no barrier to glamour," given she will represent L'Oreal along-side celebrities less than half her age.[1] To explore this further, we offer a review of the theoretical underpinnings of our understandings, sexual script theory, and how acceptable norms might be changing. Then, we explore trends in the way women are portrayed in the media, paying particular atten-tion to portrayals that include (or ignore) the sexuality of women over age forty. When older women are sexualized, we analyze how they are shot and framed. We use two classic films to frame that discussion: *The Graduate* (1967) and *Harold and Maude* (1971). Next, we review a wide range of films starring Mirren, from *The Cook, the Thief, His Wife, and Her Lover* (1989) to *Calendar Girls* (2003) to *Shadowboxer* (2005), and discuss how the lighting and editing in those scenes serve as interpretive cues about the nature of sexuality in later life. Together, these cues support sociocultural ideas about what it means to be admired and emulated by others.

Traditionally, in the rare instances in which older adults are portrayed in sexual situations in the media, they are not portrayed as heroes, but as absurd, comical, and unsightly. Older bodies are often marked for shame because of wrinkles and folds or presented as humorous for their mere expression as naked bodies. An example of this can be seen in *Bad Grandpa* (2013) as the forty-two-year-old Johnny Knoxville pretends to be an eighty-six-year-old grandfather. He performs a strip tease while a wrinkled and droopy prosthetic scrotum dangles from his underwear. For women, this issue might be more serious. For example, after fifty-four-year-old Kathy Bates appeared nude in a hot tub in *About Schmidt* (2002), the scene was ridiculed in many online lists, including "10 Nude Scenes We Didn't Need to See!"[2] That list also included a scene with Julie Andrews (then age forty-six) baring a breast in the 1981 movie *S.O.B.* These images serve as powerful scripts for the way people are "supposed" to conduct themselves in real life. Thus, we next explore the concept of sexual script theory to elaborate on ways that media images influence sexual mores.

SEXUAL SCRIPT THEORY

Sexual script theory proposes that people gauge which behaviors are allowed and expected of them, largely by observing the behavior of people around them and in the media.[3] In other words, we are taught to "act our age," "be a man," "act ladylike," and so on. People who deviate from the scripts risk being ostracized as weak or immoral.[4] Although personal preference is a factor, one implication of sexual script theory is that people's behavior—and even their sexual identity—is likely to be influenced by societal norms. By the same token, as social expectations change, sexual scripts are likely to morph as well.

Another implication of prescriptive sexual scripting is that what is considered appropriate for members of one social group may be forbidden among another group. One such way in which appropriateness is determined in groups is age. For example, adolescents and young adults tend to emulate the sexual encounters they see enacted by youthful actors in the media.[5] The sexual script is fairly clear in this regard: youthfulness is sexy. Provocative clothing and behaviors by young people, particularly if they live up to society's standards of beauty, are expected and admired. However, those same actions may be considered inappropriate at different stages of life. At the other end of the age spectrum, for example, the message has long been the opposite. Older adults have traditionally been underrepresented in the media, and when they are portrayed, they are typically cast as physically and sexually unattractive.[6]

Sexual scripts also vary by gender. Boys and men have traditionally been encouraged to follow a script in which they initiate sex, are always interested

Figure 14.1.   In her late sixties, Helen Mirren plays the type of strong, sexy roles once reserved for women in their twenties. Taken from *RED 2*, directed by Dean Parisot, 2013.

in sex, and seek out a variety of partners.[7] If a man does these things, he might be considered a stud. Conversely, the traditional script for females is that sex is more emotional than physical, and women should limit and choose their partners carefully.[8] If a woman acts counter to the script, she may be considered a slut. A third implication is that sexual scripts give rise to assumptions and stereotypes. It is a short leap of logic from a script that says "older people should not display an interest in sex" to the assumption that "older people are not *interested* in sex." Therefore, based on the images around them, college students might assume that young women's interest in sex is greater than older women's interest, and that men of all ages are more interested than women in experimental sex.[9]

With this in mind, the concept of sexual scripts is important in our exploration of Mirren. Additionally, texts such as films in mass media reflect and influence what is considered to be the social realities in which we live and interact.[10] This is important, as this perception of media underscores the power of films to reflect and influence what is "normal" in regard to sexuality. For example, if sexuality is culturally revered and linked only to youth, then aging is cast as distinctly "asexual" and inherently "less than" the ideal. This has resulted in an overwhelming number of portrayals that depict older adults as asexual or sexually unappealing. The binary nature of these assumptions—young and sexy or old and asexual—is not absolute, because those same media texts also allow for challenges to those dominant scripts. Thus, we next discuss how the sexual norms, as scripts, may be undergoing a revolution of sorts.

FORESHADOWING A SEXUAL REVOLUTION

Sexual script theory recognizes that, despite the social risks involved, norms *are* sometimes challenged and rewritten. The sexual revolution of the 1960s is a good example of these evolving norms: by the late 1980s, college students had remarkably different ideas about sexuality than their grandparents before them. For example, the younger generations endorsed the idea that premarital sex was acceptable, and three out of four of them reported that men and women should feel equally comfortable initiating sexual relationships.[11] Thus, as society evolves, a second sexual revolution might be brewing to challenge the notion that sex is only for the young.

For one, people entering their sixties today were teens or young adults during the 1960s. Again, during this sexual revolution, the birth control pill, the women's movement, and civil disobedience reshaped American society.[12] As such, these aging adults are no strangers to challenging the status quo. For another, Baby Boomers (born between 1946 and 1964) are better educated and wealthier than any generation before them.[13] With their greater numbers, Baby Boomers make up about one-third of the U.S. population and may expect to live nearly thirty years longer than their grandparents.[14] Books such as Margaret Gullette's *Declining to Decline*[15] engage Baby Boomers in redefining what it means to grow old. She proposes that, despite traditional beliefs to the contrary, youth is not the only arena for beauty, growth, excitement, sex, and fun. Additionally, the potential for profit from these Baby Boomers is immense. Advertisers and entertainment writers are savvy to the fact that the fifty-plus crowd is from the wealthiest generation in U.S. history, and thus a lucrative market for media messages and products that appeal to them.[16] "Sex appeal is part of the sell," advises *USA Today* marketing reporter Bruce Horovitz, who also observes that Baby Boomers are attracted to messages that portray them as hip, sexy, and smart.[17] Thus, several factors are contributing to this sexual revolution.

Like previous large-scale social changes, revolutionizing the sexual script, as it relates to older adults, will not likely be fast or smooth. In tracing history, we see that cultural ideas are notoriously slow to change, and specifically, challenges to sexual scripts are often met with disapproval. In fact, name-calling is one of the first signs that a script has been challenged. As a case in point, the term cougar was co-opted in the late 1990s to describe older women who show sexual interest in younger men. When researchers interviewed women aged twenty to sixty about the term, most of them considered the usage of cougar insulting. They reported that it casts women as sexual predators and underscores a double standard in which older men can date younger women with impunity, but women are castigated for doing the same thing.[18] At the same time, some of the women interviewed (particularly respondents thirty and older) reported that the term cougar calls useful attention to the idea that some women over age forty *are* interested in sex and are confident about their sex appeal. As one interviewee put it, "I think in some ways it refers to a woman who isn't in her reproductive prime but is still a sexual person."[19] Whether cougar is ultimately regarded as pejorative or not, it represents a fissure in a long-supported script that women above a certain age are, by nature, sexually demure and passive, as well as accepting without question that younger men will not find them physically appealing. With this in mind, we examine the role that Hollywood plays in defining what it means to be sexy as a woman.

HOLLYWOOD AND SEXUAL SCRIPTS FOR OLDER WOMEN

Both media portrayals *and* resultant public discussion, such as movie reviews and magazine articles, are reshaping sexual scripts that have condemned older women as asexual. To appreciate just how much these scripts are changing, we contrast two classic and noteworthy portrayals of older, sexual women—Mrs. Robinson in *The Graduate* and Maude in *Harold and Maude*—against characters played by the actress Helen Mirren, whose recent roles have included a retired and extremely dangerous MI6 agent, a madam, the queen of England, a ruthless assassin, and a topless "calendar girl."

Redefining "Young" and "Old"

It wasn't long ago that women "of a certain age" were expected to surrender their sensuality because sex was the domain of younger, fertile women. Dominant scripts reinforced heteronormative, reproductive sex and simultaneously discouraged middle-aged women from expressing continued interest in sexual activity and encouraging them to conceal their bodies. For example, fashion magazines routinely admonish women who "do not dress their age" and suggest that wearing a miniskirt past thirty-five is a fashion faux pas. [20] But times are changing as a bikini-clad Mirren was famously snapped by paparazzi in 2008, "revealing," according to the *Daily Mail*, "a figure that would not disgrace a 23-year-old Hollywood ingénue." [21] At that time, she was sixty-two years old. Additionally, describing middle-aged women in a controversial piece for *Esquire*, Tom Junod writes:

> There used to be something tragic about even the most beautiful forty-two-year-old woman. With half her life still ahead of her, she was deemed to be at the end of something—namely, everything society valued in her, other than her success as a mother. If she remained sexual, she was either predatory or desperate; if she remained beautiful, what gave her beauty force was the fact of its fading. And if she remained alone . . . well, then God help her. [22]

Junod points out that with our population aging and the median age advancing, "we have no choice but to keep redefining youth," and that our norms are changing. [23]

With this concept of change in mind, today women such as Cameron Diaz, Jennifer Garner, and Sofia Vergara are still considered sexy at forty-two, whereas a few decades ago they would have been perceived as "old" by Hollywood standards. Anne Bancroft's turn as forty-two-year-old Mrs. Robinson in *The Graduate* perfectly underscores this previous perception of "old." Mrs. Robinson was, in many respects, the first cougar. In the film, she seduced her neighbors' son, Benjamin Braddock, a recent college graduate not much older than Mrs. Robinson's own daughter. The irony is that Bancroft was only thirty-six when she shot *The Graduate* and Dustin Hoffman, her costar, playing Benjamin, was thirty. Her daughter, played by Katherine Ross, was twenty-seven. Thus, the age differences in real life were not that great. A film critic for the *Times-Picayune* noted that the casting choices director Mike Nichols made demonstrated "how quickly women 'age' in Hollywood." [24] (see Figure 14.2)

The fact that Nichols did not cast an older actress is interesting and worth noting. Film critic Roger Ebert writes that Bancroft, "in a tricky role, was magnificently sexy, shrewish, and self-possessed enough to make the seduction *convincing* [emphasis added]."[25] Was Ebert suggesting audiences could not have been convinced of an affair between Benjamin and Mrs. Robinson had the part been played by an older actress? Or was he simply complimenting Bancroft's enduring sex appeal, despite her age? While we can't know what Ebert intended, his suggestion reinforced a heteronormative, reproductive sexual script that an intergenerational sexual relationship that will not produce offspring cannot be convincing or believable. Junod hints that *The Graduate* was successful because of the way forty-two-year-olds were perceived in 1967—Mrs. Robinson was just young enough for the seduction to seem plausible, but also old enough that the affair was eventually and believably labeled "disgusting."[26] To illustrate, in his climactic outburst, Benjamin shouts, "This is the sickest, most perverted thing that's ever happened to me!"[27]

While some film critics argue that Benjamin's disgust (and by extension, the audience's aversion) had little to do with age but stemmed from his

Figure 14.2. Mrs. Robinson (Anne Bancroft) in *The Graduate* was perhaps the first famous cougar, in today's terms. In the movie, she beds twenty-one-year-old Benjamin Braddock (Dustin Hoffman), who is half her age. In reality, Bancroft was only thirty-six years old, and Hoffman thirty, when the film was shot, underscoring the age differential between Hollywood's version of an "older woman" and a "younger man." Taken from *The Graduate*, directed by Mike Nichols, 1967.

having had an affair with a married woman, the mother of his *real* love interest, we assert that despite their arguments, the intergenerational sexual relationship between Benjamin and Mrs. Robinson operated against the sexual scripts of that time. In contrast, the obvious and vast age difference between the title characters in *Harold and Maude* offended audiences and critics alike, and they rejected the film when it premiered in 1971.

Harold and Maude is a love story between a young man and an old woman. Harold is fresh-faced and in his early twenties, and Maude is almost eighty. Harold is obsessed with death and stages a series of "suicides" to the chagrin of his seemingly detached and disinterested mother. Maude, on the other hand, is full of life. Both characters go to strangers' funerals for fun, meet at such a funeral, become friends, and then eventually fall in love. In his film review, Ebert writes that "word has gotten out that 'Harold and Maude' is the story of a love affair between these two people. It is not, so necrophiliacs please stay cool."[28] Ebert's review is important because he basically infers that Maude is a corpse and in so doing, he completely denies that the film is a legitimate love story between a young man and an old woman. In other words, as the object of a necrophiliac's desire, Maude is not a sexually active being; rather, Ebert frames her as a passive dead body. However, this framing is inaccurate because while Maude was unquestionably old (portrayed by the seventy-five-year-old Ruth Gordon), she was obviously not a corpse. In fact, if Maude's character had been a man rather than a woman, he might have been regarded as a hero for attracting the sexual interest of a much younger woman.

As it was, Gordon's twenty-three-year-old costar, Bud Cort, convincingly played Maude's lover. This affair disgusted characters in the film as well as many in the audience. For example, in the film, Harold's priest learns that the young man plans to propose to Maude. Instead of encouraging a union of love, the priest unleashed vitriol that would be oft-quoted in the film's scathing reviews: "I would be remiss in my duty if I did not tell you that the idea of intercourse and the fact of your firm, young body comingling with withered flesh, sagging breasts, and flabby buttocks makes me want to vomit."[29] Margo Capparelli adds that viewers have difficulty with the film because the relationship between Harold and Maude "violates a basic cultural taboo against couples with a large disparity in their ages . . . [which is] intensified when it is the woman who is older than the man."[30] In other words, their sexual relationship defies the heteronormative, reproductive view of sex in that while viewers may not have objected to Harold "as a sexual being," they recoiled at his interest in Maude, who is "well past child-bearing years."[31] Capparelli concludes that "the film is forcing viewers to face their own ageism, influenced by a society that typically views the elderly as sexless, impassionate people."[32]

With regard to differences in the two films, in *The Graduate* Mrs. Robinson's lingerie-clad body and bare breasts were showcased in a series of close-up shots, but in *Harold and Maude*, the cinematic approach concealed Maude's nude body. In the film's only shot suggesting sexual intimacy between the lovers, Maude's bare shoulders are visible as she lies sleeping next to Harold. The "sex" scene follows their declaration of love, but Harold lies on the opposite side of the bed not even touching his lover (see Figure 14.3). In fact, the only overt sexual touching between them throughout the entire film is a kiss on the neck. But their lovemaking was supposed to have been much more apparent, as director Hal Ashby revealed. In an interview with Michael Shedlin for *Film Quarterly*, Ashby explained:

> I ran into trouble with Paramount (the film's distributor). We had a scene when Harold and Maude started to make love; their kissing becomes more passionate, and they lie back on the bed. . . . Paramount said it would be too tough for people. I said, "That's sort of what the whole movie is about, a boy falling in love with an old woman; the sexual aspect doesn't have to be distasteful." They said it would turn everybody off. I was crazy about the footage. But it was a losing battle.[33]

So, the footage of their passionate kissing only appeared in an early trailer for the film, but it was cut from subsequent ads and the film itself. Thus, by hiding their lovemaking and concealing Maude's nudity, the film reluctantly adhered to the sexual script that older adults, especially older women, are not sexual beings. *The Graduate* made clear that a forty-two-year-old body could be sexual, but *Harold and Maude* implied that although a eighty-year-old body could also be sexual, it should not be seen in a sexually suggestive light. It is important to question at what point women's bodies become asexual, according to the media. Nonetheless, *Harold and Maude* did shine a light on the issue by challenging ageist assumptions.

Although film distributors, audiences, and critics balked at the idea of a nude and sexually active older woman in 1971, later depictions of sensual middle-aged women were comparatively well received. Unlike Mrs. Robinson and her questionable relationship with Benjamin, her on-screen successors were neither morally corrupt nor predatory. *Animal House* (1978) and *American Pie* (1999) both showcased sexually experienced older women, albeit in a comedic light. Their presence, nonetheless, helped normalize the idea of sexually active middle-aged women. For example, Stifler's mom, played by a thirty-eight-year-old Jennifer Coolidge in *American Pie*, started the "sexy mom" trend. In the infamous scene that popularized the term MILF (an acronym for Mom I'd Like to F*ck), Stifler's awestruck classmates are mesmerized by his mother's sexy portrait. Transfixed, they stand before it, feverishly chanting "MILF! MILF! MILF!"[34] Fifteen years later, "MILF" and "mom" are among the most-searched porn categories in the United

Figure 14.3.   This is the only image from *Harold and Maude* hinting at the sexual intimacy the title characters share. Decision makers at Paramount cut a more explicit scene where they passionately kiss, fearing the public would be disgusted by intimacy between a young man and a much older woman. Taken from *Harold and Maude*, directed by Hal Ashby, 1971.

States, a genre in which the most popular star, Lisa Ann, is forty-two years old.[35] Although Coolidge did not disrobe in *American Pie*, Helen Mirren did precisely that a few years later in *Calendar Girls*.

As a comedy with dramatic undercurrents, *Calendar Girls* is based on a true story in which eleven members of the Rylstone and District Women's Institute in England posed nude for a calendar and sold copies to raise money for their local hospital. The women, who were between forty-five and sixty-five years old, were considered heroes in that the calendar was a tremendous success. While this suggests a celebration of older women's sensuality, the black-and-white images were not overtly sexual, and the women's nudity was partially obscured by carefully placed props. Ensuing press coverage lauded the bravery of those who stripped, but did not focus on their beauty nor on their sensuousness. This suggests that the bodies were not seen in a sexual light, thereby underscoring scripts that discourage middle-aged women from being, or being seen as, sexual. Four years later, a fifty-eight-year-old Mirren led an ensemble cast in the film adaptation and was the only actress to completely bare her breasts, in full color and sharp focus. Younger characters in the film laughed at the notion of older women stripping, and thus underscored the idea that older naked bodies are objects of ridicule. That theme persists in films such as *Wanderlust* (2012), as during the film's most "comedic" scene, older nudists run in slow motion while operatic music heightens the humorous effect of old bouncing breasts and bellies. Undeterred by snickers or criticism, the "calendar girls" overcome their inhibitions and disrobe, one by one. Although they remain hidden behind props, like the real women they were portraying, they also celebrate their bodies. Although Ebert reinforced an ageist stereotype by writing "thank god for the flower arrangements,"[36] the film *was* inspirational for aging women because *Calendar Girls* and Mirren's performance helped normalize the idea that middle-aged and older women *are* desirable.

Helen Mirren as Pacesetter

Defying ageist assumptions of asexuality, some of the characters Mirren portrays bed men nearly half their age. Also, Mirren herself twerks, wears "stripper heels,"[37] and has no qualms about posing nude (which she famously did in 2010, at the age of sixty-five, for *New York* magazine). But the ensuing critical response and public discussion surrounding her on- and off-screen antics have been mixed. In fact, the tone of that discussion has changed over the last ten years, as it is gradually shifting away from condemnation toward celebration. Lingering criticism notwithstanding, Mirren's unabashed sensuality is redefining "sexy" for middle-aged and older women and changing the sexual scripts we use.

Now that Mirren is nearly seventy years old, her nudity is considered groundbreaking. However, long before she appeared topless in *Calendar Girls* and more recently for *New York* magazine, she appeared nude in many other films. The first was *Age of Consent* (1969), when she was twenty-four years old, and she went on to appear nude in eight more films. For us, her most relevant roles combine nudity with raw sexuality. Two roles in particular come to mind: Georgina in *The Cook, the Thief, His Wife, and Her Lover* and Grace in *Love Ranch* (2010). As Georgina, Mirren, then forty-four, was completely naked for half of the film and had many prolonged, unedited lovemaking scenes with her costar, Alan Howard. Mirren's middle-aged body and sexuality are anything but bawdy. Critics called her performance brave, in part, because disrobing at forty-four was courageous considering that women past forty were seen as "has-beens" by Hollywood standards. Instead, Mirren gave a convincing portrayal of an abused wife and a sensuous lover who also exacts revenge against her abuser. As part of her portrayal, nudity made Georgina vulnerable and believable. For her work as Georgina, she was celebrated in critical reviews. However, twenty-one years later, when Mirren stripped for *Love Ranch*, critical reaction was mixed.

While many critics regarded *Love Ranch* as "a colossal bomb,"[38] the film inspired public debate that underscores enduring ageist and sexist stereotypes. In the film, Mirren plays Grace, a madam in the fictionalized retelling of the founding of Nevada's first legal brothel. Ironically, she revealed more skin in the *New York* magazine photo spread promoting the film than she did in the film itself, but *how* her nudity was presented, on film, is important to consider because it was realistic. The cinematographer did not use soft filters or lighting tricks, and so her bare breast is in sharp focus. Mirren was adamant that the scene would not be "a fake, romantic soft-lensed moment" and insisted that director Taylor Hackford (to whom she is married) "make it as true as possible."[39] (see Figure 14.4) Mirren also demands the same approach in her forthcoming L'Oreal ads, insisting her images not be retouched because older women *should* look their age.[40]

The type of cinematography used in *Love Ranch* is a brave and an unconventional choice. Simon Cable, a critic for the *Daily Mail*, remarks, "although most would demand the soft focus treatment, whatever their age, it seems the Oscar winner [Mirren] was happy to face reality."[41] In contrast, another *Daily Mail* writer, Carol Sarler, objected to this because Mirren "is not only seen naked in *Love Ranch* but also simulating sex while she's at it."[42] In other words, Sarler basically reinforced sexual scripts that disparage older adults' interest in sex by bemoaning Mirren's choice to film a sex scene at the age of sixty-five.[43] Other critics object to the age difference between Mirren and her on-screen lover, played by the thirty-five-year-old Sergio Pesis-Mencheta. For example, Mick LaSalle, describing Pesis-Mencheta's character, writes, "he only has eyes for a lady old enough to be his mom's older sister."[44] Thus, according to these critics, the thirty-year age difference between Mirren and Pesis-Mencheta makes the relationship improbable.[45]

However, Mirren's on-screen husband, played by a sixty-seven-year-old Joe Pesci, is not similarly chastised for an "improbable" relationship, despite the fact that his character beds a prostitute played by a twenty-one-year-old actress. The fact that this forty-six-year age difference escaped criticism while the thirty-year age difference between Mirren and Pesis-Mencheta was severely criticized underscores a sexual script that makes it permissible for older men, but not older women, to take younger lovers. In other words, "cougars," even ones played by Helen Mirren, simply are not afforded the same sexual liberties as men.

Mirren also took a much-younger on-screen lover, played by Cuba Gooding Jr., in *Shadowboxer*. Gooding was thirty-seven and Mirren was sixty at the time of the film's release. *Shadowboxer* stimulated debate about intergenerational and interracial relationships, but is especially noteworthy because it highlights Mirren's age instead of concealing it. In the film, Mirren and Gooding Jr. portray contract killers, Rose and Mikey, who merge violence and sex in one of the film's many memorable scenes. While Mikey makes love to Rose, the scene is intercut with violent flashbacks of Mikey's father beating him, along with visions of a younger Rose shooting and killing Mikey's father. While the passion on screen is palpable, nonetheless, partly

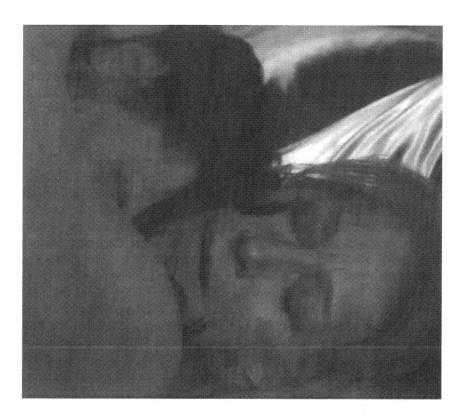

Figure 14.4. Helen Mirren was considered "brave" for appearing nude after age forty in the movie *Love Ranch*. Rather than trying to appear younger than she was, Mirren insisted on a realistic portrayal, with no filters or lighting techniques to blur the focus. (She is shown here in a scene with Sergio Pesis-Mencheta.) Taken from *Love Ranch*, directed by Taylor Hackford, 2010.

because of their age difference, they are regarded as "one of the most unlikely couples in screen history."[46] While the film was panned, Mirren was almost universally applauded for her performance. She was a convincing killer, and she looked good doing it. The director, Lee Daniels, frames her in a tight close-up after her first kill. Brightly lit, Mirren's face is radiant, and her wrinkles are not obscured by shadows, soft filters, or overexposure. By once again resisting the ubiquitous soft lighting techniques common in other films, Daniels celebrated her age, fierceness, and beauty. In comparison, consider *Alien Resurrection* (1997) and how differently the close-ups of then forty-eight-year-old Sigourney Weaver were shot. In virtually every shot of her face, Weaver is washed out or overexposed. Thus, in contrast, the "glowing" Weaver is portrayed without any wrinkles. Weaver's costars, including men and younger women, are not similarly shot. This difference draws even more attention to the obvious manipulation of Weaver's close-up shots. Mirren, on the other hand, manages to be both sexy and commanding, without camera tricks.

Although she portrayed a contract killer in *Shadowboxer*, Mirren's character is also nurturing. She carries that duality with her to the *RED* series. Both in *RED* (2010) and *RED 2* (2013), Mirren plays Victoria, a retired and extremely dangerous MI6[47] agent who is sexy and deadly, but also motherly. That she balances these divergent aspects of Victoria's nature so deftly is testament to Mirren's acting ability. Picking up "the aging action hero" trend kicked off by Sylvester Stallone's *The Expendables* (2010), *RED* followed suit with an all-star cast that included Willis, John Malkovich, and Morgan Freeman. The film was described as "an AARP-friendly *Kick Ass*"[48] and "an affirmation that life goes on after 50."[49] Mirren's Victoria appears an hour into the film, when she nurses an injured Willis and then dispenses relationship advice to him. Freeman lovingly greets her with the statement, "Sexy as ever."[50] This clues the audience in: Victoria *is* sexy, as played by the sixty-five-year-old Mirren. As with *Shadowboxer*, Mirren's age is not obscured with camera tricks. She delights, beautifully attired in an evening gown and combat boots, in taking down men less than half her age. Mirren is a full-fledged action star and plays an even bigger part in *RED 2*. But despite her ferociousness, Victoria becomes a den mother of sorts. One wonders if this is, at least in part, because of social scripts that tell us women are nurturers, even if they are assassins.

Interestingly, in real life, Mirren, like Victoria, chose career over marriage in that she did not have children. In an interview with Garth Pearce, she discusses this choice, "I put my career first right up to meeting Taylor (Hackford) in 1985, I was nearly 40."[51] She told *People* magazine, "I've never felt the need for a child and never felt the loss of it. . . . I'd always put my work before anything."[52] Thus the fact that Mirren needs to defend her work/life choices to a reporter, whereas few men justify their nonparental statuses, suggests the media's focus is driven by some lingering sexist assumptions.

CONCLUSION

Based on media portrayals, this second sexual revolution is not yet in full swing, but the pendulum is shifting. Depictions of sexually active older women are not criticized to the extent that Mrs. Robinson and Maude were during their early on-screen challenges to sexual scripts. In other words, this difference demonstrates a shift away from the normative sexual scripts that frame older women as not sexually appealing. The sexual script for older adults is also shifting partly to reflect and appeal to Baby Boomers, who are more numerous, educated, and affluent than the generations preceding them. So, many female stars are now regarded as sex symbols in their forties and beyond, which was a status previously reserved only for much younger women.

As in most social movements, people who are successful at challenging the status quo emerge as heroes because they represent a new way of thinking and behaving. Helen Mirren is such a hero. While we have focused on her more recent films in this chapter, it is important to note that Mirren has been breaking new ground since her first nude scene in *Age of Consent*. As reported in *New York* magazine, Mirren deliberately embraced the film's nudity and overt sexuality.[53] She owned both by refusing to let men dictate the terms. Mirren said that when she filmed *Age of Consent*, *Playboy* magazine and the Playboy Mansion were celebrated for liberating women's bodies. She publicly disagreed, because she controlled her own sexuality instead of allowing men to do so for her:

> It didn't seem that way to me. That was women obeying the sexualized form created by men. . . . But I was kind of a trailblazer because I demanded to do it my way. I'd say, "I'm not having it put on me by someone else."[54]

From then on out, Mirren called the shots with respect to her own sexuality and how it was depicted on film. With this in mind, she paved the way for performers like Madonna, Miley Cyrus, and Lady Gaga, or as she described them, women "claiming their sexuality for themselves."[55]

Most importantly, Mirren's choice of film roles over the last decade, her willingness to be both naked and sexual, combined with her "can't stop me" action star bravado, work together to challenge ageist and sexist assumptions about what it means to be an aging woman. Mirren embraces her age with grace, but does not succumb to sexual scripts that constrain older adults as asexual. Instead, she has made a career of pushing the limits, and because of her enduring media presence, she has helped rewrite the sexual script for what it means to be a sexy woman at any age.

NOTES

1. Sam Creighton, "Move Over Jennifer Aniston, At the Age of 69 Dame Helen Mirren is New Face of L'Oreal," *Daily Mail*, October, 26, 2014, http://www.dailymail.co.uk/femail/article-2808905/Move-Cheryl-age-69-Dame-Helen-new-face-L-Oreal.html (accessed November 11, 2014).

2. "The Naked Truth: 10 Nude Scenes We Didn't Need to See!" *MSN Entertainment*, April 24, 2009, http://entertainment.ca.msn.com/movies/galleries/gallery.aspx?cpdocumentid=19206679&page=10 (accessed September 19, 2014).

3. William Simon and John H. Gagnon, "Sexual Scripts: Permanence and Change," *Archives of Sexual Behavior* 15 (1986): 97–120, on 97; William Simon and John H. Gagnon,

196   *Barbara Cook Overton, Athena du Pré, and Loretta L. Pecchioni*

"Sexual Scripts: Origins, Influences and Changes," *Qualitative Sociology* 26 (2003): 491–97, on 491.

4. Michael W. Wiederman, "The Gendered Nature of Sexual Scripts," *The Family Journal* 13 (2005), on 496, doi: 10.1177/1066480705278729: 496–501.

5. Alison Parkes, Daniel Wight, Kate Hunt, Marion Henderson, and James Sargent, "Are Sexual Media Exposure, Parental Restrictions on Media Use, and Co-Viewing TV and DVDs with Parents and Friends Associated with Teenagers' Early Sexual Behaviour?" *Journal of Adolescence* 36 (2013), 1121–33, doi: 10.1016/j.adolescence.

6. Amanda Haboush, Cortney S. Warren, and Lorraine Benuto, "Beauty, Ethnicity, and Age: Does Internalization of Mainstream Media Ideals Influence Attitudes towards Older Adults?" *Sex Roles* 66 (2012): 668–76, on 671.

7. John K. Sakaluk et al., "Dominant Heterosexual Sexual Scripts in Emerging Adulthood: Conceptualization and Measurement," *Journal of Sex Research* 51 (2014): 516–36, on 517, doi: 10.1080/00224499.2012.745473.

8. Ibid.

9. Ibid.

10. John Fiske, *Media Matters* (Minneapolis: University of Minnesota Press, 1994), xv.

11. Ilsa L. Lottes and Peter J. Kuriloff, "The Impact of College Experience on Political and Social Attitudes," *Sex Roles* 31 (1994): 31–54, on 31.

12. Timi Gustafson, "The Second Sexual Revolution," *Food & Health and Solstice Publications*, n.d., http://www.timigustafson.com/2014/second-sexual-revolution (accessed July 1, 2014).

13. U.S. Department of Commerce and U.S. Bureau of the Census, *Aging in the United States: Past, Present, and Future*, Washington, DC: n.d., http://www.census.gov/population/international/files/97agewc.pdf (accessed July 1, 2014).

14. U.S. Department of Health and Human Services, *National Vital Statistics Report*, vol. 61, no. 4, Washington, DC, 2013, http://www.cdc.gov/nchs/data/nvsr/nvsr61/nvsr61_04.pdf (accessed May 8, 2014).

15. Margaret M. Gullette, *Declining to Decline: Cultural Combat and the Politics of the Midlife* (Charlottesville: University of Virginia Press, 1997), 222–42.

16. Emily Brandon, "Three Reasons Baby Boomers Are the Richest Generation In History," *U.S. News & World Report*, November 21, 2008, http://money.usnews.com/money/blogs/planning-to-retire/2008/11/21/3-reasons-baby-boomers-aare-the-richest-generation-in-history (accessed July 21, 2014).

17. Bruce Horovitz. "Big-Spending Baby Boomers Bend the Rules of Marketing," *USA Today*, November 16, 2010, http://usatoday30.usatoday.com/money /advertising/2010-11-16-1aboomerbuyers16_cv_n.htm (accessed September 19, 2014).

18. Beth Montemurro and Jenna M. Siefken, "Cougars on the Prowl? New Perceptions of Older Women's Sexuality," *Journal of Aging Studies* 28 (2014): 35–43, on 38.

19. Montemurro and Siefken, "Cougars," 39.

20. Tracey Lomrantz Lester, "The Cutoff Age for Miniskirts? Survey Says . . . 35!" *Glamour*, May 11, 2011, http://www.glamour.com/fashion/blogs/dressed/2011/05/the-cutoff-age-for-miniskirts (accessed August 31, 2014).

21. Christopher Hart, "Queen of Hypocrisy: Helen Mirren Is a Brilliant Talent but Her Views on Cocaine Are Daft, Naïve, and Dangerous," *Daily Mail*, September 1, 2008, http://www.dailymail.co.uk/news/article-1051593/ (accessed July 10, 2014).

22. Tom Junod, "In Praise of 42-year-old Women," *Esquire*, August 2014, http://www.esquire.com/blogs/culture/42-year-old-women (accessed July 20, 2014).

23. Ibid.

24. Michael Kleinschrodt, "Here's to You, Mrs. Robinson: Nichols, Hoffman and Company Graduate Summa cum Laude," *Times-Picayune*, September 7, 2007.

25. Roger Ebert, "The Graduate," Roger Ebert Web, December 26, 1967, http://www.rogerebert.com/reviews/the-graduate-1967 (accessed July 1, 2014).

26. Junod, "In Praise."

27. *The Graduate*, directed by Mike Nichols (1967; Hollywood, CA: MGM Home Entertainment, 1999), DVD.

28. Roger Ebert, "Harold and Maude," Roger Ebert Web, January 1, 1972, http://www.rogerebert.com/reviews/harold-and-maude-1972 (accessed July 1, 2014).

29. *Harold and Maude*, directed by Hal Ashby (1971; Los Angeles, CA: Paramount Home Video, 2000), DVD.

30. Margo Capparelli, "Harold and Maude," *Teaching Sociology* 17, no. 2 (1989): 266–67, on 266.

31. Ibid., 267.

32. Ibid.

33. Michael Shedlin, "Harold and Maude," *Film Quarterly* 26, no. 1 (1972): 51–53, on 53.

34. *American Pie*, directed by Paul Weitz (1999; Universal City, CA: Universal Studios Home Entertainment, 1999), DVD.

35. Stephen Marche, "It's Officially Time to Kill Off the Word 'MILF,'" *Esquire Blog*, July 10, 2014, http://www.esquire.com/blogs/culture/kill-the-word-milf (accessed July 14, 2014).

36. Roger Ebert, "Calendar Girls," Roger Ebert Web, December 19, 2003, http://www.rogerebert.com/reviews/calendar-girls-2003 (accessed July 1, 2014).

37. K. C. Blumm, "Helen Mirren: Don't Call Me a Sex Symbol," *People*, May 29, 2014, http://www.people.com/article/helen-mirren-sex-symbol (accessed June 1, 2014).

38. Mick LaSalle, "Love Ranch," *San Francisco Chronicle*, June 30, 2010, http://www.sfgate.com/movies/article/Movie-review-Love-Ranch-3259817.php (accessed July 1, 2014).

39. Simon Cable, "The Raunchy Sex Scenes That Prove, at 65, Helen Mirren's Not Shy about Retiring," *Daily Mail*, October 9, 2010, http://www.dailymail.co.uk/tvshowbiz/article-1318852/Helen-Mirrens-raunchy-topless-sex-scenes-prove-65-shes-shy-retiring.html (accessed July 10, 2014).

40. Katy Young and Rosa Silverman, "Same Helen Mirren: Don't Retouch My Image L'Oreal," *Telegraph*, October 27, 2014, http://www.telegraph.co.uk/news/celebritynews/11190510/Dame-Helen-Mirren-dont-retouch-my-image-LOreal.html (accessed November 11, 2014.

41. Cable, "The Raunchy Sex Scenes."

42. Carol Sarler, "Oh, Helen! Surely at Our Age It's Time to Put Them Away," *Daily Mail*, October 14, 2010, http://www.dailymail.co.uk/femail/article-1320353/Helen-Mirren-naked-Love-Ranch-Surely-age-time-away.html (accessed July 1, 2014).

43. Ibid.

44. LaSalle, "Love Ranch."

45. Roger Ebert, "Love Ranch," Roger Ebert Web, June 28, 2010, http://www.rogerebert.com/reviews/love-ranch-2010 (accessed July 1, 2014).

46. Stephen Holden, "In 'Shadowboxer,' Murder Runs in the Family (and It's a Turn-On in a Lover," *New York Times*, July 21, 2006, http://www.nytimes.com/2006/07/21/movies/21boxe.html?_r=0 (accessed July 10, 2014).

47. A branch of the British secret intelligence service, Military Intelligence Section 6.

48. Robert Wilonsky, "Killer Instincts, Bad Knees: Helen Mirren Will Cut You, and Other Awesome Old-people Things in 'Red,'" *Village Voice*, October 3, 2010, http://www.villagevoice.com/2010-10-13/film/killer-instincts-bad-knees/full/ (accessed July 10, 2014).

49. Amy Biancolli, "'Red Has Gray Hair, Colorful Characters," *San Francisco Chronicle*, October 15, 2010, http://www.sfgate.com/movies/article/Review-Red-has-gray-hair-colorful-characters-3249958.php (accessed July 15, 2014).

50. *RED*, directed by Robert Schwentke (2010; Universal City, CA: Summit Home Entertainment, 2011), DVD.

51. Garth Pearce, "I'm Much More into Nighties Than Nudity—What I Wish I'd Known at 18, Helen Mirren," *Sun*, June 27, 2011, NewsBank (13822A9D8B7A4F08) (accessed July 15, 2014).

52. Blumm, "Helen Mirren."

53. Logan Hill, "Madam Helen," New York, June 21, 2010, http://nymag.com/guides/summer/2010/66750 (accessed July 1, 2014).

54. Ibid.

55. Ibid.

Chapter Fifteen

Hellraiser, Dandy, Eccentric

The Evolving Star Persona of Peter O'Toole in the 1980s and Beyond

Anna Thompson Hajdik

For most audiences, the enduring star image of actor Peter O'Toole will forever be that of T. E. Lawrence in David Lean's epic *Lawrence of Arabia* (1962). O'Toole's transcendent performance, along with his piercing blue eyes, set against the sweeping backdrop of an endless desert, will be an indelible part of classical Hollywood cinema. However, O'Toole's career far surpassed his star turn as Lawrence. As an actor and particularly as an aging actor, Peter O'Toole consistently challenged audience expectations, at various points, by lampooning his star persona, returning to the theater and showcasing his aging body.

In the wake of the actor's death in December 2013, various news outlets lauded O'Toole as a versatile, charismatic performer. As the *New York Times* notes in its obituary for the actor, "Mr. O'Toole threw himself into what he called 'bravura acting,' courting and sometimes deserving the accusation that he was over-theatrical, mannered, even hammy. His lanky, loose-jointed build, his eyes, his long, lantern-jawed face, his oddly languorous sexual charm and the eccentric loops and whoops of his voice tended to reinforce the impression of power and extravagance."[1] A general theme to a number of O'Toole's obituaries emphasizes his magnetic attractiveness as a young man that gave way to a kind of languid sex appeal brought on by two-plus decades of bawdy behavior. Returning briefly to O'Toole's youth, these observations are significant because they emphasize his attractiveness as a key ingredient to his success. And this of course aided in his casting as Lawrence; as Noel Coward famously remarked, "If he were any prettier, they would have had to call it 'Florence of Arabia.'"² But, O'Toole always brought something be-yond simple sex appeal to the screen. Charisma in the form of "bravura acting" is crucial to understanding how he evolved his performance style in the later decades of his career, and he actively cultivated an eccentric, intel-lectual image that set him apart from many of his contemporaries.

This was evidenced between 1962 and 1982, when he was nominated for an Academy Award for Best Actor seven times. He didn't win any of them, and those losses reflected what some critics called his unfulfilled potential. In 2002, when the Academy of Motion Picture Arts and Sciences board voted to give O'Toole a lifetime achievement award honorary Oscar, the seventy-year-old actor initially turned it down. The journalist Tania Shakinovsky reported, "In a handwritten letter to the Academy, he [O'Toole] added that as he is 'still in the game and might win the lovely bugger outright, would the Academy please defer the honour until I am 80.'"³ He changed his mind and in 2003, on the stage at the Kodak Theater in Hollywood, O'Toole received his Oscar from Meryl Streep, in front of a standing ovation, with the theme from *Lawrence of Arabia* playing in the background. He remarked, "Always a bridesmaid, never a bride, my foot! I have my very own Oscar now to be with me til death do us part." However, O'Toole hardly considered himself retired. In 2006, he received his final Best Actor nod. While he did not win that Oscar, his eight nominations over a forty-four year span demonstrated his incredible longevity in a notoriously fickle industry.

During his 2003 acceptance speech, O'Toole added, "The magic of the movies enraptured me when I was a child. As I totter into antiquity, movie magic enraptures me still." It is through the magic of movies that we saw O'Toole as a maniacal director, aging matinee idol, assistant to the King of England, tutor to the last emperor of China, Sir Arthur Conan Doyle, Casano-va, Pope Paul III, and various members of English high society. Other actors have pointed to O'Toole as an influence on their careers as well. For in-stance, mega-star Tom Cruise once stated, "I remember seeing *Lawrence of Arabia*, one of my first movies, and seeing [O'Toole] going through that vast desert, and I knew I wanted to be an actor."⁴ Of course, the seemingly ageless Cruise is also aging these days, and Cruise's admiration of the actor highlights how O'Toole occupies a particularly unique space as an aging film actor in our popular culture. Through his on- and off-screen antics, O'Toole stands as a fascinating role model both during his reckless, albeit productive youth, and, as I will argue, as an aging hero, because he refused to quietly fade away. Indeed, O'Toole portrayed challenging and complex characters as we saw him age from a young British lieutenant to an elderly and dying actor.

Therefore, in this essay, I explore O'Toole as an aging actor and will conclude with why I consider him to be also an aging hero. While I cannot do justice to his considerable body of work, I will focus on two films in particular, *My Favorite Year* (1982) and *Venus* (2006), as well as include his real-life appearances on a number of talk shows in the later stages of his career. I choose these texts because they blur the lines between O'Toole as both an on-screen and a real aging star. In both films, O'Toole portrays characters who could easily be himself, an aging actor making sense of his life off screen. For example, in *My Favorite Year*, O'Toole's character attempts a stunt from a past film. He is told, "That was a movie, this is real life," to which he responds, "What's the difference?" Then, in talk show appearances, the actor frequently mined his past exploits for contemporary audiences. His seemingly endless anecdotes chronicling a colorful career along with a dramatic flair for storytelling made him a popular guest. O'Toole also possessed that extra bit of charisma that always promised a bit of old-world Hollywood glamour, and audiences embraced him because of it. Thus, O'Toole embodied the "aging hero," both in the fictional realm of these feature films and in the reality of his public life. I will return to these films in the following sections, but for now, let me first explore O'Toole as a dandy, then as an aging star. After analyzing the two films and his live talk show appearances, I will conclude the chapter with some final insights about why O'Toole fits squarely within the aging hero paradigm.

O'TOOLE AS A DANDY

O'Toole's theatricality, or the "hamminess" he was sometimes charged with, can be read as a throwback to a kind of dandy sensibility that the actor exuded and cultivated as part of his star image. As Jess Berry observes, "Dandyism is generally associated with the cult of personality and the wearing of clothes as an art form."[5] While the representation of the dandy has a long history that originates in eighteenth-century Europe, Berry analyzes contemporary manifestations of the dandy in popular culture, especially in fashion. Berry focuses in part on the "double-edged character of the dandy who is positioned as both gentleman and rogue, natural and artificial, frivolous and serious, masculine and feminine."[6] Celebrated figures such as Lord Byron or Casanova exemplify the historical definition of the dandy. Such men continue to influence literary and popular culture, and still stand as iconic representations of a more nuanced embodiment of masculinity. O'Toole even portrayed the elderly Casanova in a BBC-produced miniseries of the legendary lover's life.

O'Toole's entire star persona exemplified this "double-edged character of the dandy" and can be seen through a combination of his film roles and public image. Despite his working-class background (he was the son of a bookmaker and a nurse), O'Toole very much projected an upper-crust, gentlemanly star persona due in large part to his film roles, nationality, and training. Unlike the privileged gentleman he portrayed, he attended the Royal Academy of Dramatic Art in London on scholarship. This led to a series of fortuitous friendships and opportunities. At the young age of twenty-three, his acclaimed 1955 performance as Hamlet at the Bristol Old Vic, the famed British theater company based at the Theatre Royal, clearly demonstrated his talent and ability as an actor. But the eccentricity O'Toole exuded was also a crucial piece of how he presented himself to the public and furthered his dandified persona.

In his study of the British pop dandy, Stan Hawkins argues that the "pop dandy voyeuristically offers himself up for spectatorship" and "assumes many guises . . . demure, sensual, sexually naïve, or bold, cock-sure, rough and vulgar, passive, regressive, or a psycho-case."[7] O'Toole inhabited all of these guises throughout his career, whether the film roles he took went on to be critically acclaimed or panned mercilessly by critics. The panned performances plagued him a bit more during the later years, as roles in poorly received films like *Supergirl* (1984), *High Spirits* (1988), and *King Ralph* (1991) began to pile up. In response to these criticisms, he stated plainly, "I'm a professional and I'll do anything—a poetry reading, television, cinema, anything that allows me to act."[8] While these choices may have diminished his profile, or at bare minimum stood as evidence of O'Toole's willingness to simply cash a paycheck, for every bomb at the box office, glimmers of his past brilliance were made clear. In some instances, his very presence in a mediocre film elevated it considerably, as in the case of *The Last Emperor*, the sprawling 1987 Best Picture winner directed by Bernardo Bertolucci. While the lavish period piece claimed the most ballots among Academy voters, many critics remarked that it was an overlong and rather dull affair with the bright spot being O'Toole's performance as the young Chinese emperor's Scottish tutor.[9]

O'TOOLE AS AN AGING STAR

As O'Toole aged, his once beautiful face bore consequences of years of heavy drinking and substance abuse. But he was unapologetic. In one interview, he proclaims, "If you can't do something willingly and joyfully, then don't do it. If you give up drinking, don't go moaning about it; go back on the bottle. Do. As. Thou. Wilt."[10] While this devil-may-care attitude became an integral part of O'Toole's persona, in his younger years such behavior led to some infamous moments in the public eye. For example, late night television host Johnny Carson famously said that O'Toole was one of his most difficult guests after the actor's notorious 1970 appearance on *The Tonight Show Starring Johnny Carson*. During the appearance, O'Toole rambled incoherently through his interview after a several-days-long bender, fueled by a combination of alcohol and jet lag. Carson dismissed him early. Eight years later, O'Toole came back on the show. Carson, while polite and professional, sought and received a thorough explanation for the actor's behavior.[11]

While O'Toole's reputation as a boozer, ladies' man, and hellraiser dominated his career in the 1960s and 1970s, the last third of his career saw an added dimension to his image, that of a renaissance man. O'Toole's youthful transgressions have been well documented, most entertainingly in a joint 2008 biography that also chronicled the bawdy behavior of screen legends Richard Burton, Oliver Reed, and Richard Harris. In 1975, he allegedly gave up drinking at the age of forty-three after emergency stomach surgery revealed that alcohol had essentially eroded much of his digestive system.[12] By the 1990s, O'Toole's status as a kind of elder statesman of the acting profession allowed him the ability to frankly address such topics as his struggles with alcohol and gambling in a way that excused and even celebrated his notoriously bad behavior. He also outlived his contemporaries, beating his good friend and the other remaining hellraiser that made it into the twenty-first century, Harris (who died in 2002), by eleven years.

Richard Dyer notes that "star images have histories, and histories that outlive the star's own lifetime."[13] O'Toole's reputation as a drinker and hellraiser became a crucial part of his star image in the last third of his career. In 1982, he took on a film role that drew upon the actor's well-chronicled history with the bottle, while also channeling the star image of another beloved movie star with his own hellraiser past, Errol Flynn. The result was a charming little picture that earned O'Toole his seventh Academy Award nomination.

O'TOOLE AS THE AGING ACTION STAR IN *MY FAVORITE YEAR*

In *My Favorite Year* (1982), O'Toole portrays Alan Swann in one of his most celebrated post-Lawrence roles. Swann was loosely based on the swashbuckling matinee idol Errol Flynn, and the film could be considered a predecessor to such movies as *Scent of a Woman* (1992) and *Get Him to the Greek* (2010). Told through the perspective of young television comedy writer, Benjy Stone, earnestly played by Mark Linn-Baker (who went on to star in the long-running sitcom *Perfect Strangers* from 1986 to 1993), the film is at once sweet and complex as it seeks to nostalgically recapture the landscape of live television in the early 1950s. In the film, Stone is a junior writer for a weekly show, *The Comedy Cavalcade*, starring King Kaiser (Joseph Bologna) and filmed at the National Broadcasting Company (NBC) studios at 30 Rockefeller Center. He idolizes Swann, and in the opening scenes, we follow Stone as he carries a life-size cardboard image of Swann through New York and Rockefeller Center. Swann is scheduled to guest star on that week's broadcast.

The aging matinee idol arrives to the show's offices drunk, and passes out after flipping himself onto the table in the writer's room. Kaiser is about to fire the unconscious Swann. Stone pleads, "You're right, this is too risky, you can't take a chance with something like this . . . but suppose someday you wind up like this, I hope nobody does to you what you're doing to him." With his plea, Stone becomes responsible for Swann, and puts his job on the line to ensure that the aging actor will be sober for his rehearsals and appearance on the show. The two become close during the week as Swann shares his world with Stone. In the climax of the film, Swann refuses to perform during the show because it was a live performance. He proclaims, "I'm not an actor, I'm a movie star!"

But of course, Swann regains his confidence in the film's final reel. In the closing scenes we see Swann swing from the studio balcony and actually save Kaiser from four mob thugs. The movie closes with Swann soaking up the adoration of the live studio audience.

O'Toole devoured the role, and brought a kind of pathos to his characterization that also drew, ironically, from Flynn's well-chronicled struggles with alcohol and womanizing off the screen. He also injects the film with a humorous, breezy sensibility, skillful physical comedy containing a surprisingly high degree of physicality, and witty one-liners that are pitch perfect in their comic timing. O'Toole's portrayal of Swann also owed much to the well-worn trope of the action adventurer in Hollywood film. As Andrew Spicer has noted, the image of the action adventurer "embodied the core American masculine myth of successful, competitive individualism" that also symbolizes a "democratic and classless ideal: the adventurer's worth is proved by deeds not birth or privilege and his success celebrates gutsy resourcefulness."[14] While Swann's status as an action adventurer is a fiction, based on his star persona, O'Toole's embodiment of the role demanded the display of his physical prowess—even if his portrayal spotlighted a decidedly middle-aged physique.

In portraying Swann, O'Toole also sends up his own image, and at times in the film it is hard to tell where fiction ends and reality begins. As the film critic Janet Maslin observed, "Peter O'Toole is playing the Errol Flynn–like Alan Swann with a ravaged, sloshed manner that looks all too convincing." But, Maslin continues, "Mr. O'Toole soon rises, delightfully, from his stupor. Witty and dapper, he squires Benjy and the audience, too, on a tour through the glamour that may or may not have been New York in 1954, when the film takes place. There is a trip to an impossibly swanky Stork Club, where Swann sets all feminine hearts aflutter and woos the prettiest woman in the room away from her jealous companion."[15] With this role O'Toole seemed to channel the glamour of old Hollywood in a convincing and even heartfelt manner. And it would lay the groundwork for another role that once again allowed him to portray a character with similarities to his own life. Twenty-four years later, O'Toole once more found critical acclaim and professional success with *Venus* (2006), an independent film that unflinchingly addressed the complex themes of aging, acting, and sexuality. As with *My Favorite Year*, O'Toole's own star image was a crucial ingredient to his performance.

DESIRE AND THE INDIGNITIES OF AGING IN *VENUS*

Of *Venus*, the film critic Peter Bradshaw wrote, "It was a classic O'Toole performance in a classic O'Toole role: a little louche, witty and self-mocking, candidly disturbed by his sexual feelings—taking refuge from painful emotions in a brittle parade of erudition and affectation. It all only revealed his vulnerability more clearly."[16] This film resulted in one of the actor's most critically acclaimed performances as he embodied a character that shared many parallels to his own life. O'Toole portrays Maurice Russell, an aging, once-great actor now reduced in circumstances and suffering from prostate cancer. One of his fellow aging actors tells Russell that he has asked his grandniece to move in with him to act as a sort of caretaker. The young woman, Jessie (played by actress Jodie Whittaker) proves to be a disaster for her great uncle, but Russell is intrigued. Her rough exterior masks an emotional vulnerability that Russell is able to reach. The unlikely pair embarks upon a complicated, yet ultimately affectionate relationship.

By 2006 O'Toole was indeed in the twilight of his career, and the film again blurs the boundaries between the fiction presented on screen and the realities of his life. Russell's days are filled with bit parts in a range of films, and he enjoys the consistent camaraderie of his fellow aging actors at a local diner. The men make a habit of watching the obituaries in the newspaper and tallying up the number of columns their contemporaries receive. The reality of their lives, slowly slipping away, is never far from the surface. Physical ailments seem to be front and center as Russell endures the indignities of aging, as his body is shown steadily breaking down. He is shown at various points undergoing a prostate exam, vulnerably lying in a hospital bed, hooked up to a catheter, and impotent. The film's intimate style dwells on the uncomfortable nature of these scenes, but also portrays Russell as a vibrant and complex man who is not interested in simply fading away.

One of the most bittersweet scenes in the film takes place in St. Paul's Church, also commonly known as the Actor's Church in Covent Garden. O'Toole and costar Leslie Phillips gaze upon the memorial stones of real-life, well-known actors—friends and contemporaries. For example, the camera lingers on the name of Laurence Harvey, a fellow actor of the stage and screen and a drinking buddy who succumbed to stomach cancer at the much-too-young age of forty-five. Indeed, upon O'Toole's actual death, his will revealed that he wished to have some of his ashes interred in the very same church shown in the film. [17]

Another moving scene shows O'Toole as Russell, sonically surrounded by a cacophony of voices—they are all bits of his own dialogue from actual films and stage performances throughout his lengthy career. As the camera dwells on his body, O'Toole shuffles, almost dragging his feet, as if he is physically resisting the present. As the audience, we are provided with a profoundly intimate moment as Russell/O'Toole reflects back on his life through his body of work in this dramatic scene. With this role, O'Toole also wryly comments on the sometimes morose elements of what it is like to be an aging film actor. As Russell, he finds work easily, but the roles are less than desirable as he finds himself constantly cast as dead or dying. "I'm being typecast as a corpse," Russell cynically declares. Film critic Roger Ebert pointedly observed that O'Toole had portrayed a dying king in the big-budget fantasy epic *Stardust* a few months before the release of *Venus*. The film then ends with Russell's death, as his elderly acting friends count the columns to his obituary (he receives a whole page in the newspaper) while the image used in the article is of the real and very youthful Peter O'Toole. In the final scene, one of the characters states outright, "God, he was gorgeous," as the young waitress that served the elderly cohort each morning suddenly realizes the significance of Russell's extraordinary career. In that moment, the audience too is made aware of O'Toole's aging body through the juxta-position of that final image—the youthful obituary photograph—with Rus-sell, or O'Toole, in the present. He truly was gorgeous once, but because of alcohol and other vices, he willingly put his body through the proverbial wringer.

Beyond O'Toole as the star, *My Favorite Year* and *Venus* share several parallel themes. In both films, O'Toole's characters act as guiding lights for young people that seem to lack direction in their lives. Mark Linn-Baker's Benjy Stone and Jodie Whittaker's Jessie each act as fascinating foils, but it is O'Toole's characters that act as a transformative force in their lives. Swann inspires Benjy to become more confident so that he is able to success-fully pursue the girl he loves and gain more respect in the workplace. Rus-sell's admiration of Jessie's beauty instills a newfound sense of self-respect within the young woman, and she leaves an abusive boyfriend. In other words, O'Toole perfectly embodies the aging hero, both within the plots of these films and for audiences watching these films.

Furthermore, as a consummate actor, O'Toole brings a unique blend of confidence and insecurity to these film roles. Swann and Russell are driven by a need to perform, and each craves the adulation and accolades that have perhaps diminished somewhat as their careers have waned. O'Toole brilliantly infuses his portrayals of these men with that enduring desire for the spot-light, an inclination certainly familiar to all professional actors.

STARRING PETER O'TOOLE AS PETER O'TOOLE: TALK SHOW GUEST EXTRAORDINAIRE

Entertainment reporter Nat Jones wryly observed that "just as important in cementing the image of Peter O'Toole in the public consciousness were his decades of talk-show appearances, nearly all of them performed through a smirk, a twinkle, and just as often, a large amount of vodka."[18] Turning once again to Richard Dyer, his insight that "stars are involved in making them-selves into commodities" and are a key part of manufacturing their own image certainly applied to O'Toole.[19] In fact, his greatest character was himself—a star image and public persona carefully honed through decades of appearances on talk shows and candid interviews that were in no shortage during the latter third of his career. One can clearly witness the development of O'Toole's image as an aging, classically trained actor in his many public appearances, beginning in 1978 on *The Tonight Show* through the 2006 pub-licity tour he undertook for *Venus*. These appearances followed the tradition-al pattern of the Hollywood publicity machine in that they often accompany the release of a film.

However, one of O'Toole's most celebrated talk show appearances fol-lowed the release of the second of a pair of his memoirs, *Loitering with Intent: The Apprentice*, in 1998. That year the production of *Late Night with David Letterman* moved to London for a week, and many of the guests included performers or personalities from the United Kingdom. For example, actor Kenneth Branagh made an appearance one night, while the Spice Girls and Sarah Ferguson showed up a few nights later. O'Toole came on Letter-man's show to ostensibly promote the second volume of his autobiography, but the appearance was also an exercise in the actor's ability to live up to audience expectations by mining his past glory. As the strains of the *Law-rence of Arabia* theme song plays, O'Toole enters the stage, nattily dressed and on the back of a camel named Topsey. He then proceeds to dismount, crack open a beer, take a swig, and feed the rest to Topsey. He strolls across the stage, cigarette holder in hand. The audience cheers and applauds. The interview is filled with witty one-liners, amusing stories about old friends and costars from his younger days, and a brief mention of his memoir. Letterman and the audience seem thoroughly entertained. This 1998 appear-ance is great fun, and O'Toole is in fine form. The actor's florid magnetism is apparent as he draws on his working-class origins, rather effeminate mas-culinity, and slightly dangerous sexuality in presenting himself to the pub-lic.[20] The fact that O'Toole had not starred in a well-received, critically acclaimed film role since the mid-1980s was beside the point. Instead, the audience was more interested in O'Toole's public persona that, in this case, was more closely tied to his past exploits than his current projects.

Years later, the series of appearances O'Toole made during his promotion of *Venus* followed in a similar vein. On *Late Show with David Letterman*, he regaled the audience with the story of how he and fellow actor Peter Finch once bought a bar in Dublin during an alcohol-fueled evening out. On *The Tonight Show with Jay Leno*, O'Toole quipped that the only exercise he got was "following the coffins of friends who once took exercise." He also recounted some misadventures with a film crew in the Amazon that were "booze inspired."[21]

During these appearances O'Toole also mined, to great effect, the trope of the "English gentleman" that he so fully embodied in *Lawrence of Arabia* and his other film roles of the 1960s. Spicer notes that the "hegemony of the debonair gentleman was challenged by the emergence of the ordinary man as hero, but the image retained considerable currency with audiences through its tragic romanticism."[22] The O'Toole's portrayal of Lawrence, of course, stands as an iconic representation of the nostalgia for British colonialism. Lawrence is ultimately a tragic figure in that he represents a vanishing breed of a particular form of British nationalism. But we can also apply this observation to the reality of O'Toole's star persona—in one sense the actor's image, his behavior, and his way of being—seemed to belong to an earlier era.

Nowhere did this seem more evident than when the writers and comedians at *Saturday Night Live* satirized O'Toole. In a sketch from 2007, cast member Bill Hader plays O'Toole as a lovable drunk who meets Drew Barrymore (playing herself) at an elegant bar as the two of them reminisce about the "good old days" of Hollywood, when she was drunk at the age of nine and he "drove a car through David Niven's living room." Coming on the heels of O'Toole's Academy Award nomination for *Venus*, clearly it possesses a kind of unwarranted nostalgia for a self-indulgent, reckless Hollywood glamour, but it is done in a lovable and affectionate way.[23]

In the youth-obsessed industry of show business, the career and star trajectory of Peter O'Toole is particularly fascinating because he remained highly visible in his old age. He was viewed by the culture industry at large through the lens of nostalgia—a rogue, a rapscallion, and, simply, a survivor from an earlier era. And he in turn played up that aspect of his image. Perhaps the best evidence of that comes from an exchange in *My Favorite Year* between O'Toole's Swann and Linn-Baker's Stone. Swann has just learned that the much-touted appearance he'll be making will be on *live* television, and he gets cold feet:

Swann: I'm afraid . . .

Stone: Alan Swann, afraid? The Defender of the Crown? Captain from Tortuga? The Last Knight of the Round Table?

Swann: Those are movies, damn you! Look at me! I'm flesh and blood, life-size, no larger! I'm not that silly God-damned hero! I never was!

Stone: To ME you were! Whoever you were in those movies, those silly goddamn heroes meant a lot to ME! What does it matter if it was an illusion? It worked! So don't tell me this is you life-size. I can't use you life-size. I need Alan Swanns as big as I can get them! And let me tell you something: you couldn't have convinced me the way you did unless somewhere in you, you had that courage! Nobody's that good an actor! You ARE that silly goddamn hero!

Stone's response to Swann is a testament to the power of the hero on film—the larger-than-life appeal that has not diminished in the slightest, with the added complexity of the hero needing his audience in order to be successful. Of course, this is a fictional representation that plays to audience expectations. In *My Favorite Year*, O'Toole was an aging movie star portraying an aging movie star.

Moreover, O'Toole's dandy sensibility was a crucial ingredient of his star image.

His reputation as a ladies' man and hellraiser worked in tandem with an appeal that drew on a heady blend of dramatic flair, dangerous sexuality, and the trope of the English gentleman. While these elements of O'Toole's image led to great success in his youth, they also served him well in his old age. At the same time, however, O'Toole embraced the reality of aging and adjusted accordingly, whether that meant regaling fans with tales mined from the past glory of his youth, or taking on a slew of varied projects that kept him active and employed in his chosen profession until his retirement in 2012, just one year before his death. And perhaps therein lies the answer to why we value actors like Peter O'Toole so highly, and need him as an aging hero. His diverse body of work speaks for itself along with his ability to infuse any role he took with electric dynamism and an unparalleled vitality, no matter his age.

NOTES

1. Benedict Nightingale, "Peter O'Toole, Whose Acclaim Began with 'Lawrence of Arabia,' Dies at 81," *The New York Times*, December 15, 2013, http://www.nytimes.com/2013/12/16/movies/peter-otoole-lawrence-of-arabia-is-dead-at-81.html (accessed June 15, 2014).

2. "Tributes Paid to 'Lawrence of Arabia' Star Peter O'Toole," CBS News, December 16, 2013, http://www.cbsnews.com/news/tributes-paid-to-lawrence-of-arabia-star-peter-otoole/ (accessed June 17, 2014).

3. Tania Shakinovsky, "O'Toole Turns Down Honorary Oscar," *Daily Mail,* January 30, 2003, http://www.dailymail.co.uk/tvshowbiz/article-157501/OToole-turns-honorary-Oscar.html (accessed October 10, 2014).

4. Scott Bowles, "Peter O'Toole Raised Hell – and Standards," *USA Today*, December 15, 2013, http://www.usatoday.com/story/life/people/2013/12/15/peter-otoole-dead-81/4031623/ (accessed October 10, 2014).

5. Jess Berry, "Show Ponies and Centaurs: The Male Dandy Revisited," in *Fashion Forward*, edited by Alissa de Witt and Paul and Mira Crouch (London: Interdisciplinary Press, 2011), 85–97, on 85.

6. Berry, 85–87.

7. Stan Hawkins, *The British Pop Dandy: Masculinity, Popular Music, and Culture* (Burlington, VT: Ashgate Publishing Company, 2009), 5.

8. Nightingale, "Peter O'Toole."

9. Todd McCarthy, "Review: *The Last Emperor*," *Variety*, October 7, 1987, http://variety.com/1987/film/reviews/the-last-emperor-1200427361/ (accessed September 1, 2014).

10. "Tributes Paid to 'Lawrence of Arabia' Star Peter O'Toole."

11. *The Tonight Show with Johnny Carson*, YouTube video, January 13, 1978. http://www.youtube.com/watch?v=JuhHThAaymQ (accessed June 20, 2014).

12. Robert Sellers, *Hellraisers: The Life and Inebriated Times of Richard Burton, Richard Harris, Peter O'Toole, and Oliver Reed* (New York: St. Martin's Press, 2008).

13. Richard Dyer, *Heavenly Bodies: Film Stars and Society* (New York: St. Martin's Press, 1986), 3.

14. Andrew Spicer, *Typical Men: The Representation of Masculinity in Popular British Cinema* (London: I. B. Tauris, 2001), 65.

15. Janet Maslin, "Movie Review: My Favorite Year," *New York Times*, October 1, 1982, http://www.nytimes.com/movie/review?res=9B01EFD8123BF932A35753C1A964948260 (accessed July 20, 2014).

16. Peter Bradshaw, "Peter O'Toole: A Star Who Sprang from Nowhere," *Guardian*, December 15, 2013, http://www.theguardian.com/film/2013/dec/15/peter-otoole-career (accessed June 17, 2014).

17. Andrew Young, "Peter O'Toole's 4M Will—and a Mystery over Why He Left One Child with Nothing," *Daily Mail*, July 19, 2014, http://www.dailymail.co.uk/news/article-2698584/Peter-OTooles-4m-mystery-left-one-child-Actors-dying-wishes-Assistant-200-000-daughter-Kate-1-1m-son-Lorcan-760-000-daughter-Patricia-0.html (accessed August 1, 2014).

18. Nat Jones, "Peter O'Toole: The Ultimate Talk Show Guest," *People*, December 16, 2013, http://www.people.com/people/article/0,,20766901,00.html (accessed June 20, 2014).

19. Dyer, *Heavenly Bodies*, 5.

20. *Late Show with David Letterman*, YouTube video, January 14, 1998. https://www.youtube.com/watch?v=K561m7Nq7kk (accessed June 20, 2014).

21. *The Tonight Show with Jay Leno*, YouTube video, February 21, 2007. http://www.youtube.com/watch?v=Bm8tcoilW0o (accessed June 20, 2014).

22. Spicer, *Typical Men*, 28.

23. "Formosa Café," *Saturday Night Live*, February 3, 2007.

Chapter Sixteen

The Betty White Moment

The Rhetoric of Constructing Aging and Sexuality

Kathleen M. Turner

There is even a funny side to aging, if one has a warped sense of humor. If one has no sense of humor, one is in trouble.[1]

—Betty White

Betty White is listed in the 2014 *Guinness World Records* as having the longest television career for a female entertainer: seventy-five years of working in the industry.[2] Her acting career in television includes such notable roles as Sue Ann Nivens in *The Mary Tyler Moore Show* (1973–1977), Rose Nyland in *The Golden Girls* (1985–1992), and, most recently, Elka Ostrovsky in *Hot in Cleveland* (2010–2014). Her career began long before portraying Nivens, however, and her credits extend far beyond these three shows. In fact, White is credited as being one of the first women in television to gain "creative control in front of and behind the camera," for her starring role in *Life with Elizabeth* (1953–1955), which she coproduced.[3]

When White was given a Lifetime Achievement Award by the Screen Actors Guild, she addressed the longevity of her career: "71 years ago when I sang on an experiment thing, and it was called television, who would have dreamed it would culminate in an evening like this?"[4] No other actor or actress in her age group has had as long a career or as prominent a place in the cultural imagination of multigenerational audiences. When fans, critics, and the general population talk about Betty White, their rhetorical choices always show a great affection for her, even as they disparage the works in which she appears. Some of the most interesting backlash has occurred recently in response to her portrayal of a sexual older woman in her role in *Hot in Cleveland* and as host of *Saturday Night Live*. I argue in this chapter that

211

Betty White is a hero and that criticism of her performances in shows with sexually explicit dialogue and narratives is a reflection of intersecting sexism and ageism in contemporary culture.

BETTY WHITE AS HERO

Betty White clearly has star power, given her prolific and long-lasting career. Stuart Hall claims that many ideologies must be marginalized in order for one ideology to be dominant,[5] and Dyer claims that stars challenge and reinforce prevailing cultural norms.[6] The roles of stars in our cultural consciousness are important because they play multiple roles in establishing and shifting ideology. These roles do not stop with the sanctioned canonical texts, but also extend to transformative texts created by fans. When we add to these ideas about how ideology and stars function in our culture, the fact that we are in a culture of convergence where fans increasingly play with—often poaching or transforming—star texts and star power, it becomes important to consider how fans interact with and respond to stars. In this sense, what we see with the longevity of a star like Betty White is an expansion beyond a typical single text/reader relationship, similar to what Michel de Certeau describes as *poaching*.[7] But instead of poaching or transforming a single text or line of narratives across similar texts in a single story-world, as Henry Jenkins discusses with *Star Trek*, fans' textual poaching and creation centering around a single star develop slightly differently, as they can interact with the entire career trajectory of a single actor or actress. As Jenkins points out, "fans operate from a position of cultural marginality and social weakness."[8] Therefore, when an older female actor, like White, exists on the margins of culture, she is more likely to inspire the kind of poaching that subverts the dominant cultural ideology. This poaching in turn creates star power, wherein the star will be able to simultaneously challenge cultural norms and reinforce them. Currently, White—as an actress in her nineties with a prolific career—stands in a liminal cultural position, able to challenge ideologies of ageism and sexism. Her consistent use of blue humor and her multiple portrayals of sexually active older characters, combined with her star power, allow Betty White a special position to ignore people who are critical of her work.

Betty White is clearly a groundbreaking female entertainer and an incredibly accomplished woman who has made a name for herself across multiple media. The Screen Actors Guild honored her for her achievement as an actress, but she started in radio and has also written six books, performed stand-up comedy, and made a name for herself as an animal-rights activist. White has performed in so many spheres and for so long that she has made a lasting name for herself. Betty White is very much an old media figure, and she rejects social media. However, she has been embraced by younger fans who use new media, which was clearly demonstrated in the successful Facebook campaign to have Betty White host *Saturday Night Live*.[9] She claims that she hosted the 2010 show because her agent told her that she must.[10] In Dan Faltesek's essay on this Facebook campaign, he argues that it is not the "flashy digital media, but relatively old-fashioned media" that has made Betty White such an important figure.[11] Realistically, White's prolific career and syndication of her shows is what has kept her popularity and star power at the forefront of social consciousness.

Because White's shows now air in syndication, she has been able to reach fans of several different age groups. This has led to myriad fan discourses and transformative texts, which have expanded her reach further. For example, *The Golden Girls* has been co-opted and transformed in the LGBTQA community, where it appeared in several transformative texts, including Jim Colucci's *The Q Guide to the Golden Girls*, and numerous fan-art transformations, especially those connected with pride events.[12] As fans have transformed Betty White's shows and characters, she has become a central figure in the dominant public discourse as well as expanded her reach into the cultural consciousness of counterpublics. These noncanonical texts have created an alternative textual discourse that both aligns with Robert Asen's definition of counterpublic,[13] and that also exemplifies Michael Warner's discussion of how counterpublics are created through conflict with dominant norms and cultural contexts.[14] Because these transformative texts are created as textual representations in the spheres of counterpublics (i.e., in the spaces on the margins and in opposition to dominant norms), they are spaces of transformation and defiance that extend Betty White to new audiences and new ideological spheres.[15] Part of this process is the attribution to White of sexually explicit quotations that she has denied saying. One example, widely circulated on the Internet, is: "Why do people say 'grow some balls'? Balls are weak and sensitive. If you wanna be tough, grow a vagina. Those things can take a pounding." White has said in an interview that she would not say that, and credits this misattribution to the rise of Facebook and the Internet.[16] The quotations and the misattributions persist, however, despite these denials. Thus, not only is White the Betty White that people imagine based on the roles that she has played and the shows she has been a part of, but she is also the Betty White of these various counterpublic re-creations. Fan engagement with her work has given her persona multiple meanings in the cultural consciousness.

THE RHETORIC OF CONSTRUCTING BETTY WHITE

Betty White's public and counterpublic persona has thus led to an interesting fan rhetoric surrounding her. She is often referred to in popular media as a "golden girl," which is a moniker tied not only to her role on the show *The Golden Girls*, but also to the idea of her star power and her role as a cultural icon. To advance this concept, it is productive to consider the rhetoric that fans and critics use in talking about her.

Fans write about Betty White in multiple media and through multiple texts. Here I will use a small sampling of texts that demonstrate common themes in how her fans describe her. For the purposes of this discussion, I will focus less on social media and more on print forms and texts. Andrew E. Stoner's biography of White reads, at first glance, more like a fan letter as he talks about his lifelong dream of being able to interview White. Stoner writes, "We feel this special love and affection that runs as deep as the dimples adorning Betty's lovely smile; and she fulfills without question, for many of us, the role of beloved aunt, cousin or even grandmother. She's that fun person you are hoping you will see at the reunion; and the one you make a special effort to sit near."[17] Stoner calls his subject by her first name, exhibiting a familiarity that he reinforces by discussing her as a surrogate member of his family. When he describes affection as deep as her dimples, his fan letter almost turns into a love letter to Betty White. Stoner is supposed to be a biographer, but his passion for his subject is clear and by using the first-person plural, he makes the reader complicit in his fantasy of Betty White as family. Similarly, when Faltesek writes about the Facebook campaign to have White host *SNL*, he calls the character she played, Rose, "infinitely likeable" and later claims "the figure of Betty White has evolved over the years to incorporate the best features of the characters she played."[18] Faltesek otherwise seems to have kept an objective view of White; however, in these two instances, he admits an admiration of her, and he begins to conflate her with her characters. Additionally, he implies that she has become a better person as she has played these roles. In *Bossypants*, Tina Fey talks about her own admiration for Betty White as an aging female comedian:

> I've known older men in comedy who can barely feed and clean themselves, and they still work. The women, though, they're all "crazy." I have a suspicion—and hear me out, 'cause this is a rough one—I have a suspicion that the definition of "crazy" in show business is a woman who keeps talking even after no one wants to fuck her anymore. The only person I can think that has escaped the "crazy" moniker is Betty White, which, obviously, is because people still want to have sex with her.[19]

Fey not only brings up the idea that White is still performing well as she ages, but she also softens her word choice from "fuck" when talking about aging female comedians in general to "have sex with" when she discusses White in particular, thereby implying respect and admiration even in her word choice. Naturally, fans of White glow about her. What is interesting here is the way that all of these people write about her as though they know her personally, even though only one of the three has met her. It is also interesting how many times her appearance and her attractiveness come up as fans talk about her.

What is perhaps more intriguing than fan rhetoric, though, is the way in which people who are critical of White's sexually explicit lines and the sexual innuendo discuss White. These writers will criticize the roles, the shows, the writers, and the other actors, but they always write about Betty White in positive terms. Hank Stuever titles a review, "Even Betty White's Spark Can't Make 'Hot in Cleveland' Sizzle."[20] Stuever criticizes the show throughout his review, but his title suggests that he attributes none of the blame to Betty White. Laura Bennett's article criticizes both *Hot in Cleveland* and the *SNL* episode that White hosted: "Betty White has always been saucy, but her dirty old lady act is a recent development. . . . The story of how such a versatile actress was reduced to an adorable receptacle for penis jokes is also the story of the condescending way we treat old people on television today."[21] While Bennett criticizes both shows and the portrayals of "dirty old women" on television, she writes about these events as though White has no agency or choice in portraying these roles on television, and how she is a *receptacle* rather than an agent. Through her rhetorical choices, she implies that Betty White is forced to work in these types of roles if she wants to work at all, portraying White as a helpless victim. Likewise, Deborah Macey critiques the role White plays in *Hot in Cleveland* for not being feminist enough, while still expounding on the virtues of White herself:

> While White's star persona has pushed boundaries sexually as Sue Ann Nivens in a 1970s sitcom and even today with her bawdy risqué comments as herself and Elka Ostrowsky [sic], White has not threatened status quo patriarchy, unlike Bea Arthur and Roseanne Barr. We see White as the sweet, optimistic, if at times eccentric, old woman, who we all wish were our grandmother. At ninety, White demonstrates that you can still be happy and healthy and best of all working, because with the economic uncertainty of our times, Baby Boomers might be forced to work well beyond retirement.[22]

Macey again refers to a familiarity with Betty White and makes the reader complicit in the hope of having Betty White as a family member. So even as she criticizes White for not pushing against patriarchy enough, Macey also extols her virtues, calling her *sweet* and *optimistic*. All of these critics reprove the shows and the narratives, rather than level any ad hominem attack against Betty White; simultaneously, they conflate the actress with her roles on television.

Another reccurring theme as people write about White and her roles is discussion of her age. Tina Fey's commentary about Betty White, for example, is in direct reference to her age. And White herself constantly brings her age to the forefront in her roles. She jokes about her age in her opening monologue for *SNL*, and in the pilot episode of *Hot in Cleveland*, her character (who is the only character whose age is discussed without lies) says a few times that she is eighty-eight. In other early episodes of the show, she frequently says, "I'm old" or "I'm like a hundred." In addition to these fictional narratives, she also writes about her age in her most recent book: "Somewhere along the line there is a breaking point, where you go from not discussing how old you are to bragging about it. I have never lied about my age, but these days I seem to work it into the conversation at the drop of a hat."[23] It seems that everyone is obsessed with Betty White's age, including White herself. Clearly, as a record holder for several career firsts, White is justly lauded for her age. But within all these comments there is also a sense of awe that Betty White defies the norms for retirement and for slowly moving out of the public view as she ages.

NOTHING NEW HERE—IT'S JUST SEX, FOLKS

Critics of Betty White being cast in the role of Elka, or making sexual jokes on *Saturday Night Live*, ignore the fact that White has been using blue humor and sexual innuendo for a good part of her career. When White played Sue Ann Nivens in *The Mary Tyler Moore Show*, she played the role of sex object. Something that we might forget watching the show in syndication now is that her character was sexually progressive in the 1970s. Sue Ann has an affair with a married character, Lars Lindstrom, and she is unwilling to end the relationship when his wife, Phyllis, approaches her about the tryst, changing her mind only when Mary levels a threat to make the affair public and ruin Sue Ann's career because being a home wrecker does not align with the image of the "Happy Homemaker."[24] Additionally through Sue Ann, White delivers many double entendres and sexual one-liners throughout the show, she seduces Lou Grant, and she implies that she had sex with the program manager to get her show.[25] Because her character in *The Mary Tyler Moore Show* was a sexually promiscuous woman, and her lines on the show were often filled with innuendo and sexual dialogue, I cannot help but think that the backlash against White's more recent portrayals of sexually active characters has less to do with her personally, as some of these critics have claimed, than with the intersection of gender and age.

Complicating the situation is the fact that Betty White is often conflated, especially by younger generations, with her character of Rose on *The Golden Girls*, who was naïve and afraid of sexual intimacy because her late husband,

Charlie, died from a heart attack during sex, and a subsequent boyfriend died in a similar fashion.[26] Rose is therefore represented as the celibate member of the household; she had sex when she was younger, but is no longer sexually active for most of the show's run.

In 2010 White began her role on *Hot in Cleveland* as a guest star, agreeing initially to only one episode, but appearing throughout all six seasons of the show until its recent cancellation.[27] When her character, Elka, first appears in the pilot episode, she asks, "Why are you renting to prostitutes?" As Melanie, Elka's new housemate, waits for and takes a phone call from a man she had sex with the night before, Elka says, "That's shameful. I haven't even looked at another man since 1949. When the husband dies, you die. . . . Inside you die. You still maintain the shell."[28] As the series unfolds, however, Elka goes to the local bar with her new housemates and, on her first trip, gets three phone numbers from men. Elka subsequently dates multiple men, is fought over by men, and, when she is on trial, even has sex with a juror in an attempt to sway the verdict.[29] Elka thus changes in her sexual activity and her openness to relationships and sex as the show unfolds. The women she initially calls "prostitutes" help her leave the house and become the kind of woman that men fight over. As Elka begins to date multiple men on the show and her double entendres become single entendres, viewers and reviewers of the show began to criticize the fact that Betty White was portraying a sexually active character at her age. Bennett is one reviewer among many who claims that the show's portrayal of Elka demeans older women.[30]

WHAT'S WRONG WITH SEX?

A multitude of reasons for this backlash exist. Fans of White have conflated the characters she portrays with Betty White the person. Therefore her character, who begins the show as essentially celibate, like Rose Nyland, is also compounded with White's previous roles, and the memory of Rose affects the cultural reading of Elka in interesting ways. But these reactions are also a direct result of a society where sexism is compounded by ageism in an interlocking system of oppression. As discussed elsewhere in this book, our society has a sexual script, and older adults are mostly cast as being physically and sexually unattractive.[31] Because in our society youth is fetishized and aging is a cause for anxiety, a female character in her late eighties and early nineties, portrayed by a woman of the same age, serves to make people uncomfortable when the character acts against society's norms. Yvonne Tasker and Diane Negra discuss the compounding result of ageism and sexism in terms of *postfeminism*, arguing that "postfeminism evidences a distinct preoccupation with the temporal. Women's lives are regularly conceived of as time starved; women themselves are overworked, rushed, harassed, subject to their 'biological clocks' and so on to such a degree that female adulthood is defined as a state of chronic temporal crisis."[32] The essays in Negra and Tasker's edited volume discuss women in adulthood, but do not move into the realm of older adulthood; thus, White is marginalized further by being in an age group that often is not discussed. One of the issues is that, in the rhetoric of the fans and critics, it is acceptable for Betty White to be desired as family member, as aunt or grandmother at her age, but it is unacceptable for her to remain sexually desirable at her age.

Because of cultural backlash to representation of aging women, even Elka's clothing is mostly tracksuits. As Julia Twigg explains, "Clothing, particularly for older women, is often embedded in moral prescriptions that act to police their bodies and entrench the micro-social order."[33] Twigg also discusses the role of leisure clothing for older adults, claiming that it allows for the expansion and movement of bodies, but it also connotes extreme youth. She calls sportswear similar to what Elka is dressed in "asexual" and "toddler-like" in its shapes and colors.[34] This desexualization is subverted, however, in the most recent sixth season, as Elka runs for political office and becomes a Godfather-esque figure in Cleveland, donning more fashionable and dressy costumes, which are more akin to what Betty White wears in public appearances and photo shoots.

Part of the reason for this cultural reaction is the concepts and stereotypes that we tend to have about sexuality and aging. The stereotype of old people disappearing into the margins after a certain age is pervasive in our culture, and the idea that they have sexual activity has not been frequently studied or discussed in either academic or popular discourses. Most academic research on adults over fifty and the aging process focuses on illness.[35] Few academic studies have examined sexuality and aging in adults over fifty.[36] However, more recent studies seek to understand how people over fifty think about, discuss, and engage in sexual activity.[37] Older adults still have sex and still have sexual drives. The perception that Elka embodies in the pilot episode—that there is no sex after widowhood or divorce at a certain age—is dispelled in these studies as well; additionally, these studies reveal that older people now seem to be more comfortable than before in discussing sexuality. The fact that no other woman character on television in her late eighties/early nineties is entwined in romantic and sexual relationships, particularly in dramatic roles, is also indicative of the fact that older people's sexual and romantic relationships are something that we ignore in our cultural consciousness, and this, in turn, can lead to some of the outrage at older women being sexually explicit and active on television shows. As a comedian and a star, Betty White does defy some of the patriarchal norms of society merely by being an older woman in media and by being a woman who uses sexually explicit humor into her older years. For decades, numerous studies have determined that older women are virtually invisible across media in comparison to younger women and older men.[38] Betty White has remained visible as a star in the cultural consciousness.

"THE BETTY WHITE MOMENT"

Betty White's characters in *Hot in Cleveland* and *Saturday Night Live* sketches could be seen as negative portrayals of aging. They are sexually active and portrayed as objects of desire in their late eighties and early nineties, but this is done for comedic affect and therefore labeled absurd. It is tempting to think that this seemingly progressive portrayal of aging and sexuality is thus doing nothing to change public notions of beauty and desire in the aging, or to promote the idea that sexual activity at any age is perfectly normal. I was ready to write just that as a possible conclusion to this chapter, until a recent phone conversation with my mother.

A widow now in her early seventies, my mother spent most of my life holding very conservative ideas about sexuality. Raised as a Roman Catholic, she became a nun at a young age, but eventually felt called to a secular life and left the order. I can count on one hand the number of times my mother has discussed sex with me. Yet, just a few evenings ago, she called me and told me a story about an older man who hit on her in the grocery store, and she referred to this as her "Betty White moment." She explained that for a short time she again felt desirable and attractive, and she joked with me that she thought about a liaison.[39] My mother joked about being attractive and having a relationship because society has passed down a dominant ideology wherein only youth is considered beautiful; therefore, she does not feel attractive. This moment convinced me that while certain individuals might indeed find this portrayal to be "unseemly" or to merely reinforce negative stereotypes about aging and older people, I choose to believe that it might at the same time be liberating for some older people. I think perhaps an interesting future study would be to examine perceptions of the show *Hot in Cleveland* and its portrayal of Elka across generations. Perhaps what younger people find offensive, older people find to be liberating. One thing I do know is that Betty White is my hero if she can inspire my mother to joke about sex, and to feel beautiful.

NOTES

1. Betty White, *If You Ask Me (And of Course You Won't)* (New York: Berkley Books, 2011), 4.

2. Randee Dawn, "Betty White, 'Breaking Bad' Earn Guinness World Record Titles," *NBC News Today Show*, September 6, 2013, http://www.today.com/popculture/betty-white-breaking-bad-earn-guinness-world-records-titles-8C11089734 (accessed November 17, 2014).

3. "Pioneers of Television, 'Betty White,'" PBS, http://www.pbs.org/wnet/pioneers-of-television/pioneering-people/betty-white/ (accessed November 17, 2014).

4. Betty White, "Screen Actors Guild's 46th Annual Life Achievement Award Acceptance Speech," Screen Actors Guild, January 24, 2010, http://www.sagawards.org/awards/life-achievement-award-recipient/46th (accessed November 17, 2014).

5. Stuart Hall, "Encoding/Decoding," in *Media and Cultural Studies: Key Works*, edited by Meenakshi Gigi Durham and Douglas M. Keller (Malden, MA: Blackwell Publishing, 2006), 163–67.

6. Richard Dyer, *Stars* (London: British Film Institute, 2004).

7. Michel de Certeau, *The Practice of Everyday Life* (Berkeley and Los Angeles: University of California Press, 1984).

8. Henry Jenkins, *Textual Poachers: Television Fans and Participatory Culture* (New York: Routledge, 1992), 26.

9. Vivek Bajpai, Sanjay Pandey, and Shweta Shriwas, "Social Media Marketing: Strategies and Its Impact," *International Journal of Social Science and Interdisciplinary Research* 1, no.7 (2012): 216, doi: 10.1111/j.1468-2885.2000.tb00201.x.

10. White, *If You Ask Me*, 42.

11. Dan Faltesek, "Betty's Back? Remembering the Relevance of the Rerun in the Age of Social Media," FLOW, September 10, 2010, http://flowtv.org/2010/09 /bettys-back/ (accessed November 17, 2014).

12. Faltesek, "Betty's Back"; Jim Colucci, *The Q Guide to the Golden Girls* (New York: Alyson Books, 2006).

13. Robert Asen, "Seeking the 'Counter' in Counterpublics," *Communication Theory* 10, no. 4 (2010), doi: 10.1111/j.1468-2885.2000.tb00201.x.

14. Michael Warner, *Publics and Counterpublics* (New York: Zone Books, 2002).

15. Throughout this chapter, I discuss Betty White as both a concept and a person interchangeably. Obviously, she is a person beyond her characters and what fans write about her, but here I do not distinguish or separate as it is difficult to separate a public persona, fan creations and attributions, and the woman as a person. Therefore, I focus on the rhetoric that surrounds her as a public figure.

16. Michael Craig, "Betty White: TV's Golden Girls on 63 years in Show Business," *Guardian*, November 9, 2012, http://www.theguardian.com/tv-and-radio/2012/nov/10/betty-white-golden-girl (accessed November 20, 2014).

17. Andrew E. Stoner, *Betty White: The First Ninety Years* (Indianapolis, IN: Blue River Press, 2013).

18. Faltesek, "Betty's Back."

19. Tina Fey, *Bossypants* (New York: Reagan Arthur, 2011), 271.

20. Hank Stuever, "Even Betty White's Spark Can't Make 'Hot in Cleveland' Sizzle," *The Washington Post*, June 16, 2010, http://www.washingtonpost.com (accessed August 10, 2014).

21. Laura Bennett, "Betty White Is Not a Sex Machine: Our Culture's Cruel Obsession with Dirty Old Women," *The New Republic*, June 10, 2013, 6, http://www.newrepublic.com/article/113296/betty-white-and-our-cruel-obsession-dirty-old-women (accessed September 10, 2014).

22. Deborah A. Macey, "Eighty Is Still Eighty, But Everyone Else Needs to Look Twenty-Five: The Fascination with Betty White Despite Our Obsession with Youth," in *Television and the Self: Knowledge, Identity, and Media Representation*, edited by Kathleen M. Ryan and Deborah A. Macey (Lanham, MD: Scarecrow Press, 2013), 254.

23. White, *If You Ask Me*, 4.

24. "The Lars Affair," *The Mary Tyler Moore Show*, first broadcast September 15, 1973.

25. "A New Sue Ann," *The Mary Tyler Moore Show*, first broadcast October 26, 1974.

26. "In a Bed of Rose's," *The Golden Girls*, first broadcast January 11, 1986.

27. James Hibbard, "'Hot in Cleveland' Cancelled," *Entertainment Weekly*, November 17, 2014, http://insidetv.ew.com/2014/11/17/hot-in-cleveland-canceled/ (accessed November 17, 2014).

28. "Pilot," *Hot in Cleveland*, first broadcast June 16, 2010.

29. "Law and Elka," *Hot in Cleveland*, first broadcast March 23, 2011.

30. Bennett, "Betty White is Not a Sex Machine."

31. See Barbara Cook Overton, Athena du Pré, and Loretta L. Pecchioni, "Helen Mirren and Media Portrayals of Aging: Women's Sexuality Concealed and Revealed (chapter 14, present volume)."

32. Yvonne Tasker and Diane Negra, *Interrogating Postfeminism: Gender and the Politics of Popular Culture* (Durham, NC: Duke University Press, 2007), 10.

33. Julia Twigg, "Clothing, Age and the Body: A Critical Review," *Aging and Society* 27 (2007): 286, doi: 10.1017/S0144686X06005794.

34. Ibid., 294.

35. Elisabeth O. Burgess, "Sexuality in Midlife and Later Couples," in *The Handbook of Sexuality and Close Relationships*, edited by John H. Harvey, Amy Wenzel, and Susan Sprecher (Mahwah, NJ: Erlbaum, 2004), 437–54.

36. John DeLamater and Sara M. Moorman, "Sexual Behavior in Later Life," *Journal of Aging and Health* 19, no. 6 (2007): 921, doi: 10.1177/0898264307308342.

37. DeLamater and Moorman, "Sexual Behavior in Later Life"; Merryn Gott and Sharron Hinchliff, "How Important Is Sex in Later Life?: The Views of Older People," *Social Science and Medicine* 56 (2003): 1617–28, http://www.ncbi.nlm.nih.gov/pubmed/12639579 (accessed November 17, 2014).

38. Craig Aronoff, "Old Age in Prime Time," *Journal of Communication* 24, no. 4 (1974): 86–87, doi: 10.1111/j.1460-2466.1974.tb00412.x; Gerbner et al., "Aging with Television: Images on Television Drama and Conceptions of Social Reality," *Journal of Communication* 30, no. 1 (1980): 34–47, doi: 10.1111/j.1460-2466.1980.tb01766.x; Bradley S. Greenburg, F. Korzenny, and C. K. Atkin, "Trends in the Portrayal of the Elderly," in *Life on Television: Content Analysis of US TV Drama*, edited by Bradley S. Greenburg (Norwood, NJ: Ablex, 1980), 23–33; Nancy Signorielli, "Marital Status in Television Drama: A Case of Reduced Options," *Journal of Broadcasting* 26, no. 2 (1982): 85–97, doi: 10.1080/08838158209364027; James D. Robinson and Thomas Skill, "The Invisible Generation: Portrayals of the Elderly on Prime-Time Television, *Communication Reports* 8 (1995): 111–19, doi: 10.1080/08934219509367617.

39. Bernadette Turner, personal communication, November 2014.

Chapter Seventeen

The Recharacterization of Age and the Aging *Bricoleur*

Danny Trejo's Reinvention of Aging in Acting

Salvador Jimenez-Murguia

Of the few Latino actors who have broken into mainstream Hollywood, even fewer have commanded an on-screen presence such as Danny Trejo (1944–). With his disheveled long hair, brawny tattooed frame, gritted teeth, and the rough contours of his pockmarked leathery skin, Trejo's appearance alone is enough to distinguish him from dozens of other unsavory-looking actors that play the bad-guy roles. In fact, his look is characteristically one that makeup production artists would struggle to duplicate. With a career spanning over three decades, Trejo has been involved in everything from film and television to voice-overs and lip-syncing in music videos. Despite his early professional accomplishments, however, these feats pale in comparison to Trejo's true successes later in life. Unlike many actors in the youth-obsessed Hollywood, his later-life successes have arrived on the coattails of his performances as an aging actor. Now in his seventies, Trejo has not only reinvented himself as the face of freakish intimidation, but, in combination with the eccentric roles for which he is often cast, has also recharacterized the image of aging actors.

Trejo's work is representative of a somewhat larger trend in film today. While the roles for aging actors and actresses are commonly riddled with notions of docility and passivity that reinforce stereotypes of the elderly, select roles for the aging demographic among recent Hollywood productions appear to tell a different story. In an interview for the *New York Post*, Reed Tucker suggests, "Instead of aging being a disease, it's now portrayed as faster and stronger. It's no longer a hindrance. It's seen as a source of wisdom."[1] For example, major motion pictures that feature aging characters in central roles, such as the *Space Cowboys* (2000), the *Expendables* trilogy (2010, 2012, and 2014), and the *RED* franchise (2010 and 2013), suggest the presence of an audience that accepts and will pay for such portrayals. Yet some of these roles still appear to remain well within the boundaries of aging by drawing attention to the characters' limited range of motion, hearing and memory loss, and impotence (even if only to incorporate humor). Moreover, despite what appears to be a positive turn for aging actors, this trend does not necessarily suggest that the movies in which they star are popular because the films challenge common understandings of aging. Indeed, some of the best-known names in Hollywood fail to direct, produce, or act in box office hits along these lines.[2] Moreover, despite casting big names in the throes of aging, like Sylvester Stallone in *Bullet to the Head* (2012), Arnold Schwarzenegger in *The Last Stand* (2013), and Bruce Willis in *A Good Day to Die Hard* (2013), these films, by most accounts, bombed at the box office.

For Trejo, however, his performances are anything but limited to these characteristics; rather, his unique look and masterful improvisation have garnered a considerable amount of attention and recognition in equal light to that of his aging. Indeed, in the acting roles of Trejo—some of the most violent and bizarre performances in film today—he challenges these boundaries on a hyper-real scale. For example, in such films as *Machete* (2010), *Bad Ass* (2012), *Bro'* (2012), *Machete Kills* (2013), and *Bad Ass 2: Bad Asses* (2014), Trejo has reinvented the dynamics of aging within performance. In addition to the reappropriation of objects and actions among a battery of hyperviolent scenes, Trejo acts as a *bricoleur* of popular culture, recharacterizing what it is to be old in an almost surrealistic fashion. In other words, by improvising with props and using his "bad-guy" image, Trejo alters the more traditional roles played by aging actors, effectively substituting much more rugged, as well as sensational, performances for those that might otherwise be associated with the slow pace of the late-aging process. Building on the theoretical framework of bricolage as a form of social innovation, in this chapter I document some of Trejo's performances as a case study of this recharacterization of age in film. I will delve into bricolage later, but in brief, I use the concept to mean something created from a mosaic of other things, such as using a coat hanger to unclog a sink drain or applying socks over one's shoes to gain traction in the snow. The action of the popular television series *MacGyver* was centered entirely around the notion of bricolage, and the innovative capabilities of the protagonist, secret agent Angus MacGyver. With a keen understanding of the physical sciences and an abundance of everyday items at his disposal, MacGyver managed to do everything from making and defusing bombs to rigging elaborate getaway vehicles.

Notwithstanding research within the social sciences and humanities that has explored such phenomena, such research has only been executed in a somewhat limited scope. This volume, and the subject matter it explores, is not only making notable contributions to the fields of aging and acting respectively, but is doing so at a time when relatively little research exists. Despite, for example, a considerable amount of research on life-outcome disparities associated with ascriptive characteristics such as sex and race,[3] the same type of research models that explore the characteristic of age are few and far between[4]—something that, in part, this very volume seeks to rectify. In other words, although considerations of how one's life opportunities are affected by one's sex or race, there has been little of consideration for how age affects such life opportunities. In tandem with the other chapters in this book, this case study is intended to contribute to a broader discussion of the social dynamics found at the intersection between the inevitable process of aging and the professional world of acting.

INTRODUCING DANNY TREJO

Danny Trejo was born in 1944 to Alice Rivera and Dan Trejo in Echo Park, California. A hotbed of Chicanismo, the *barrios* of Echo Park were considered by locals to be some of the toughest neighborhoods in Los Angeles. Among many cultural definitions, the concept of Chicanismo is centered on a sense of pride in one's Mexican heritage, combined with a commitment to realizing social justice and the civil rights guaranteed through citizenship in the United States—something that is quite often accompanied by anger and resentment toward American institutions. Despite the hardworking examples that Trejo's parents provided, the peer pressures of the rough streets drew Trejo into trouble. From school truancy and drug use to theft and violence, Trejo reaped the consequences of his defiant activities by spending much of his coming-of-age years in and out of California jails and prisons.

In a twist of irony, however, Trejo's multiple stints in correctional facilities may have been the single most important contributing factor to his later successes in Hollywood. Of his time in prison, Trejo remarked:

> Prison is the only environment in the world where you're gonna be either predator or prey. You go crazy yourself so that they don't make you crazy. You've gotta get that fear and turn it totally into madness. You start realizing real quick that only the strong are gonna survive. Now how do I become a "strong guy" . . . grab somebody by the neck and bite 'em![5]

In many ways the experience of prison was a laboratory for refining the talents that would make Trejo so famous. Indeed, while serving a sentence in San Quentin, Trejo put these tough talents to the test, becoming both a lightweight and welterweight boxing champion. Additionally, Trejo attributes part of his success to his recovery from drug and alcohol addiction—the "twelve-step program" that he completed while incarcerated.

Upon his release from his final prison term, Trejo began making life changes, including a brief college career at Pomona Pitzer College in California and becoming a drug counselor for youth struggling with addiction. It was in this latter role that Trejo had his big break. In 1985, while counseling an individual with a drug problem on the set of the film *Runaway Train* (1985), Trejo was discovered by screenplay writer and former San Quentin inmate, Edward Bunker. Having recalled Trejo's boxing skills in prison, Bunker offered him a position as a boxing trainer for actor Eric Roberts. Shortly thereafter, director Andrei Konchalovsky found Trejo's talents and looks to be worthy of a part in the film and offered him work as an extra, as well as a small role as a boxer.

From his initial break on the *Runaway Train*, Trejo went on to act in hundreds of film and television roles. Naturally, some roles have been more acclaimed than others, and along these lines, his recurring performances in Robert Rodriguez films are arguably those that have been the most important in building his "tough-guy" image. Of note, he was Navajas in *Desperado* (1992), Razor Charlie in *From Dusk till Dawn* (1996), and Machete in *Spy Kids* (2001). Yet as his body began to age, Trejo made his most considerable advances as an action star in Rodriguez's *Machete* (2010) and *Machete Kills* (2013). Both of these films, and a host of others not directed by Rodriguez, seem to have generated a typecasting of Trejo as the likable bad guy or even lovable good guy that simply looks bad. In an interview that illustrates this point, Trejo was asked if he wasn't at all averse to being subject to typecasting as "the mean Chicano dude with tattoos."[6] Trejo responded: "I am the mean Chicano dude with tattoos! I'm using what God gave me! For the first half of my life my looks got me in trouble and now it's paying off."[7]

BRICOLAGE

The term "bricolage" refers to a form of innovative engineering whereby individuals (as the *bricoleur*) piece together various objects—often disregarding their originally intended uses—in the creation of an entirely new mechanism. Examples might include using a book to prop open a door, suspending an automobile tire with rope from a tree to make a child's swing, or even using a pencil eraser as a makeshift earring back. Notwithstanding these examples, however, bricolage need not necessarily take the form of simple innovation, but it additionally encompasses a much more complex form of production. Take, for example, the artistic expressions found among the Chicano subculture of low-rider vehicles. As such, the automobiles are ornately painted and decorated like moving canvases, and are less associated with transportation than adapted for presentation; with these cars, individuals are seeking to make a positive impression on onlookers. Of this subculture, George Lipsitz writes:

> Low riders are themselves masters of postmodern cultural manipulation. They juxtapose seemingly inappropriate realities—fast cars designed to go slowly, "improvements" that flaunt their impracticality, like chandeliers instead of overhead lights. They encourage a bi-focal perspective—they are made to be watched but only after adjustments have been made to provide ironic and playful commentary on prevailing standard of automobile design. [8]

In this way the combination of dissonant materials, and features of artistic expression out of what may be considered conventional time and space, is a form of innovation that has the potential to engender an incredible degree of creativity.

Perhaps the first use of bricolage, as it is commonly understood today, was introduced by the anthropologist Claude Lévi-Strauss in his 1962 seminal study of structural thought entitled *The Savage Mind.* In brief, Lévi-Strauss used bricolage to describe a form of thinking and production that organized one's creative capabilities (e.g., artistic design, innovation, appropriation). Lévi-Strauss explains that "in our own time the 'bricoleur' is still someone who works with his hands and uses devious means compared to those of a craftsman."[9] Such description, however, wasn't simply a designation between the skilled and unskilled, but rather something more attuned to how the social fabric of a given people constructed its reality. In his discussion of bricolage, for example, Lévi-Strauss distinguished between the *bricoleur* who used "primitive" forms of arriving at solutions in the creation of culture, and the engineer who employed "scientific forms" of solving problems in a much more precise and technical fashion in the service of advancing a given society. In the former, Lévi-Strauss argued that the *bricoleur* operated in a closed system where mythology could be constructed, while in the latter, the engineer operated in an open system where science could be used to navigate a multitude of possibilities. As he explains,

> The "bricoleur" is adept at performing a large number of diverse tasks; but, unlike the engineer, he does not subordinate each of them to the availability of raw materials and tools conceived and procured for the purpose of the project. His universe of instruments is closed and the rules of his game are always to make do with "whatever is at hand," that is to say with a set of tools and materials which is always finite and is also heterogeneous because what it contains bears no relation to the current project or indeed to any particular project, but is the contingent result of all the occasions there have been to renew or enrich the stock or to maintain it with the remains of previous constructions or destructions. [10]

Nearly two decades after Lévi-Strauss introduced bricolage into discussions of structural anthropology, cultural studies theorist Dick Hebdige retooled its use through a much more sociological approach. In his classic 1979 book titled *Subculture*, Hebdige went to great lengths to interpret the meanings behind the culture of defiant British youth and their various uses of fashion. Critical to his analysis was the way that bricolage served to inform meaning. As he notes,

> Objects borrowed from the most sordid of contexts found a place in the punks' ensembles: lavatory chains were draped in graceful arcs across chests encased in plastic bin-liners. Safety pins were taken out of their domestic "utility" context and worn as gruesome ornaments through the cheek, ear or lip. "Cheap" trashy fabrics (PVC, plastic, lurex, etc.) in vulgar designs (e.g., mock leopard skin) and "nasty" colours, long discarded by the quality end of the fashion industry as obsolete kitsch, were salvaged by the punks and turned into garments (fly boy drainpipes, "common" miniskirts) which offered self-conscious commentaries on the notions of modernity and taste. [11]

For Hebdige, bricolage among youth was more than simply a fashion, but a redefining of one's image that indicated resistance to the homogeneity of middle- and upper-class bourgeois culture. Both the objects and the context in which they were redefined through bricolage engendered a highly significant statement about what could be viewed as their developmental values—something quite contrary to the norms of mainstream youth.

In this way, bricolage has both an object-based component that operates on the inventory of available resources, as well as a subject-based component for which these resources can be appropriated through innovation. In other words, bricolage is a combination of physical items and human interaction with these items that results in creating a new item or a new action altogether. Telephones, for instance, were originally designed to operate as communication devices, or merely physical objects used to talk to others. Yet after years of technological development they are now mechanisms offering any number of multimedia capabilities that lend themselves to new forms of human interaction. Individuals no longer simply call people with phones, but may also choose to take photographs, watch movies, track their heart rates, pay their bills, listen to music, check the time, organize their calendars, and the like. In the context of acting—a profession that is largely organized around the imitation of real social interaction—bricolage may be viewed as a limitless mechanism for enhancing creative abilities. For example, the widely celebrated film *Forrest Gump* (1994) transformed the witty talents of lead actor Tom Hanks into an intellectually challenged character who found luck and fortune virtually around every corner of life. Although Hanks's performance was remarkable, the technology and special effects used by the production staff enhanced the role Hanks played. By splicing real footage of actual events from the twentieth century, Hanks charmed audiences by teaching Elvis how to dance, assisting in desegregation, shaking hands with various Presidents, causing the Watergate scandal, and influencing the songwriting of John Lennon. The combination of scripts, props, direction, special effects, and Hanks's interactive performance made for a lucid demonstration of bricolage. With this in mind, viewing Danny Trejo's performances in his later years of acting, one may see more clearly how his own interaction with scripts, props, direction, and special effects is actually a form of bricolage that has led to his success as an aging actor.

DANNY TREJO . . . THE *BRICOLEUR*

> It is conventional to call "monster" any blending of dissonant elements. . . . I call "monster" every original, inexhaustible beauty.
>
> —Alfred Jarry [12]

The monster to which the French Symbolist Alfred Jarry refers is the beautiful sum of all that is unconventionally concocted—perhaps an aesthetic that has not yet found true appreciation. To create a mishmash of symbols and actions out of objects and ideas that were originally intended for very different outcomes is to break away from tradition, reconfigure the status quo, and deviate from the long-established customs of everyday life. This monstrous creation, a bricolage, is by its very definition a reinvention. The monstrosity of this type is what drives Danny Trejo's performances—a piecing together of all that *doesn't* fit in order to create the *perfect* fit.

At the age of seventy, many actors could be framed and portrayed as losing their edge. However, Trejo's looks and moves have only become more enhanced over time. His graying long hair and sagging skin folds across his tattooed body—a body that is often exposed in film, weathered and beat up—giving off a certain air about him that smacks of a life hard-lived. Though his flexibility appears to lack the range of motion that he once had, his struggles to punch, kick, wrestle, or wield a machete have an endearing quality about them, perhaps in a way that audiences somehow appreciate more than from a performance by a younger actor. Yet the obvious shortcomings that accompany aging have no apparent negative bearing on Trejo's performances, as his are always riddled with the clever allure of bricolage. That is, rather than having these quirks of aging work against him, Trejo manages to rework the image of actions associated with aging to his advantage, as some of his actions are so outlandishly violent and grotesque that audiences are, at the very least, surprised that someone of his age can pull such scenes off. The expectations of limits imposed by aging are exceeded, not by the nature of performances that defy the aging process, but instead by *how* these performances are enacted and redirected to new and innovative heights.

As an onscreen *bricoleur*, Trejo overcomes the "old man" image by delivering some of the most outlandish fight scenes in film today. In the opening scene of *Machete*, for example, Trejo uses a car as a battering ram to run over a line of automatic-rifle-firing bad guys and then smash through a two-story warehouse. Carrying no gun of his own, he valiantly charges up the stairs swinging what appears to be a foot-and-a-half-long machete. In a most unbelievable fashion, Trejo then slices off a hand, cuts clear through a few bodies, divides a head in half with one stroke, and finally decapitates three other individuals in a roundhouse move. The use of the car and the machete, however, are only minor examples of objects being employed beyond their intended uses. In a later scene, Trejo maneuvers an escape from the back seat of a police patrol car by using his machete to pierce through the front seat and the abdomen of the police officer who is driving. Then, using that same machete, he steers the juggernaut of a patrol car in distress by twisting his machete left and right—directions for which the police officer correspondingly steers until the automobile finally crashes. Through the remaining film, Trejo wields unlikely weapons. He uses shards of glass to cut across throats, flings kitchenware (including a meat thermometer) through heads, swings an improvised morningstar made up of razor-sharp medical equipment across faces, and shoots a half-dozen men with a Gatling gun attached to a motorcycle while in mid-air. Yet above all of these implausible scenarios, none come close to a scene set in a hospital where Trejo gouges out a piece of an oncoming combatant's intestines, strings it out across a corridor, and smashes through a window, all while using the intestine as a rope to rappel to another floor.

The bricolage-at-play in such scenes are certainly creative (though gory) and add to the overall bizarre character that Trejo often portrays. Yet in some ways such improvisation works as a diversion away from what audiences might recognize as a performance hindered by aging. That is, with so much focus on the strange way objects and actions are being recast for their parts in hyperviolent scenes, it is not so easy to notice that Trejo may be losing a step or two to the aging process. Yet this isn't always the case. In the 2012 film *Bad Ass*, Trejo plays the role of Frank Vega, a struggling hot-dog-cart vendor and Vietnam veteran turned senior-citizen vigilante. Explicitly focused on Vega's age, the movie revolves around the ironies posed by an aging and washed-up man who can still deliver a violent beating, all in the name of good. Although Trejo uses some improvisation in this film as well, including swinging pool sticks, driving a bus like a tank, and slamming people through windows, the more complex role as a *bricoleur* is found in his use of age itself. In other words, tapping into what it is to be old, harnessing its semantics, and putting these into action is an artistic endeavor of the *bricoleur*.

In *Bad Ass* and its sequel *Bad Ass 2: Bad Asses*, in which he teams up with veteran actor Danny Glover, Trejo in the role of Vega displays a number of qualities associated with aging. He is slow stepping, at times even hobbling. His look is replete with passé fashions, including the white athletic socks and ever-present fanny pack strapped to his hip. In his oral performance, Vega complains of his aches and pains, talks about the regrets in his long life (in particular his disdain for failed opportunities), and always seems to have an "old-fashioned" nuance about him with regard to everything from the use of technology to pursuing the opposite sex. As a *bricoleur*, Trejo takes what is available to him in terms of references to aging and animates them with his acting. The unique look of Trejo and his tough-guy personality work in tandem, with these references mentioned above forming something of a novel phenomenon in acting bound to the concept of assembling dissonant material. In this way, it is the appropriation of scripts, props, and looks (object-based resources), and Trejo's interaction with them (subject-based innovation), that makes his acting such a success.

Of course there are a number of factors outside of Trejo's control that add to his performances. These include some of the very resources mentioned above, such as the script, the direction, the props, and the organization of the set. Yet within the theoretical framework of bricolage, these would be considered mere parts of the object-based resources that Trejo puts into action. Moreover, if Trejo were replaced by any other actor—one who does not have Trejo's looks and history—then audiences might simply see a tough guy brandishing a weapon. So, Trejo has managed to master his skills in such a way that he may indeed be irreplaceable. For all this, Danny Trejo has become a model of recharacterizing acting at the late stages of life—something audiences may be seeing more of, in part due to what Trejo has contributed to the image of aging through bricolage.

NOTES

1. Reed Tucker, "Hollywood Loves Its Aging Acting Heroes," *New York Post,* February 16, 2014, http://nypost.com/2014/02/16/ready-aim-retired/ (accessed November 1, 2014).

2. Christopher Rosen, "Aging Stars Sylvester Stallone and Arnold Schwarzenegger Face Trouble at the Box Office," *Huffington Post,* March 28, 2013, http://www.huffingtonpost.com/2013/03/28/aging-stars-box-office_n_2958883.html (accessed November 1, 2014).

3. Anne E. Lincoln and Michael Patrick Allen, "Double Jeopardy in Hollywood: Age and Gender in the Careers of Film Actors, 1926–1999," *Sociological Forum* 19, no. 4 (2004): 611–30, on 611.

4. Barbara F. Reskin, "Including Mechanisms in Our Models of Ascriptive Inequality," *American Sociological Review* 68 (2003): 1–3.

5. *Champion,* directed by Joe Eckardt (Los Angeles: The Film Emporium, 2005), Film.

6. Steven MacKenzie, "Danny Trejo Interview: My Looks Used to Get Me in Trouble But Now They're Paying Off," *The Big Issue,* February 13, 2014, http://www.bigissue.com/features/interviews/3505/danny-trejo-interview-my-looks-used-to-get-me-in-trouble-but-now-theyre# (accessed November 1, 2014).

7. MacKenzie, "My Looks Used to Get Me in Trouble."

8. George Lipsitz, "Cruising around the Historical Bloc: Postmodernism and Popular Music in East Los Angeles," in *The Subcultures Reader,* edited by Ken Gelder and Sarah Thornton (New York: Routledge, 1997), 358.

9. Claude Lévi-Strauss, *The Savage Mind* (Chicago: University of Chicago Press, 1966), 16–17.

10. Ibid., 17.

11. Dick Hebdige, *Subculture: The Meaning of Style* (New York: Routledge, 1979), 107.

12. Quoted in Hebdige, *Subculture*, 102.

Index

About the Editors and Contributors

Norma Jones is a University Fellowship and David B. Smith Award recipient as well as a doctoral candidate in the College of Communication and Information at Kent State University. She examines heroic narratives in popular culture as they relate to cultural identities and representations of various groups. She is an associate editor for *The Popular Culture Studies Journal*, the official publication of the Midwest Popular Culture Association. With Bob Batchelor and Maja Bajac-Carter, she is also the coeditor of two companion volumes on heroines of popular culture (*Heroines of Film and Television: Portrayals in Popular Culture* and *Heroines of Comic Books and Literature: Portrayals in Popular Culture*). In addition to contributing to popular press books about business and nontraditional student experiences, Norma has authored or coauthored eight chapters/entries in edited volumes. Earlier in her career, Norma spent over a decade working in the media as well as consulting for international companies in a variety of fields, including public relations, marketing, sales, high-end jewelry, and international telecommunications. Jones received her master's degree from the University of North Texas in communication studies, focusing on gender, race, and mass media. Her bachelor's degree is also in communication studies, from the University of California, Santa Barbara.

Bob Batchelor, a noted cultural historian and biographer, has published widely on popular culture, modern American literature, and mass communications. Among his many books are *John Updike: A Critical Biography* and *Gatsby: The Cultural History of the Great American Novel*. Batchelor edits several book series for Rowman & Littlefield, including the *Contemporary American Literature* and *Great Authors/Great Works* series. He is the founding editor of *The Popular Culture Studies Journal*, published by the Midwest

Popular Culture Association, and is a member of the editorial advisory board of *The Journal of Popular Culture*. Batchelor also serves as director of marketing and media for the John Updike Childhood Home Museum in Reading, Pennsylvania. Visit him on the web at www.bobbatchelor.com.

* * *

Jace Allen received his BA from the University of Montana, and is currently a graduate student in the Communication Studies Department at San Francisco State University. His research focuses on sexuality and communication, representations of non-normative sexual identities in video games and new media, and sexual identity in cross-cultural settings, especially gay male identity in Japan, Korea, and the United States, within and outside of various forms of media.

Patrice M. Buzzanell is a professor in the Brian Lamb School of Communication, and the School of Engineering Education by courtesy, at Purdue University. She is coeditor of three books and the author of numerous articles and book chapters. Her research centers on the everyday negotiations and structures that produce, and are produced by, the intersections of career, gender, and communication. Her research has appeared in such journals as *Communication Monographs*, *Management Communication Quarterly*, *Human Relations*, *Communication Theory*, *Human Communication Research*, and *Journal of Applied Communication Research*, as well as handbooks on professional, organizational, gender, applied, family, ethics, and conflict communication. A Fellow of the International Communication Association, she has received awards for her research, teaching/mentoring, and engagement.

Guillaume de Syon teaches European history and the history of technology at Albright College in Reading, Pennsylvania. He is also a research associate at Franklin & Marshall College in Lancaster, Pennsylvania. He is the author of *Zeppelin! Germany and the Airship, 1900–1939* (2002, reprinted 2007) as well as articles on the cultural history of aviation ranging from gender and flight to advertising and airline food. More recently he published works on government censorship of comics and caricature in France, and on the role of the postcard in the creation of a European mass culture of technology in the early twentieth century.

Suzy D'Enbeau, who received her PhD in organizational communication from Purdue University, is an assistant professor in the School of Communication Studies at Kent State University. Her research explores how social-change organizations navigate competing goals in domestic and transnational contexts; problematizes dominant ways of thinking about, constructing, and performing gender in different organizational contexts and in popular culture; and unpacks some of the challenges of qualitative inquiry in terms of analysis and researcher identity. She is the author of numerous book chapters, and her work has appeared in leading journals such as *Communication Monographs, Feminist Media Studies, Human Relations, Journal of Applied Communication Research, Qualitative Inquiry, Qualitative Communication Research*, and *Women's Studies in Communication.*

Athena du Pré, who earned a PhD in communication from the University of Oklahoma in 1995, is a professor at the University of West Florida, where she directs the undergraduate Communication and Leadership programs as well as the Strategic Communication & Leadership master's degree program. She is author or coauthor of numerous books, including *Communicating About Health: Current Issues and Perspectives* (4th ed.), *Understanding Human Communication* (12th ed.), *Essential Communication*, and *Humor and the Healing Arts*. Du Pré is a two-time recipient of the UWF Distinguished Teaching Award, bestowed annually by the student body, and was recently named Distinguished University Professor.

Itir Erhart studied philosophy and Western languages and literatures at Boğaziçi University. She completed her MA in philosophy at the same university and her MPhil at the University of Cambridge. In 2006 she earned her PhD in philosophy from Boğaziçi University. She is the author of the book *What Am I?* and several articles on gender, sports, human rights, and media, including "Ladies of Besiktas: Dismantling of Male Hegemony at the Inönü Stadium," and "United in Protest: From Living and Dying with Our Colours to Let All the Colours of the World Unite." Erhart is also the cofounder of Adim Adim (Step by Step), Turkey's first charity running group. In 2009 she was featured on CNN Türk's "Turkey's Changemakers," which is sponsored by the Sabanci Foundation. She received the Ten Outstanding Young Persons (TOYP) award in 2010. In 2014, she was selected as an Ashoka Fellow for her work with Adim Adim. Ashoka Fellows are innovative social entrepreneurs who find and implement creative solutions to social problems. Currently, she is an assistant professor at Istanbul Bilgi University where she teaches courses on gender, human rights, and sports.

Hande Eslen-Ziya received her doctorate at the Polish Academy of Sciences IFIS PAN, Warsaw. She also received a PhD in Gender Studies at the Central European University in Budapest in 2002. Her research is theoretically informed by social psychology, feminist psychology, and sociology, as well as gender role strain, conceptions of femininity and masculinity, and gendered migration. Since 2011, she is the project coordinator for Construction of

Femininity and Masculinity in Friday Prayers in Turkey. Her most recent publications are "Unpacking Masculinities in the Context of Social Change: Internal Complexities of the Identities of Married Men in Turkey" in the *Journal of Men and Masculinities* (2014), and "Janissary: An Orientalist Heroine or a Role Model for Muslim Women?" in *Heroines of Comic Books and Literature: Portrayals in Popular Culture.* Eslen-Ziya is an external visiting fellow of the Institute for Society and Social Justice at Glasgow Caledonian University.

Amanda Gallagher worked in public relations, advertising, and marketing prior to going to graduate school, for clients including the City of Charlotte Department of Transportation and Willamette Industries. She also works as an independent communications consultant, and past clients have included a major health care provider in the state of Texas. For the past eight years, Mandy has held faculty positions at Elon University and Texas Tech University, where she taught courses in strategic writing, graphic design and layout, research, communication campaigns, and several introductory courses. She recently concluded a two-year term as coordinator of the Women's and Gender Studies Program at Elon University. Currently, Mandy is working in research and consulting, while teaching courses at the University of North Carolina–Chapel Hill. She is an active member of the cycling community, especially in the Raleigh, Durham, and Chapel Hill areas.

Dustin Bradley Goltz received his doctorate from Arizona State University from the Hugh Downs School of Human Communication, and is currently an associate professor of Performance Studies at DePaul University. His research focuses on gay male aging, queer media, and cultural discourses of future. He is the author of *Queer Temporalities in Gay Male Representation: Tragedy, Normativity, and Futurity* (2009). His work has been published in *Text and Performance Quarterly*; *Critical Studies in Media Communication*; *Qualitative Inquiry*; *Review of Education, Pedagogy, and Cultural Studies*; and *Liminalities.*

Paul Haridakis is professor and director in the School of Communication Studies at Kent State University. His research focuses particularly on media use and effects, and issues related to freedom of speech and access to information. His published research covers a wide array of topics such as the effects of television violence on aggression, the use of social media and YouTube videos for news and political information, the role of sports viewing on social identity, the protection of online privacy, the influence of media coverage of terrorism, and Internet addiction—to name a few. Paul has coauthored or coedited four books and approximately fifty articles, chapters, and encyclopedia entries. His books are: *Sports Fans, Identity, and Socialization:*

Exploring the Fandemonium (with Adam C. Earnheardt and Barbara S. Hugenberg); *Research Methods: Strategies and Sources,* 7th ed., (with Rebecca B. Rubin, Alan M. Rubin, and Linda J. Piele); *War and the Media: Essays on News Reporting, Propaganda, and Popular Culture* (with Stanley T. Wearden and Barbara S. Hugenberg); and *Sports Mania: Essays on Fandom and the Media in the 21st Century* (with Lawrence W. Hugenberg and Adam C. Earnheardt).

Salvador Jimenez-Murguia is associate professor of sociology at Akita International University and Paul Orfalea Center Fellow in Global Studies at the University of California, Santa Barbara. His current research interests include deviant behavior in popular culture; new religious movements; and visions, apparitions, and spirit possession. His work has appeared in over a dozen edited volumes, as well as in peer-reviewed journals including the *American Behavioral Scientist, ESSACHESS—Journal for Communication Studies,* the *Journal for the Scientific Study of Religion,* and *Preternature: Critical and Historical Studies on the Preternatural.* He is currently working on four book manuscripts including one for Intellect Press titled, *Epic Fails! Crystal Pepsi, Mullets, and the Icons of Unpopular Culture,* set for publication in 2015.

Emily S. Kinsky, assistant professor in the Department of Communication at West Texas A&M University, earned her graduate degrees in mass communications from Texas Tech University and her bachelor's degree through the University Scholar program at Baylor University. Her research interests include children and media, social media, crisis communication, and portrayals of public relations. In 2013, she received an award from the Sybil B. Harrington College of Fine Arts and Humanities for her intellectual contributions. She helps advise WTAMU's chapters of the Public Relations Student Society of America, American Advertising Federation, and National Broadcasting Society. In March 2014, she was named National Advisor of the Year for the latter (NBS). She currently serves as the Vice Head Elect for the Public Relations Division of the Association for Education in Journalism and Mass Communication.

Ryan Lescure received his MA from San Francisco State University and is currently a lecturer in Communication Studies at San Francisco State University and an adjunct instructor in Communication Studies at Skyline College in San Bruno, California. His research falls within the field of critical cultural studies, primarily focusing on the intersections between communication, gender, sexuality, queer theory, media, culture, and power.

Mei-Chen Lin, who received her PhD from the University of Kansas, is an associate professor in the School of Communication Studies at Kent State University. Her current research focuses on communicative issues in intergroup relationships, with an emphasis on elder abuse, aging-related decision making and discussion within the family, and political communication between political parties. Her work has appeared in *International Psychogeriatrics, Handbook of Family Communication, Journal of Language and Social Psychology*, and *Journal of Aging Studies*.

Nathan Miczo is a professor of communication in the Department of Communication at Western Illinois University. He received his BA in broadcasting from Arizona State University, and both his MA and PhD in communication from the University of Arizona. His primary area of teaching and research is interpersonal communication. He also teaches courses in health communication, research methods, and message production. Nathan has published articles in *Journal of Family Communication, Communication Studies, Health Communication, Human Studies, Journal of Communication Studies, Journal of Intercultural Communication Research, Communication Reports*, and *Qualitative Health Research*, as well as several book chapters. His work crosses multiple disciplines and has garnered him awards in the areas of interpersonal communication, communication theory, health communication, and language and social interaction.

Cynthia J. Miller is a cultural anthropologist, specializing in popular culture and visual media. Her writing and photography have appeared in edited volumes and journals across the disciplines. She is the editor of *Too Bold for the Box Office: The Mockumentary from Big Screen to Small* (2012), and coeditor of *Cadets, Rangers, and Junior Space Men: Televised "Rocketman" Series of the 1950s and Their Fans* (with A. Bowdoin Van Riper, 2012); *Undead in the West: Vampires, Zombies, Mummies and Ghosts on the Cinematic Frontier* (with A. Bowdoin Van Riper, 2012); the award-winning *Steaming into a Victorian Future: A Steampunk Anthology* (with Julie Anne Taddeo, 2012); *Border Visions: Identity and Diaspora on Film* (with Jakub Kazecki and Karen A. Ritzenhoff, 2013); *Undead in the West II: They Just Keep Coming* (with A. Bowdoin Van Riper, 2013); and *International Westerns: (Re)Locating the Frontier* (with A. Bowdoin Van Riper, 2013). Cynthia serves as series editor for Rowman & Littlefield's *Film and History* series, as well as on the editorial board of the *Journal of Popular Television*.

Carlos D. Morrison received his doctorate from Howard University (1996) and is currently a professor of communications in the Department of Communications at Alabama State University. His research and publications focus on black popular culture and communication, African American rhetoric, black masculinity and the media, and social movement rhetoric. He has authored or coauthored eight chapters in edited volumes and seven encyclopedia entries. Additionally, he has authored popular works in publications such as *Media Ethics, The CAU Panther*, and *Beyond Research.*

Caryn E. Neumann is a lecturer in integrative studies and an affiliate in history at Miami University of Ohio. She is a past interim director of the Integrative Studies Department. She has published three books and numerous essays, including a piece on Wonder Woman coauthored with Sharon Zechowski. Neumann won the Miami University at Middletown award for scholarly achievement in 2014. She earned bachelor's and master's degrees from Florida Atlantic University before completing her doctorate in U.S. women's history at The Ohio State University. She has taught at Florida Atlantic University, The Ohio State University, and Ohio Wesleyan University.

Ayoleke David Okeowo is a professor of communications and the chair of the Department of Communications at Alabama State University. He earned his bachelor's degree at Alabama State University and his master's and doctoral degrees at the University of Tennessee in Knoxville. His professional experiences are in the areas of journalism and public relations. In addition to authoring and coauthoring research articles, he has written for the Gannett daily newspaper, *Montgomery Advertiser*, in Montgomery, Alabama. His research interests are in the areas of media coverage patterns, international media performance, and public relations.

Barbara Cook Overton is a doctoral candidate studying health communication at Louisiana State University. She earned an MFA in film and television production from the University of New Orleans in 1999. As an assistant professor, she taught film and video production, editing, cinematography, film history, horror and science fiction studies, screenwriting, television news reporting, and mass communications. Overton is also a documentary filmmaker. Her research interests include mass media, communication and aging, ageism and health outcomes, persuasion, public health campaigns, pharmaceutical advertising, sexual health, patient education, and patient-provider communication.

Loretta L. Pecchioni, earned a PhD in communication from the University of Oklahoma in 1998, and is currently an associate professor at Louisiana State University. Her research interests focus on interpersonal relationships across the life span, particularly in relation to family care-giving dynamics. She is coauthor of *Communication and Aging* (2nd ed.) and *Life-Span Communication,* and has published book chapters and journal articles regarding family care giving, aging stereotypes in family relationships, and aging and health status in *The SAGE Family Communication Handbook, The SAGE Handbook of Interpersonal Communication, The Routledge Handbook of Health Communication, The Journal of Social and Personal Relationships, Health Communication, The Journal of Communication, The Journal of Family Communication, Research on Aging,* and *The Journal of Gerontology: Social Science.*

Anna Thompson Hajdik is a lecturer in the Department of Languages and Literatures and the Film Studies Program at the University of Wisconsin–Whitewater. She earned her PhD in American studies from the University of Texas at Austin in 2011. She teaches a range of composition and film studies courses through the lens of popular culture, race, class, and regional identity. She has authored or coauthored several articles, chapters, encyclopedia entries, and reviews in publications such as *Agricultural History, Southwestern Historical Quarterly,* and *The Encyclopedia of Movies and American Culture.*

Jacqueline Allen Trimble has taught American literature, African American literature, women's literature, creative writing, Southern literature, composition, and critical theory for almost three decades. She has won numerous teaching awards, and her work on playwright Adrienne Kennedy was named Outstanding Dissertation of the Year by the University of Alabama. She serves as president of the Alabama Writers Forum and on the board of directors of the Fitzgerald Museum. For seven years she chaired the English department at Huntingdon College, and she currently chairs the Department of Languages and Literatures at Alabama State University. Her poetry collection, *American Happiness,* is forthcoming from New South Books.

Kathleen M. Turner is currently an assistant professor of communication at Aurora University in Illinois, where she teaches a variety of classes in media and communication. She has loved getting lost in narratives for as long as she can remember, and feels privileged to be able to indulge in the worlds she loves and call it work. You can frequently find her saying with a sly smile, "I have to watch television this weekend; it's my job." And she firmly believes that one of the most wonderful things about human nature is how we are absorbed and captivated by stories and how we use stories to make meaning out of life. She is also the executive secretary of the Midwest Popular Culture Association/American Culture Association because she believes that it is important to study the world around us.

A. Bowdoin Van Riper is a historian who specializes in depictions of science and technology in popular culture. He received his PhD in the history of science from the University of Wisconsin–Madison, and is currently web coordinator for the Center for the Study of Film & History, and editor of the Rowman & Littlefield *Science Fiction Television* series. He is the author or editor of ten books, including *Rockets and Missiles: The Life Story of a Technology* (2004; reprinted 2007); *A Biographical Encyclopedia of Scientists and Inventors in American Film and Television* (2011); *Cadets, Rangers, and Junior Space Men: Televised "Rocketman" Series of the 1950s and Their Fans* (2012, coedited with Cynthia J. Miller); and *(Re)Locating the Frontier: International Western Films* (2013, coedited with Cynthia J. Miller).

Gust A. Yep received his PhD from the University of Southern California, and is currently professor of communication studies, core graduate faculty of sexuality studies, and faculty in the EdD Program in Educational Leadership at San Francisco State University. His research focuses on communication at the intersections of culture, gender, sexuality, and health. In addition to three books, he has published over seventy articles in (inter)disciplinary journals and anthologies. He is the recipient of the 2006 NCA Randy Majors Memorial Award for Outstanding Lesbian, Gay, Bisexual, and Transgender Scholarship in Communication, and the 2011 San Francisco State University Distinguished Faculty Award for Professional Achievement (Researcher of the Year).

CPSIA information can be obtained at www.ICGtesting.com
Printed in the USA
BVOW07*1208280415

397684BV00003B/3/P